COWGIRLS

100 Years of Writing the Range

EDITED BY

THELMA POIRIER

First Printed in 1997 5 4 3 2 1
Printed in Canada

The Publishers

Lone Pine Publishing
206, 10426 – 81 Avenue
Edmonton, Alberta T6E 1X5
Canada

Lone Pine Publishing
1901 Raymond Avenue SW
Suite C
Renton, Washington USA 98055

Canadian Cataloguing in Publication Data
Cowgirls
(Roundup books)
Co-published by Red Deer College Press and Lone Pine Pub.
ISBN 0-88995-168-3 (Red Deer College) — ISBN 1-55105-117-6 (Lone Pine)
1. Cowgirls. 2. Ranch life—North America—Anecdotes.
3. Women in rodeos. I. Poirier, Thelma. II. Series: Roundup books (Red Deer, Alta.)
F596.C69 1997 636.2'13'097 C97-910532-5

Credits
Cover art and design by Parkland Illustrators.
Text design by Dennis Johnson.
Cover photo courtesy of the Glenbow Museum.
Printed and bound in Canada by Webcom Limited for Lone Pine Publishing.

Acknowledgments
The publisher gratefully acknowledges the assistance of Alberta Community Development and the Department of Canadian Heritage, the support of the Canada/Alberta Agreement on the cultural industries, and the financial support provided by the Alberta Foundation for the Arts.

COMMITTED TO THE DEVELOPMENT OF CULTURE AND THE ARTS

Editor's Note:
To acknowledge the historical signficance of the writing styles reproduced in this collection, all originally published spellings, punctuation and grammar have been preserved.

Contents

A Common Range: The American and Canadian West

Rodeo and Other Arenas

Acknowledgments

"Old Ranch Mother" from *Poems of a Ranch Woman* by Sharlot Hall. Copyright © by Sharlot Hall. Used by permission of Sharlot Hall Museum Library/Archives.

"Scalawag" from "Queen Ann of Brown's Park" by Ann Bassett Willis from the *Colorado Magazine,* 1956. Reprinted in *A Family Remembered* by Frank McKnight. Copyright © 1996 by Cindy Paskett. Used by permission.

"Bucking Bronco" by Belle Starr from Lula Price's scrapbook. Used by permission of Thelma Poirier.

"Love Finds Its Hour" by B.M. Bower from *Chip of the Flying U,* originally published by G.W. Dillingham Company (1906) and then by Grosset and Dunlap, 1906.

"Snow: The Adventures of a Woman Homesteader" by Elinore Pruitt Stewart from *Atlantic Monthly,* December 1923. Used by permission of *Atlantic Monthly.*

"The Man Who Shot Liberty Valance" by Dorothy M. Johnson. Copyright © 1949 by Dorothy M. Johnson. Used by permission of McIntosh and Otis, Inc.

"The 'Cowgirl' in Montana" by Evelyn J. Cameron from *Country Life,* 1914. Copyright © 1914 Evelyn Cameron. Used by permission.

"Please Excuse the Pants" by Eulalia Bourne from *Woman in Levis.* Copyright © 1961 Eulalia Bourne. Used by permission of the University of Arizona Press.

"A Lady and Her Ranch" by Mary E. Inderwick from *Alberta Historical Review.* Autumn 1967. Used by permission of the Historical Society of Alberta.

"A Pioneer Gentlewoman" Reprinted with permission of the publisher of *A Pioneer Gentlewoman in British Columbia: The Recollections of Susan Allison.* Edited by Margaret A. Ormsby © UBC Press 1976, rpt. 1991. All rights reserved by publisher.

"A Sheep Herder's Bride" by Catherine Neil from "Recollections of a Sheep Herder's Bride" in *Alberta History* 35 No 2, 3, 4 and 36 No. 1. 1987. Used by permission of the Historical Society of Alberta.

"Lost Child Creek" by Augusta Hoffman. Used by permission of Wood Mountain Historical Society.

"Log Cabin and We Two" by Monica Hopkins. Copyright © 1910 Monica Hopkins. Used by permission of the Glenbow–Alberta Institute.

"High River Cook Book," originally published in 1907 by Ladies' Aid of Chalmer's Church, High River. Used with permission of Friends of the Bar U Historical Ranch Association, 1994.

1990 by Mary Clearman Blew. Reprinted by permission of Confluence Press, Lewis–Clark State College, Lewiston, Idaho 83501–2698.

"Moonlight Ride" by Mela Mlekush. Copyright © by Mela Mlekush.

"Effie's Garden" by Teresa Jordan first published in *Boulevard* No. 15 & 16, Spring 1991. Copyright © by Teresa Jordan.

"Sewing Circle," "The Barren Mare," and "The Blue Filly" by Linda Hussa from *Where the Wind Lives.* Copyright © 1994 by Linda Hussa. Used by permission of Gibbs–Smith, Salt Lake City.

"From a Sheepherder's Notebook: Three Days," from *The Solace of Open Spaces* by Gretel Ehrlich. Copyright © 1985 by Gretel Ehrlich. Used by permission of Viking Penguin, a division of Penguin Books USA Inc.

"Somebody" by Doris Bircham from *Calving and the Afterbirth.* Copyright © 1992 by Doris Bircham.

"Foreclosure" by Doris Bircham previously printed in *Riding the Northern Range,* edited by Ted Stone. Copyright © 1993 by Doris Bircham. Used by permission of Red Deer College Press.

"Breaking Horses" by Sharon Butala from *The Queen of Headaches.* Copyright © 1985 by Sharon Butala. Used by permission of Coteau Books, Regina, Saskatchewan.

"Cow-Less" and "Let Life" by Katie Kidwell. Copyright © Katie Kidwell.

"A Letter From Mary" by Mary Daley and "From Mary's Window" and "Bossy's Profits" by Doris Daley from the *The Daley Grind* by Doris Daley. Copyright © 1995 by Doris Daley.

"To Everything A Season," by Marilyn Halvorson excerpted from *To Everything A Season.* Copyright © 1991 by Marilyn Halvorson. Used by permission of Stoddart Publishing.

"Lesson # 1" and "What I'd Do in Paris" by Terri Mason from *Livin' on Cowboy's Wages.* Copyright © 1996 by Terri Mason.

"Home Ranch Cattle Drive: Fall 1981" by Judy Alsagar from *The Gang Ranch the Real Story.* Copyright © 1994 by Judy Alsagar. Used by permission of Hancock House, Surrey, B.C.

"Figure Eights" by Sarah Trusler previously published in *Ten Year's Gatherings Montana Poems and Stories,* edited by Gwen Petersen, Sandy Seaton, Afton Bloxham, Betty Lynne McCarthy, 1995. Copyright © Sarah Trusler. Used by permission.

A tough and tender range.

Old Corrals and New Ranges

FOR MORE THAN ONE HUNDRED YEARS ranch and rodeo women have been a vital part of the North American range. On the range, in the corrals, in the ranch house kitchens and nurseries, they have contributed to the growth of a distinctly cowgirl culture. Most North Americans do not live on or near ranches, so they have learned what they know of cowgirl culture through literature, music, film and sometimes rodeo. Until recently, cowgirl literature was not usually written by cowgirls.

While it may never be known how many women were "writing the range" a hundred years ago, it is known that only a few were published before the midtwentieth century. Today that has changed, and many ranch and rodeo women are not only writing their stories, but the stories are being widely published. The growth of cowgirl literature in the past decade is a phenomenal story. In *Cowgirls: 100 Years of Writing the Range* it was my intent that old literature would find a new range, and new literature would ride beside it, celebrating a rich but previously unheard history.

Cowgirls: 100 Years of Writing the Range rounds up the old and the new from the United States and Canada. Women's ranch life on the American frontier differed in many aspects from ranch life on the ranges of the Canadian North-West. Many American cowgirls were daughters of frontier families. They were capable and determined, they participated in long cattle drives, they branded cattle and they rode broncs in the rodeo arena. These experiences are reflected in the book's first section "American Frontiers." By contrast, many of the women on Canadian ranches were of British origin and had embraced Victorian manners and modes long before their arrival in the West. Most of them rode side-saddle years after their American counterparts had abandoned such tack and slipped into Levi's. The Canadian women sometimes helped with roundups, but mostly they cooked and washed and cleaned. Their experiences are reflected in the book's second section: "The Canadian North-West."

The differences between Canadian and American ranch and rodeo women gradually disappeared. In the early 1900s two groups of cowgirls entered the Canadian scene: ranch women who emigrated with husbands and family, as did my mother, and cowgirls who entered Canadian rodeos such as the first Calgary Stampede in 1912. Then came the western music and films. Each of these would soon influence the styles and behavior of Canadian cowgirls. By the end of World War II, most Canadian cowgirls were buying American jeans and western shirts and entering the same rodeo events as their American counterparts.

This shared culture inevitably affected their literature. The contemporary stories of Sharon Butula and the poems of Linda Hussa, except for regional vernacular, are as true in one country as in the other. Those shared experiences are reflected in the book's third section: "A Common Range: The American and Canadian West."

Finally, the book's fourth section, "Rodeo and Other Arenas," presents the literature of rodeo women—not nearly as large a body of literature, but it is distinguished by its focus and by the history of this subculture. As the experiences of ranch women grew to include rodeo life, this new aspect of their lives was also reflected in their writing.

My exploration and discovery of writing by ranch and rodeo women has been a rewarding experience. It did not happen in a year or just a few years, although the creation of this anthology intensified my search. My first experience with women writing was in the ranch home in southwestern Saskatchewan where I grew up. My mother, Mary Aquina Anderson, scribbled her recipes for baked beans and bread pudding in the back of a *Blue Ribbon Cook Book.* At the same time, the recipes of Alberta ranch women were being collected and published in the *High River Cook Book.* My mother's grocery lists were made out on the backs of discarded envelopes. They never did become part of a book of memoirs as did Ann Clifford's list, "Bar U Storehouse." Recipes and grocery lists were part of everyday life, and they were among the earliest recorded writings of ranch women.

Letters were more deliberate. For years my mother wrote long and detailed letters to her relatives in South Dakota. The letter writing began years before I was born, when my mother, as a girl of fourteen, moved with her parents to Canada in 1911. My mother bore thirteen children and raised twelve of them on the ranch. I marvel how she found time to write so many letters, and in later years I found out she didn't always have that time. There were years when my grandmother, Lula, as we called her, carried on the family correspondence. By coal-oil lamps and later by dim electric lights, mother and daughter shared the replies from Ohio, Minnesota, Texas, Montana, Nebraska and South Dakota. When the first of my older sisters left home, a trail of letters criss-crossed the Canadian prairies between Calgary and Fir Mountain. And when I left to attend Mount Royal College in Calgary in 1955, I became another recipient of the letters.

Letters were part of a larger body of informal writing, a genre that has engaged most ranch women all over North America. Early ranch women often lived isolated lives fifty or more miles from the nearest town. How they reacted to that isolation varied. While Mary Daley of southern Alberta wrote out of a sense of isolation and loneliness in "A Letter From Mary," Mary Inderwick ("A Lady and Her Ranch") and Monica Hopkins ("Log Cabin and We Two") generally wrote of exhilarating experiences. Most of them, like my grandmother and mother, wrote to distant relatives and friends without intending to be published. Others launched a writing career with their letters. Elinore Pruitt Stewart's detailed adventures of life on a remote Wyoming ranch were passed on for their literary value, and she was contracted to write for such prominent magazines as the *Atlantic Monthly*. For the first few decades of the century, it was considered fashionable for small literary magazines to include tales of distant adventures from the remote West. Sometimes the letters became books. Monica Hopkins' "Log Cabin and We Two" was published nearly eighty years later as *Letters of a Lady Rancher.*

Occasionally my grandmother and her sister Blanche wrote with a view to publication in local newspapers. Both of them published poetry, usually in the style of the traditional ballad, such "Bucking Bronco," a favorite by Belle Starr, lady outlaw and cowgirl of the last century. But sometimes my family published in more complex forms, which often seemed to be of their own invention. Overall, their poetry was reminiscent of that of Sharlot Hall—realistic, quick and witty, somewhat nostalgic, but not overly so. The work of other cowgirl poets of the time differed in that it was formally crafted with careful attention to form and meter. In the 1930s when Sharlot Hall self-published her first poetry chapbook in Arizona, others did likewise in Alberta. Whether formal or informal, these styles of writing rarely made their way into published books. What did appear was self-published in small circulation chapbooks and newspapers.

Aside from letters and poetry, many ranch women wrote their memoirs. My mother wrote her memoirs, including "Wedding on Rock Creek," in the 1950s, several years before it became popular to write memoirs in local history books. Other detailed memoirs reached a wider readership: Catherine Neil's story "A Sheep Herder's Bride" was published in *Alberta Historical Review;* Ann Bassett Willis's, "Queen Ann of Brown's Park" was originally published by the *Colorado Historical Society.* Susan Allison's memoirs were compiled by Margaret Ormsby into a single volume and published as *A Pioneer Gentlewoman in British Columbia: The Recollections of Susan Allison* in 1976, although they were written years earlier. Her memoirs have been acknowledged nationally in Canada just as those of Eulalia Bourne have been recognized across the United States.

Not all ranch women, however, have been willing or able to tell their stories through autobiography. The first short stories and novels written by ranch women date from the last century. While it is known that Lizzie Johnson, one of the first independent ranchers of Texas, wrote stories for weekly magazines in the 1870s, none of her writing has been specifically identified to date. At the turn of the century several women writers, including Bertha Muzzy Sinclair (B.M. Bower), were writing a popular form of ranch romance. Johnson, Sinclair and others wrote under pseudonyms—an indication of the lack of acceptance of women's writing. Perhaps because of simplistic, predictable plots the romances lost their appeal. Some works, like Bower's, were relegated to the shelves of the children's libraries. However, that genre is once again flourishing. Two chapters from romance stories—*Chip of the Flying U,* written in 1904, and *Twisted Heart,* written in 1996, have been included to allow you to make comparisons.

While I was interested in what the women of my family were writing about from early childhood, it was not until the 1980s, when I was an adult with a grown family, that I first became interested in the writings of ranch women in more than a casual way. When I was a child, my father had always subscribed to the *Saturday Evening Post.* I was about eight when I started reading the fiction in it, and I may have read "The Man Who Shot Liberty Valance" when that story was first published. I'm sure I paid little attention to the fact that it was written by a woman, Dorothy M. Johnson from Montana. About the same time, a country school teacher introduced me to B.M. Bower's *Chip of the Flying U.* I did not read these stories because I saw the authors as ranch women; all that I identified with and really wanted was a great western experience. Still, as I read more and more, I began to ask, Where are the writings of ranch women? As I matured I began to want books and stories to authenticate my own experience.

For years, however, my everyday life on the ranch included a busy schedule of calving, spring and fall roundups for branding or marketing, fencing during the summer and feeding livestock daily in the winter—hardly enough time for all these activities let alone reading or writing. But in the 1980s, when my children were grown, I found more time for myself, more time to read and finally some time to write.

Some of the writing I encountered at this time had been published. One writer was Sharon Butula, whose first fictional stories of southwestern Saskatchewan made their way into print. One by one I read them, sometimes agreeing with her perceptions of ranch life, sometimes disagreeing, always acknowledging her craft. I also became aware of the reflections of Linda Hasselstrom, her South Dakota legacies. About the same time, I came to terms with my own ranch story, part of which was eventually published as a book of poetry called *Grasslands* in 1991. If Linda and Sharon and I were writing the range, and if we had discovered one another, then I thought others must be doing likewise.

In 1992 I went to Elko, Nevada, to the National Cowboy Poetry Gathering, and there I began to see the event as more than just a meeting of "cowboys." Women were present along with the men—women who shared their stories in song and poetry. The poetry I heard was a mirror of their lives. Through it I could identify the ways ranch women coped: with humor, tenderness, honesty, sometimes irony and even bitterness. I heard the stories of Sue Wallis, Elizabeth Ebert and Linda Hussa. I laughed and I wept. That year and the next year, the women broke down the bunkhouse doors and confronted the cowboy poetry world with a new reality: their own.

It was also at Elko that I discovered Teresa Jordan's *Cowgirls* and Joyce Gibson Roach's *The Cowgirls.* After 1980, as never before, it seemed publishers, especially American publishers, were finally anxious to print ranch women's stories. Each season a new slate of cowgirl and ranch women books appeared on the shelves, and at the same time old books were reprinted. In Canada, the publication of writing by ranch women lagged, but not significantly. Both Gertrude Minor Roger and Judy Alsagar's contemporary biographies have been printed since 1979 by a Vancouver publisher, Hancock House. Marilyn Halvorson has experienced national success with *To Everything A Season.*

After Elko, I moved on to the Alberta Cowboy Poetry Gathering, and there I also heard women's voices, the unique stories of their ranch experiences. Doris Bircham, Rose Bibby, Doris Daley and Christine Ewert told their own stories from their own point of view in their own ways—through poetry and song, conventional and unconventional, and it was the honesty and courage of their voices that made my heart applaud. When Doris Bircham published her own chapbook of poetry, *Calving and the Afterbirth,* the title left no room for doubt: women were standing with both feet in the corral and writing from that vantage point.

Finally, the 1990s also saw the publication of the first anthology of cowgirl poetry, *Graining the Mare.* Teresa Jordan was editor. About the same time, the first book of ranch women's poetry was published, *Where the Wind Lives* by Linda Hussa. Put all the cowgirl poets together and they are a big bunch. Each year there are more and more.

Contemporary cowgirl poets, I discovered, are a mixed bunch. Some like Gwen Petersen write mainly traditional ballads, others like Mela Mlekush write open verse (as in open range) and some like Doris Daley cross back and forth from one range to the other. The best of the cowgirl poetry authenticates ranch and rodeo experience, bristles with honesty or bubbles with a wry humor. Many of the poems blossom by oral performance. The very best poems work on the page as well as the stage. In Canada and the United States, cowgirl poets have published (and continue to publish) their writing in the form of chapbooks illustrated by ranch artists. In the last decade anthologies have become a popular way of presenting ranch poetry, and ranch women have been included in several collections along with ranch men and cowboys. Women on the ranches have found their own voice. The writers selected for this book represent the broad range of experiences of many ranch women, past and present.

Aside from those writers who have direct links with ranches and rodeos, there is a group of writers who have always lived on the edge of the range—women like Dorothy M. Johnson and Helen Clark, keen observers of human relationships in a western context. Although my original intent was to include only writings by ranch and rodeo participants, other writers presented such poignant experiences that I felt compelled to include them, too. Rosalee van Stelten is one of these writers; Edna Alford is another.

Today, ranch and rodeo writers draw inspiration not only from their own lives but from the women writers who preceded them. Peggy Simson Curry, Mary Clearman Blew, Sharon Butula and most recently Pam Houston follow the tough stance of Dorothy Johnson. They dare to tell the realities of relationships, the ways ranch women sometimes patch their lives together and start again. Their stories resonate with authentic experience, not just because they dare to write about themselves, but because their stories join what is now a one-hundred-year tradition of women writing the range.

Many of the women included in this book have also helped me find material for this book. To those who sent work that was not included I can only say I regret the physical limitations of the book. Many fine writers were not included, and if in any way this anthology is successful it will lead readers to them. Besides Teresa Jordan, Joyce Gibson Roach and Candace Savage, I would like to acknowledge the assistance of ranch women Judy Kjos, Doris Bircham, Anne Slade; Donna Livingstone of the Glenbow–Alberta Institute; Diane Lavallee at the Museum of the Highwood; the Colorado State Historical Society; the Montana Historical Society; the County Library of Glasgow, Montana; the Badlands Regional Library; the Medicine Hat Library; my niece, Marion Wolfe of Calgary; Karen Clark of Cochrane, Alberta; B.M. Barss of Calgary; Gwen Petersen of Big Timber, Montana; Pamela Banting of Calgary; Cindy Paskett of Salt Lake City; as well as Ted Stone, George Parry and my husband, Emile Poirier. I would also like to thank my friend Donna Boisvert for her considerable help with proofreading. I have had so much assistance I am sure I have forgotten someone. If I have, you know who you are and I extend my thanks to you, too.

Whether I am sorting cattle, opening and closing gates, or tallying brands I carry the stories of other ranch women into the corral with me. In *Cowgirls: 100 Years of Writing the Range* I invite you to join me in the ranch house, corral, rodeo arena and on to the range.

–Thelma Poirier

AMERICAN
FRONTIERS

SHARLOT HALL

Sharlot Hall was born in Kansas when Indians were a very real threat to settlers. She was still a girl when she herded horses along the Santa Fe Trail to a ranch near Prescott, Arizona. Early in her life a horse accident left her with a serious spine injury. In the 1890s, her mobility limited by her injury, she began to write while managing the family ranch. Poems of a Ranch Woman *was published in 1993. At Prescott, Arizona, an historical society and a library have been named in her honor.*

The Old Ranch Mother

Long time ago I used to say to Jim
('Fore any children come to call him Paw):
"Oh, Jim, Oh, Jim, let's leave this sorry place
An' go where trees is, an' green grass,
An' water springs. This desert here
Burns up my heart an' makes me so afraid.
Let's go where folks is—Jim. Oh, Jim, let's go."
An' Jim, he'd chaw an' spit an' chaw,
An' say: "Aw, Lizy, this place, it's all right;
Th' cattle's company better'n too much folks."

I set here on this hill right smart that year—
A-waitin' and' a-waitin'—plum scared wild
To hold some woman's hand, an' hear her talk.
I made Jim put th' baby 'way up here—
An' sometimes yit I see her scared, dead face.

Jodie, he come nex' year. I walked them trails

Fer weeks an' months—seemed like I had to fly
To git away—to go an' be with folks.
That there ain't Jodie's grave. It's got his name
But God, He only, knows where Jodie is.
'Fore he could walk he'd roll an' crawl to git
Out o' th' door—jist had to git away—
Like everywhere was callin' him to come.
Las' year I made-believe that grave o' his
When he was killed 'way down in Mexico.
Seemed like I felt him comin' on them trails
Back to his Maw.

When th' rest come, I didn't think so much.
Th' cattle, like Jim said, was company.
Th' cows with little calves, cute little tricks,
I turned 'em in to water at the trough
An' talked to 'em. When Piedy's calf, it died
An' she went wild a-mooin', I jes took
Th' little thing an' buried it up here
Right by my baby—an' she seemed to know—
An' her an' me was frien's fer many year
Like human folks.

I took a heap o' comfort in them cows.
It never done no good to talk to Jim—
He'd jes' set dum an' chaw, an' spit, and' chaw.
My, them was workin' times! Me waterin' cattle—
Childern comin' fast, an' growin' fast—
An' Jim off ridin', mostly, on th' range.
That's John there, close to Babe.
Come, once, a runnin' horse, a-thunderin' down
Th' water trail—an' somethin' draggin' caught
Into th' stirrup.

Even yit
A runnin' horse jes' shets my heart up tight.
That's Lulie—she was so afraid o' storms.
Th' lightnin' got her, bringin' up th' cows—
Me, goin' to meet her, saw the big flash hit.
I ain't never let no rain storm fall
On Lulie, there. I put that roofin' iron
All over her, an' always kep' it close—
Storms scared her so.

ANN BASSETT WILLIS

Ann Bassett grew up on a ranch in Brown's Park, a remote range in northwest Colorado. In 1952 she wrote her memoirs, Queen Ann of Brown's Park, *which told of rustlers, range wars and desperadoes. Her childhood and life on the frontier was tough and rough but never quite as bad as some chroniclers, or even Ann, would have it. Her great niece Cindy Paskett claims Ann was given to exaggeration. In the fall of 1996 the Bassett family story was published in Utah. The story "Scalawag," about Dixie Burr, a maverick calf, gives a glimpse into Ann Bassett's version of her life. It was also published in* Colorado Magazine *and in* A Family Remembered.

Scalawag

IN THE SPRING OF 1883 I found a dogie that was left by the mother when the drive passed our ranch. This calf had wandered into our pasture and located itself near a clump of protective willows where it could nip the soft green grass.

But it required milk, it could not live entirely on grass, and was about at the folding-up stage when I found it. The wild little brute was full of fight, but I managed to get it to the house, over a distance of a mile, which took most of the day and a lot of relays.

After I fed the calf milk—a forced feeding—I went to Mother and told her about my find. When she saw the starved, tiny creature that had been branded and ear-marked at that tender age, she immediately made it clear to me that I could feed and care for the calf, but as soon as it could eat grass and grew strong enough to rustle its living without milk, I must "turn it on the range, for I knew very well that it belonged to Mr. Fisher." He was general manager for the Middlesex at that time. The calf of the long horned Texas breed, covered with burrs and emaciated from starvation, was not a very promising looking critter.

With constant attention and kindness it learned to drink milk, and started to grow into something resembling a calf. The fact of ownership being definitely announced from the start caused much grief and secret planning on my part. I decided that I never would give the precious creature up—such a thing was unthinkable, for the little waif was as fond of me as I was of it.

I did not take my troubles to anyone, but decided to lay my case before Mr. Fisher, whose office was in Rock Springs, a hundred miles away. So when Father went to this town for supplies, I begged to go with him. He consented and raised the question of who should care for the calf during my absence. I had arranged all that. Knowing how my brother and sister had referred to the wonderful calf as a "lousy, ugly little runt, unfit for coyote bait," I would not give them the chance to let it starve nor ever over feed it. Father and mother were amazed at my wanting to go on this trip. I had refused to leave "Dixie Burr" for any reason longer than a few hours at a time during the six weeks since finding her. I kept my reasons a deep secret, only confiding in Slippery Jim, one of the ranch hands, who had shown great understanding and had spoken encouragingly of my treasure, declaring in a most flattering manner: "This will be a big herd of cattle some day, good uns too, the kind that have sense and can find their own feed, not like them old Durhams. I don't like 'em no-how" (referring to the kind of cattle Father and Mother were raising).

So, by arrangement and with promises of extra chewing tobacco, and some candy for good measure, Slippery became caretaker of Dixie Burr during my ten days' trip to and from town by wagon. While in Rock Springs I asked Father to take me to Mr. Fisher's office, which he did without question, somewhat to my surprise. Father may have suspected my errand, but was plainly quite taken back when I boldly offered to swap one of his purebred, yearling steers for the common little scalawag. He could only be polite in presence of Mr. Fisher, so he gave his approval. Then Mr. Fisher said he would not accept such an unequal trade, but would gladly give the calf to me. He added that the calf would have died anyway, since it had no mother, and also declared that he was indebted to Father for many accommodations.

With great exaltation I returned home to exercise ownership of valuable live stock. My happiness was complete, actually owning, even in miniature a Texas cow, which, according to Slippery's opinion meant something of indescribable value.

My childish love and affection became centered on that mite of tangled hair and bone, which soon possessed a private corral and shed, built by the combined efforts of Slippery and me. This was a work of art, and proudly exhibited to all comers. I disregarded Mother's amused and mildly disapproving attitude. It was I who slept in the little bedroom adjoining the calf's shelter, and it did not show from the front of the house—that is, not much. Almost at once I had become sole occupant of what my sister termed "a combination calfshed and bedroom." She promptly moved to other quarters, for some reason beyond by comprehension. When Dixie Burr was a yearling and showing unmistakable signs of being a true "scalawag," she was turned out in the pasture with other cattle. During the year Mr. Fisher had resigned as general manager of the Middlesex Cattle Company, and another man held the position.

The new manager had been informed by Mr. Fisher of the ownership of that certain yearling bearing the company's brand. But there were many cowpunchers in an outfit of the size owned by this company, who could not possibly have this information. It was customary to ride through pastures among cattle, inspecting brands for any stock belonging in the show-up, which, as often happened, might have slipped through a fence into the enclosure. I was on the job when the round-up neared our ranch, for my Dixie Burr still bore the Two Bar brand. Such brand being the only means of identification, some uninformed puncher could easily make the mistake of driving my pet away. When I supposed all was well, as the herd had been started on, I went home.

The Bassett ranches contained hundreds of acres stretched along the foot hills out of sight of the home buildings. It was my habit to drive Dixie Burr to the house each night. When I rode to the pasture for that purpose, she was not there. Upon careful examination of tracks at the gate, I knew she had been driven away. It was too late to follow the herd, so I went back to the house. I found Slippery and told him what had happened. He seemed as hurt as I was. We pow-wowed for a time, then he said, "git out and find that herd and stay on the job 'til you ride it from end to end. Yore dogie is there, so wash the tear tracks ofe'n yore face, git to bed, and be ariden at the crack o' day."

I did just that, finding the herd already on its way, and a rider bringing up the drag, lashing my Dixie Burr with a raw hide rope. I went berserk, "hog wild," and flew at him in outraged fury. Before he noticed my wild intent, I began whipping him over the head with my quirt. Evidently he was not feeling too good himself. My slashing him over the head and face turned him plum sour, and he took on the work of properly educating and chastising me. I must have acted somewhat like a bear trap, jumpy and vicious. As I look upon the incident now, I can scarcely blame him for what he did. He refused to let me take the calf, which in a sense was right, because it bore only the brand of the Middlesex Company. I knew the calf was mine, and fought with the intensity born of that knowledge. I was outraged, and each minute more terror stricken lest this man, who seemed to me the meanest of brutes, would be able to hold my calf, that I might be losing Dixie Burr forever. He must have finally gone too far in the enforcing of his authority. Eventually the onlookers became restive.

Among the cowhands gathered around to watch the fracas, was Joe Martin, a Texas puncher, repping for himself and his neighbors, to gather cattle strayed from the Bear River range. At the start he was merely a disinterested spectator, concerned only in seeing what would happen as a result of this misunderstanding between Roark, the foreman of the Middlesex outfit, the man I had quirted, and myself. Finally Joe Martin spoke. "Why not just let the kid take the calf and settle the ownership later. It's evident the calf and the girl know each other." That remark touched off the fireworks. The foreman went for his gun, saying, "You son of a——, who asked for your advice?" Joe was a live hand and he beat the foreman to the draw. Roark was just a would-be gunman anyway, so Joe took his gun. Joe did not seem a bit excited. He laid his weapon aside with Roark's gun, and got ready for the fight. These men were about equal in size and age. The fight began fast, with furious blows. For a while I was uncertain which way the victory would go, but Joe came on faster than ever, and soon the foreman was down and out for the final count.

I jumped off my pony and started to kick him. Joe grabbed me by the arm, and said: "Shame on you, Ann, that's cowardly. Don't you know you should never jump on a man when he is down?" Those words brought me up standing, and I have never forgotten them. "Never jump on a man when he is down."

I took my dogie calf, drove it home and kept the whole affair to myself. When mother asked me where I had been, I simply said that I had been up in the pasture getting Dixie Burr. I had already curried my horse and cleaned away the sweat stains just as I had been taught to do by Slippery and his "book of knowledge." When I got Slippery off alone, I told him the facts. He muttered, more to himself than to me, "I'll do something about that brand. " This gave me an idea. It could not be erased like the letters and numbers we placed on our slates, but there was nothing to prevent me from adding a few more marks to those already on the calf. After considering the matter for some time, the idea took a definite form and I favored it.

When I had made up my mind, I thought it best to keep the decision to myself, and did not tell Slippery, for, child though I was, I understood what changing of brands meant. I knew what the consequences might be, for such acts were strictly outside range ethics in Brown's Park, yet I had to protect Dixie Burr.

A few days after I had reached the decision that something drastic must be done about the brand, I took her into an out of the way place, up a draw, and tied her tight. While I hated to hurt her, I felt it was much better than to have her driven away and abused, as I had already witnessed. I built a fire and put a branding ring in it. When the ring was white hot I made the Two Bars into a pig-pen brand by adding two more lines at right angles to the bars.

Then I left Dixie Burr where she would be undisturbed while the new burns healed into scars and two more bars. The nearby spring which was seldom visited would provide water for her, the grass grew thick and tall, and the air was refreshingly cool. My conscience must have wakened, for as I was riding away I commenced to feel the inclination to tell somebody. This feeling deepened to an urge that caused me, a few hours later, to confide what I had done to my brother, Sam. He at once became a fellow conspirator. He was eleven, I eight years old, two younsters who were white for fear of what mother would say and do if she discovered what I had done.

We finally decided it would be best to remove the calf to our summer place in Zenobia Basin, about a dozen miles from the home ranch. Father was doing some building and mother readily gave permission for us to "visit father." A very early start was required to get Dixie Burr from her hiding place unseen by anybody on the ranch. We were out by streak o' day. But the calf was decidedly stubborn and hard to drive. We had only reached the "Hogback" by sundown, and were still several miles from our goal. We tied Dixie Burr securely to a tree and built a fire at some little distance, to frighten off mountain lions. Then we left her for the night and rode on to father's camp. He suspected nothing out of the ordinary. And when we caught our horses the next morning there was nothing unusual in that act, so we got away without questioning. We moved Dixie Burr safely into Zenobia Basin, and established her as far from the cabin and father as possible. Father never did pay much attention to the cattle. We were safe for the present.

Roark of the Middlesex was a stranger to the people of Brown's Park, and he undoubtedly wanted to make a good showing with his company. He developed a grudge against the granger class in our section after he took the beating from Joe Martin in the presence of the cow punchers at the roundup. This had added nothing to his prestige. He had a score to settle and his resentment grew. His secret malice was directed toward all grangers but *my* family in particular. It should be remembered, none of them had heard even a whisper about the Martin–Roark fight.

Roark had a habit of riding over the settler's ranges when owners were engaged elsewhere. He never showed up to talk matters over, just coyoted through the brush. After Father left the Basin, Roark began to snoop around. He found Dixie Burr. The job I had done was a sloppy imitation of brand blotting. (Me heap savy now). When he found the calf with the brand so obviously changed, he lit out on horse back, making hot tracks to Hahn's Peak, the county seat of Routt County, considerably over a hundred miles from Zenobia Basin. He swore out warrants of arrest for everyone in Brown's Park but Father, who was one of the County Commissioners and was attending a board meeting at the county seat. Roark made no other exceptions in his wholesale arrests. He included men and women alike.

Sam Walker, of Hayden, was sheriff at the time. He came to the Park with his bundle of warrants, and was treated as any guest would have been. But the serving of warrants was received with amazement. A roving Englishman, who roamed the world seeking enjoyment in strange or isolated spots, happened to be in the Park at the time. He had build himself a cabin and shared the life without being a real part of the community. He was astounded when presented with his warrant, and hadn't the least idea what it meant. That most innocent and law-abiding lady, Mrs. Sears, viewed hers with a mingling of astonishment and consternation.

However, all the recipients of those warrants reacted as any good citizens naturally would, and appeared in court when the case was called for hearing. This was immediately dismissed for lack of evidence. Its instigator may have foreseen this conclusion, but a deeper purpose, no doubt, lay behind his move, a hope to discourage the occupants of the Park remaining there.

As a result of my child efforts to protect a cherished pet from brutality, Brown's Park was branded as a home for rustlers, and the lying rumor was widely circulated that "no good can come from Brown's Park."

The Middlesex were not successful in their hope-for grab. They sold out to Ed Rife. He at once stocked the range with sheep, and small cow outfits adjoining lived in peace. This state of serenity continued for many years, or until the Haley Two–Bar commenced to harrass them from the East.

"Scalawag" though she was, Dixie Burr continued to firmly hold her position in my regard, and I kept her until she died of old age, still bearing her scars and two bars.

BELLE STARR

Infamous groups of women were a peripheral part of life on the range, but some unique individuals made names for themselves. Of them none left a legend like Belle Starr's.

Bucking Bronco

My love is a rider, wild broncos he breaks,
Though he's promised to quit it, just for my sake.
He ties up one foot, the saddle puts on,
With a swing and a jump he is mounted and gone.

The first time I met him, 't was early one spring,
Riding a bronco, a high-headed thing.
He tipped me a wink as he gayly did go,
For he wished me to look at his bucking bronco.

The next time I saw him, 't was late in the fall,
Swinging the girls at Tomlinson's ball:
He laughed and he talked as we danced to and fro,—
Promised never to ride on another bronco.
He made me some presents, among them a ring;
The return that I made him was a far better thing;
'T was a young maiden's heart, I'd have you all know
He'd won it by riding his bucking bronco.

Now, all you young maidens, where'er you reside,
Beware of the cowboy who swings the rawhide,
He'll court you and pet you and leave you and go
In the spring up the trail on his bucking bronco.

B.M. BOWER

Like many women writers at the end of the nineteenth and beginning of the twentieth century, Bertha Muzzy Sinclair wrote under an assumed name: B.M. Bower. The initials concealed her gender at a time when it was not acceptable for women to be published writers. Sinclair was raised in Montana, she never fully understood the realities of the American frontier and barely acknowledged ranch women of the West. Her heroines were almost always beautiful young women from the eastern United States, or they had been educated at eastern schools. The plots were invariably a simplistic mix of adventures—rustlers captured or a range feud intertwined with a predictable romance. The style was light, often humorous. Sinclair's novels have managed to stay on the library shelves for almost one hundred years. She intended her stories for adult audiences, but by midcentury they became more popular among young adults. "Love Finds Its Hour" is the last chapter of her first and best-known novel, Chip of the Flying U.

Love Finds Its Hour

"BAY DENVER'S BROKE OUT UH THE LITTLE PASTURE," announced the Old Man, putting his head in at the door of the blacksmith shop where Chip was hammering gayly upon a bent branding iron, for want of a better way to kill time and give vent to his surplus energy. "I wish you'd saddle up an' go after him, Chip, if yuh can. I just seen him takin' down the coulee trail like a scared coyote."

"Sure, I'll go. Darn that old villain, he'd jump a fence forty feet high if he took a notion that way." Chip threw down the hammer and reached for his coat.

"I guess the fence must be down som'ers. I'll go take a look. Say! Dell ain't come back from Denson's yit. Yuh want t' watch out Denver don't meet her—he'd scare the liver out uh her."

Chip was well aware that the Little Doctor had not returned from Denson's where she had been summoned to attend one of the children, who had run a rusty nail into her foot. She had gone alone, for Dr. Cecil was learning to make bread, and had refused to budge from the kitchen till her first batch was safely baked.

Chip limped hurriedly to the corral, and two minutes later was clattering down the coulee upon Blazes, after the runaway.

Denver was a beautiful bay stallion, the pride and terror of the ranch. He was noted for his speed and his vindictive hatred of the more plebian horses, scarcely one of which but had, at sometime, felt his teeth in their flesh—and he was hated and feared by them all.

He stopped at the place where the trail forked, tossed his crinkly mane triumphantly and looked back. Freedom was sweet to him—sweet as it was rare. His world was a roomy box stall with a small, high corral adjoining it for exercise, with an occasional day in the little pasture as a great treat. Two miles was a long, long way from home, it seemed to him. He watched the hill behind a moment, threw up his head and trotted off up the trail to Denson's.

Chip, galloping madly, caught a glimpse of the fugitive a mile away, set his teeth together, and swung Blazes sharply off the trail into a bypath which intersected the road further on. He hoped the Little Doctor was safe at Denson's, but at that very moment he saw her ride slowly over a distant ridge.

Now there was a race; Denver, cantering gleefully down the trail, Chip spurring desperately across the prairie.

The Little Doctor had disappeared into a hollow with Concho pacing slowly, half asleep, the reins drooping low on his neck. The Little Doctor loved to dream along the road, and Concho had learned to do likewise—and to enjoy it very much.

At the crest of the next hill she looked up, saw herself the apex of a rapidly shortening triangle, and grasped instantly the situation; she had peeped admiringly and fearsomely between the stout rails of the little, round corral too often not to know Denver when she saw him, and in a panic turned from the trail toward Chip. Concho was rudely awakened by a stinging blow from her whip—a blow which filled him with astonishment and reproach. He laid back his ears and galloped angrily—not in the path—the Little Doctor was too frightened for that—but straight as a hawk would fly. Denver, marking Concho for his prey and not to be easily cheated, turned and followed.

Chip swore inwardly and kept straight ahead, leaving the path himself to do so. He knew a deep washout lay now between himself and the Little Doctor, and his only hope was to get within speaking distance before she was overtaken.

Concho fled to the very brink of the washout and stopped so suddenly that his forefeet plowed a furrow in the grass, and the Little Doctor came near going clean over his head. She recovered her balance, and cast a frightened glance over her shoulder; Denver was rushing down upon them like an express train.

"Get off—your—*h-o-r-s-e!*" shouted Chip, making a trumpet of his hands. "Fight Denver off—with—your whip!"

The last command the Little Doctor did not hear distinctly. The first she made haste to obey. Throwing herself from the saddle, she slid precipitately into the washout just as Denver thundered up, snorting a challenge. Concho, scared out of his wits, turned and tore off down the washout, whipped around the end of it and made for home, his enemy at his heels and Chip after the two of them, leaning low over his horse as Blazes, catching the excitement and urged by the spurs, ran like an antelope.

The Little Doctor, climbing the steep bank to level ground, gazed after the fleeing group with consternation. Here was she a long four miles from home—five, if she followed the windings of the trail—and it looked very much as if her two feet must take her there. The prospect was not an enlivening one, but she started off across the prairie very philosophically at first, very dejectedly later on, and very angrily at last. The sun was scorching, and it was dinner time, and she was hungry, and hot, and tired, and—"mad." She did not bless her rescuer; she heaped maledictions upon his head—wild ones at first, but growing perceptibly more forcible and less genteel as the way grew rougher, and her feet grew wearier, and her stomach emptier. Then, as if her troubles were all to come in a lump—as they have a way of doing—she stepped squarely into a bunch of "pincushion" cactus.

"I just *hate* Montana!" she burst out, vehemently, blinking back some tears. "I don't care if Cecil did just come day before yesterday—I shall pack up and go back home. She can stay if she wants to, but I won't live here another day. I hate Chip Bennett, too, and I'll tell him so if I ever get home. I don't know what J.G.'s thinking of, to live in such a God-forgotten hole, where there's nothing but miles upon miles of cactuses—" The downfall of Eastern up-bringing! To deliberately say "cactuses"—but the provocation was great, I admit. If any man doubts, let him tread thin-shod upon a healthy little "pincushion" and be convinced. I think he will confess that "cactuses" is an exceedingly conservative epithet, and all too mild for the occasion.

Half an hour later, Chip, leading Concho by the bridle rein, rode over the brow of a hill, and came suddenly upon the Little Doctor, sitting disconsolately upon a rock. She had one shoe off, and was striving petulantly to extract a cactus thorn from the leather with a hat pin. Chip rode close and stopped, regarding her with satisfaction from the saddle. It was the first time he had succeeded in finding the Little Doctor alone since the arrival of Dr. Cecil Granthum—God bless her!

"Hello! What are you trying to do?"

No answer. The Little Doctor refused even to lift her lashes, which were wet and clung together in little groups of two or three. Chip also observed that there were suggestive streaks upon her cheeks and not a sign of a dimple anywhere. He lifted one leg over the horn of the saddle to ease his ankle, which still pained him a little after the ride, and watched her a moment.

"What's the matter, Doctor? Step on a cactus?"

"Oh, no," snapped the Doctor in a tone to take one's head off, " I didn't step on a cactus—I just walked all over acres and acres of them!"

There was a suspicious gurgle from somewhere. The Little Doctor looked up.

"Don't hesitate to laugh, Mr. Bennett, if you happen to feel that way!"

Mr. Bennett very evidently felt that way. He rocked in the saddle, and shouted with laughter. The Little Doctor stood this for as much as a minute.

"Oh, no doubt it's very funny to set me afoot away off from everywhere—" Her voice quivered and broke from self-pity; her head bent lower over her shoe.

Chip made haste to stifle his mirth, in fear that she was going to cry. He couldn't have endured that. He reached for his tobacco and began to make a cigarette.

"*I* didn't set you afoot," he said. "That was a bad break you made yourself. Why didn't you do as I told you—hang to the bridle and fight Denver off with your whip? You had one."

"Yes—and let him gnaw me!"

Chip gurgled again and drew the tobacco sack shut with his teeth. "He wouldn't 'gnaw' you—he wouldn't have come near you. He's whip trained. And I'd have been there myself in another minute."

"I didn't want you there! And I don't pretend to be a horsetrainer, Mr. Bennett. There's several things about your old ranch life that I don't know—and I don't want to know! I'm going back to Ohio tomorrow, so there!"

"Yes?" He drew a match sharply along his stamped saddle skirt and applied it to the cigarette, pinched out the blaze with extreme care, and tossed the match-end facetitiously against Concho's nose. He did not seem particularly alarmed at her threat—or, perhaps, he did not care. The Little Doctor prodded savagely at her shoe, too angry to see the thorn, and Chip drove another nail into his coffin with apparent relish, and watched her. After a little while, he slid to the ground and limped over to her.

"Here, give me that shoe; you'll have it all picked to pieces and not get the thorn, either. Where is it?"

"*It!*" sniffed the Little Doctor, surrendering the shoe with hypocritical reluctance. "It? There's a dozen, at the very least!"

Chip emptied his lungs of smoke, and turned the shoe in his hands.

"Oh, I guess not—there isn't room in this little bit of leather for a dozen. Two would be crowded."

"I detest flattery above all things!" But, being a woman, the brow of the Little Doctor cleared perceptibly.

"Yes? You're just like me in that respect. I love the truth."

Thinking of Dr. Cecil, the Little Doctor grew guiltily red. But she had never said Cecil was a man, she reflected, with what comfort she could. The boys, like Dunk, had simply made the mistake of taking too much for granted.

Chip opened the smallest blade of his knife deliberately, sat down upon a neighboring rock and finished his cigarette, still turning the shoe reflectively—and caressingly—in his hand.

"I'd smile to see the Countess try to put that shoe on," he remarked, holding the cigarette in some mysterious manner on his lip. "I'll bet she couldn't get one toe in it."

"I don't see that it matters, whether she could or not," snapped the Little Doctor. "For goodness sake, hurry!"

"You're pretty mad, aren't you?" inquired he, shoving his hat back off his forehead, and looking at her as though he enjoyed doing so.

"Do I look mad?" asked she, tartly.

"I'd tell a man you do!"

"Well—my appearance doesn't half express the state of my mind!"

"Your mind must be in awful state."

"It is."

Two minutes passed silently.

"Dr. Cecil's bread is done—she gave me a slice as big as your hat, with butter and jelly on it. It was out of sight."

"The Little Doctor groaned, and rallied.

"Butter and jelly on my hat, did you say?"

"Not on your hat—on the bread. I ate it coming back down the coulee—and I sure had my hands full, leading Concho, too."

The Little Doctor held back the question trembling on her hungry, parched lips as long as she could, but it would come.

"Was it good?"

"I'd tell a man!" Chip said, briefly and eloquently.

The Little Doctor sighed.

"Dr. Cecil Granthum's a mighty good fellow—I'm stuck on him

myself—and if I haven't got the symptoms sized up wrong the Old Man's *going* to be."

"That's all the good it will do him. Cecil and I are going somewhere and practice medicine together—and we aren't either of us going to get married, ever!"

"Have you got the papers for that?" grinned Chip, utterly unmoved.

"I have my license, " said the Little Doctor, coldly.

"You're ahead of me there, for I haven't—yet. I can soon get one, though."

"I wish to goodness you'd hurry up with that shoe! I'm half starved."

"Well, show me a dimple and you can have it. My, you are cranky!"

The Little Doctor showed him two, and Chip laid the shoe in her lap—after he had surprised himself, and the doctor, by planting a daring little kiss upon the toe.

"The idea!" exclaimed she, with a feeble show of indignation, and slipping her foot hurriedly into its orthodox covering. Feeling his inscrutable, hazel eyes upon her, she blushed uncomfortably and fumbled the laces.

"You better let me lace that shoe—you won't have it done in a thousand years, at that gait."

"If you're in a hurry," said she, without looking at him," you can ride on ahead. It would please me better if your did."

"Yes? You've been pleased all summer—at my expense. I'm going to please myself, this time. It's my deal, Little Doctor. Do you want to know what's trumps?"

"No, I don't!" Still without looking at him, she tied her shoelaces with an impatient twitch that came near breaking them, and walked haughtily to where Concho stood dutifully waiting. With an impulsive movement, she threw her arms around his neck and hid her hot face against his scanty mane.

A pair of arms clad in pink-and-white striped sleeves went suddenly about her. Her clasp on Concho loosened and she threw back her head, startled—to be still more startled at the touch of lips that were curved and thin and masterful. The arms whirled her about and held her against a heart which her trained senses knew at once was beating very irregularly.

"You—you ought to be ashamed!" she asserted feebly, at last.

"I'm not, though." The arms tightened their clasp a little.

"You—you don't *seem* to be," admitted the Little Doctor, meekly.

For answer he kissed her hungrily—not once, but many times.

"Aren't you going to let me go?" she demanded, afterward, but very faintly.

"No," said he, boldly. "I'm going to keep you—always." There was conviction in the tone.

She stood silent a minute, listening to his heart and her own, and digesting this bit of news.

"Are you—quite sure about—that?" she asked at length.

"I'd tell a man! Unless"—he held her off and looked at her—"you don't like me. But you do, don't you?" His eyes were searching her face.

The Little Doctor struggled to release herself from the arms which held her unyieldingly and tenderly. Failing this, she raised her eyes to the white silk handkerchief knotted around his throat; to the chin; to the lips, wistful with their well defined curve; to the eyes, where they lingered shyly for a moment, and then looked away to the horizon.

"Don't you like me? Say!" He gave her a gentle shake.

"Ye—er—it doesn't seem to matter, whether I do or not," she retorted with growing spirit—witness the dimple dodging into her cheek.

"Yes, it does—it matters a whole heap You've dealt me misery ever since I first set eyes on you—and I believe, on my soul, you liked to watch me squirm! But you do like me, don't you?"

"I—I'd tell a man!" said she, and immediately hid a very red face from sight of him.

Concho turned his head and gazed wonderingly upon the two. What amazed him was to see Chip kissing his mistress again and again, and to hear the idolatrous tone in which he was saying "*My Little Doctor!*"

ELINORE PRUITT STEWART

Elinore Pruitt Stewart is best known for her letters, which were originally published between 1909 and 1933. They are a series of adventures that reveal her life as a homesteader in a remote part of Wyoming. Her indomitable spirit led her to manage her own small ranch, but faced with extreme poverty, she turned to writing a series of letters for various eastern magazines to supplement her meager income. "Snow: An Adventure of the Woman Homesteader" was first published by the Atlantic Monthly *in December 1923.*

Snow: An Adventure of the Woman Homesteader

My Dear Friend,—

When Mr. Stewart asked me to behave myself while he was gone, I promised. I really thought I should. He cautioned me over and over not to go on any wild-goose chase and get lost or frozen, and I had no desire to do so.

But no objections have ever been made to my helping out when a neighbor is in need; so when young Melroy Luke came for me very early one bitter morning I felt no guilt in going. It was not until we were well on the way that he told me he had moved and now lived ten miles farther on. 'I thought maybe you would not want to go so far to help and we need you so!' he pleaded. Any twinge of anger that might have stirred me left when I saw the concern and anxiety on his boyish face. We made our way with what grace we could; but grace is a scarce quality on such a ride. I had a very likely tale outlined to tell Dad to account for the toes I felt sure would be missing when all that seemed frozen were off.

At last the frozen miles were over, and we took our cold stiffened bodies into a cabin in a remote cañon that I had never seen before. Another neighbor was with young Mrs. Luke, and later the baby came. The neighbor had already been gone from her home longer than she should have stayed; so next morning she left, saying she would send someone to stay on. So I stayed that day and the next. I knew that at my home bread would be out, and the boys would be with the men who were feeding for us, so I felt that I must go.

Luke could not leave his wife, but he said the way was perfectly plain. 'Just you follow the telephone poles after you get over the first hogback. They are right along the mail road to Linwood, and you have only to go west along the road to Burntfork. You can't possibly miss the road, and if you did get off there are plenty of houses along to set you right.'

We had taken a short cut in going, and I had not noticed the way at all; it was so cold that I had kept my face as much covered as possible. I set out with all confidence. I should not have minded at all if the weather had been pleasant, but it was still very cold, with a veil of frost hanging over the mountain. A sudden gust of wind swept over the bare mountain, carrying with it a sheet of snow. My horse and I were enveloped in a whirling, driving mist of snow. It was strangling, smothering. It penetrated my clothing; it drove down my back, I gasped for breath. It struck us from all points at once. In a flash it was gone. I turned to look as the flying mist of snow swept on down the valley. 'If it were not broad daylight, the sun shining brightly, I should think that a snow-wraith, a ghost of a storm long dead. But no respectable ghost would be so unconventional as to stir out in the day!' Almost before I had so assured myself, another ghost of a storm assailed me. I was not alarmed, I had been to Linwood, to Manilla; I knew the road once I reached it. The sun shone with a gleaming lustre owing to the flying snow. I don't know how I could have been so careless, but I rode along enjoying the scene, the snow-wraiths traveling down the valley.

I had been conscious of a muffled roar for some time—wind in the mountains; but the full meaning did not strike me until suddenly the sun went out; I was caught in a whirling, blinding gust that did not pass on down the valley. I could not force my horse against the storm; he turned tail to whatever direction the capricious wind came from, and in so doing must have turned round many times.

I saw to my dismay that the snow now flying was not old snow. A storm was now on that might last for hours, days even. To remain there meant to freeze, so I urged my horse down the hill, intending to go back to Luke's. When we reached the bottom, I could see in patches where the snow had blown off what seemed to be an old road; better yet, in a lull I saw a telephone pole. I started to follow that, but the storm increased and I could not see a yard ahead of me and it was growing darker every minute. I believe that I am as courageous as most women, but at last I almost gave up. Wherever my clothes touched me I was wet with snow. All outside clothes were frozen stiff. I hadn't an idea where I was and I could not force my horse to move when the wind bore down upon us. I was so tired and sleepy that I began to wonder dully what would happen if I never came home. I felt a decided relief that Jerrine was safe in Boulder, but, foolish as it sounds, my chief worry was that the children might not let Whiskers, my cat, sleep in the house.

I don't know how long it was, but it seemed ages that we plodded on. I must have been half asleep when something brushed my head and at the same time scratched my leg. I was stiff with the cold and my frozen garments, so I tumbled off. For a moment I lay in delicious drowsiness, and then I remembered that freezing people always go to sleep. I bestirred myself with whatever energy is possible in a half-frozen state. To my surprise I saw the roof of a shed. We had come back to Luke's, I supposed, so I called and called for help, but only the roar of the storm replied.

My horse went to the shed, and I tried to follow, but I was a long time getting there. However, I made it; but my gloves were so frozen that I couldn't unsaddle, couldn't even take the bridle off. I went to the door and called, but no answer. I saw a cabin only a few feet away and, filled with anger, I staggered out to it. The storm hurled me down, but I crawled to the door and pounded. I couldn't lift the latch, but I kicked and pounded till the door opened and I fell into the room. A rat scampered across the floor but there was no one else there.

I closed the door and leaned against the wall, panting and sobbing, with a sharp pain in my throat and in my chest. A trickle of water crept down my face. The snow in my hair had begun to melt. I walked over to a stove in the corner. It was rusted with disuse. I began a search for matches, but there were none to be found. All this was my salvation, had I but known it. If I had been able to get a fire at once, I might have lost some portion of my hands, face, or feet.

Failing to find matches, I decided to go to bed. I couldn't get in with my frozen clothes and I couldn't get the clothes off. I began another search for matches, and after I had looked the cabin over again I remembered that I wore Clyde's macakanaw. (That is wrong I know, but you will understand.) Clyde never is without matches; so, after getting my now sodden gloves off, I began to search the inside pockets of the coat. I was rewarded with two matches and a piece. I had little use of my hands, so I wasted the two matches, and was about to weep when I remembered a piece of candle that the rats had partly eaten. I waited as long as I dared, slapping and rubbing my numb hands trying to get them so they would be a little more steady.

At last I succeeded in getting the candle lighted. In a few minutes I had a roaring fire, and was foolish enough to get as close to it as I could. As my fingers limbered, I removed my frozen skirts and hung them to thaw and dry. When I began to thaw, I was in agony. Of all the itching, burning, and stinging! I suffered terribly every time I went near the fire. Some snow had blown in through the ill-fitted window-frame, and by accident I touched it. At once a soothing relief came over that part of my arm. I had begun to think a little more rationally now, so I took great handfuls of the snow and rubbed myself over and over. At last, after what seemed hours of work, I was able to move about in moderate comfort as long as I stayed away from the fire. I didn't dare let the fire go out; there were no more matches. It was long since dark, so I filled the stove with the largest pieces of wood, closed all the drafts, and made the bed so as to be sure that not a rat shared it, then crept into bed, thanking God and my unknown benefactor for plenty of dry wood.

My bed was dusty and smelled of rats, but was not otherwise uncomfortable. I had not expected to go to sleep; I thought I should get up at times and replenish my fire; but when I awoke it was morning, and the sullen, gray light told that the storm was still on. I was tender and sore, but not so badly off as I had expected to be. Enough of my fire remained for me to kindle. I soon had a roaring fire; then I thought I had better see how my horse had fared.

The snow was waist-deep and still falling steadily. I made my way to the shed, but was unable to get in, the snow had drifted around it so; but I peeped in through a crack, and saw that Brownie was very comfortable indeed. He had rubbed the bridle off and helped himself to someone's oats which were stacked in one end of the shed. I knew that if he were very thirsty he would lick the snow that had drifted in, so I went to the house with a clear conscience.

It is strange that when we are under great stress we are mindful of small comforts, but when we are not under stress we are more mindful of small discomforts. When I was really in danger of death, I was thankful even to fall from the horse; but now I began to fret because I could see no place to get water. When I was safe in the cabin once more, I remembered that I had had nothing to eat since breakfast the morning before; and as I have never cared for much breakfast the memory was not very filling. I was hungry. A ransacking of the shelves revealed no food, and the cupboard might have been Old Mother Hubbard's.

But I found plenty to divert me. By the fuller light of day I saw a card tacked over a shelf. 'Welcome, friend. You are at home. Help yourself. All I have to eat is in the cellar. I may never need. I am off to war. EMIL GENSALEN.' But where was the cellar? The drifting snow covered the ground so that none could be seen out of doors, even if by any chance any of the mentioned refreshments remained. I knew that I could never find the cellar, so I sat down to read a battered magazine that the rats had spared. I guess they were not literary, or else they preferred the *Atlantic Monthly.* Certainly almost all of an old copy of *Everybody's* was there to help.

I read, I viewed the storm, I wondered what it was all for. I explored the cabin and wondered about the friendly Emil. I had not known any Emil. But I reflected that it was not necessary for me to know him for him to exist. After a while I noticed a ring in the floor. A ring meant a trapdoor. Of course! The cellar. How bright I felt! Ring in the floor. Cellar. Food. Who says a woman is not logical? Who says we cannot make deductions!

The door yielded unwillingly and I was half afraid to descend the mouldy steps; but I did and saw a neat set of shelves almost empty, but with enough cans to awaken hope in my stomach. The labels had long ago given up the fight with rust and mould. I selected two cans and sought the upper world. I have known for a long time that breakfast need not begin with an iced melon or a grapefruit. I have even suspected that oatmeal and toast might be omitted, but I should hardly have supposed that coffee was superfluous. I found no coffee, but I found a hatchet with which I opened my cans, one of corn and one of Vienna sausage. The frying pan was ratty; I had to take time to scrub it out with snow, but I did not dally at my work, I can tell you.

I expect that you have had better breakfasts, but I never did. Even the thought of ptomaine did not scare me. But, true to my former assertion, no sooner was I comfortable than I thought of four more discomforts. How long would I have to stay? What if the wood gave out? Maybe I was snowed in. Would anyone ever think to look for me? Would they be in time? I knew perfectly well that the children would be cared for. The two men would be there and both men could cook. I was restless as a mule colt being weaned. I tried to see out of the window, to see if the snow was too deep for me to try. As I leaned against the rough casing, I saw some written words.

'When you make any charge against Providence, consider, and you will learn that the thing has happened according to reason.'

'Well sang the Hebrew Psalmist. "If I take the wings of the morning and dwell in the uttermost parts of the universe, God is there."'

'Nothing happens to any man which he is not formed by nature to bear.'

Every bit of available surface was covered with such writings, English on one facing and some other language on the other. The door the same way. I hunted for a pencil, a piece of paper, to copy it down, but none could be found. The three I send you seemed to fit my case so exactly that I memorized them. All that day I tried to picture to myself what Emil would be like. Not old, else he could not go to war. Not young, for no young man is wise. Kind and learned. That of course. An ideal host, for he attended to his guest's needs even when he was no one knew where. I was astonished to see dusk gathering. I knew that I should lack courage to go into the cellar after dark, so I brought up another can. I tried again to get to Brownie, but could not get in.

As night settled, the wind rose, and such a tumult as was outside! I ate a can of tomatoes and banked my fire and went to bed. Except for being dreadfully sore, I seemed to be none the worse for wear. I lay in the dark listening to the unearthly noises and thinking of the absent philosopher whose guest I was. . . .

. . . I must stop this long jumble. You won't love me pretty soon. Perhaps I shall never get to mail this to you. The postmaster has had no envelopes for a month or more. That happens often. With much love to you and tenderest remembrance of the day.

Your friend,
Elinore P. Stewart

DOROTHY M. JOHNSON

Dorothy M. Johnson grew up in Whitefish, Montana. She developed close friendships with ranchers and cowboys, and wrote many short stories that were published in such popular magazines as The Saturday Evening Post. *Several of her stories, including "The Man Who Shot Liberty Valance," "A Man Called Horse" and "The Hanging Tree," were made into movies. Johnson was always concerned with "righting" the western mythology by presenting the realities of the western frontier. Many of her stories, including "The Man Who Shot Liberty Valance," were published in* Flames on the Frontier.

The Man Who Shot Liberty Valance

Bert Barricune died in 1910. Not more than a dozen persons showed up for his funeral. Among them was an earnest young reporter who hoped for a human-interest story; there were legends that the old man had been something of a gunfighter in the early days. A few aging men tiptoed in, singly or in pairs, scowling and edgy, clutching their battered hats—men who had been Bert's companions at drinking or penny ante while the world passed them by. One woman came, wearing a heavy veil that concealed her face. White and yellow streaks showed in her black-dyed hair. The reporter made a mental note: Old friend from the old District. But no story there—can't mention that.

One by one they filed past the casket, looking into the still face of old Bert Barricune, who had been nobody. His stubbly hair was white, and his lined face was as empty in death as his life had been. But death had added dignity.

One great spray of flowers spread behind the casket. The card read, "Senator and Mrs. Ransome Foster." There were no other flowers except, almost unnoticed, a few pale, leafless, pink and yellow blossoms scattered on the carpeted step. The reporter, squinting, finally identified them: son of a gun! Blossoms of the prickly pear. Cactus flowers. Seems suitable for the old man—flowers that grow on prairie wasteland. Well, they're free if you want to pick 'em, and Barricune's friends don't look prosperous. But how come the Senator sends a bouquet?

There was a delay, and the funeral director fidgeted a little, waiting. The reporter sat up straighter when he saw the last two mourners enter.

Senator Foster—sure, there's the crippled arm—and that must be his wife. Congress is still in session; he came all the way from Washington. Why would he bother, for an old wreck like Bert Barricune?

After the funeral was decently over, the reporter asked him. The Senator almost told the truth, but he caught himself in time. He said, "Bert Barricune was my friend for more than thirty years."

He could not give the true answer: He was my enemy, he was my conscience; he made me whatever I am.

Ransome Foster had been in the Territory for seven months when he ran into Liberty Valance. He had been afoot on the prairie for two days when he met Bert Barricune. Up to that time, Ranse Foster had been nobody in particular—a dude from the East, quietly inquisitive, moving from one shack town to another; just another tenderfoot with his own reasons for being there and no aim in life at all.

When Barricune found him on the prairie, Foster was indeed a tenderfoot. In his boots there was a warm, damp squidging where his feet had blistered, and the blisters had broken to bleed. He was bruised, sunburned, and filthy. He had been crawling, but when he saw Barricune riding toward him, he sat up. He had no horse, no saddle and, by that time, no pride.

Barricune looked down at him, not saying anything. Finally Ranse Foster asked, "Water?"

Barricune shook his head. "I don't carry none, but we can go where it is."

He stepped down from the saddle, a casual Samaritan, and with one heave pulled Foster upright.

"Git you in the saddle, can you stay there?" he inquired.

"If I can't," Foster answered through swollen lips, "shoot me." Bert said amiably, "All right," and pulled the horse around. By twisting its ear, he held the animal quiet long enough to help the anguished stranger to the saddle. Then, on foot and like any cowboy Bert Barricune hated walking—he led the horse five miles to the river. He let Foster lie where he fell in the cottonwood grove and brought him a hat full of water.

After that, Foster made three attempts to stand up. After the third failure, Barricune asked, grinning, "Want me to shoot you after all?"

"No," Foster answered. "There's something I want to do first."

Barricune looked at the bruises and commented, "Well, I should think so." He got on his horse and rode away. After an hour he returned with bedding and grub and asked, "Ain't you dead yet?"

The bruised and battered man opened his uninjured eye and said, "Not yet, but soon." Bert was amused. He brought a bucket of water and set up camp—a bedroll on a tarp, an armload of wood for a fire. He crouched on his heels while the tenderfoot, with cautious movements that told of pain, got his clothes off and splashed water on his body. No gunshot wounds, Barricune observed, but marks of kicks, and a couple that must have been made with a quirt.

After a while he asked, not inquisitively, but as one who has a right to know how matters stood, "Anybody looking for you?"

Foster rubbed dust from his clothes, being too full of pain to shake them.

"No," he said. "But I'm looking for somebody."

"I ain't going to help you look," Bert informed him. "Town's over that way, two miles, when you get ready to come. Cache the stuff when you leave. I'll pick it up."

Three days later they met in the town marshal's office. They glanced at each other but did not speak. This time it was Bert Barricune who was bruised, though not much. The marshal was just letting him out of the one-cell jail when Foster limped into the office. Nobody said anything until Barricune, blinking and walking not quite steadily, had left. Foster saw him stop in front of the next building to speak to a girl. They walked away together, and it looked as if the young man were being scolded.

The marshal cleared his throat. "You wanted something, Mister?" Foster answered, "Three men set me afoot on the prairie. Is that an offense against the law around here?"

The marshal eased himself and his stomach into a chair and frowned judiciously. "It ain't customary," he admitted. "Who was they?"

"The boss was a big man with black hair, dark eyes, and two gold teeth in front. The other two—"

"I know. Liberty Valance and a couple of his boys. Just what's your complaint, now?" Foster began to understand that no help was going to come from the marshal.

"They rob you?" the marshal asked.

"They didn't search me."

"Take your gun?"

"I didn't have one."

"Steal your horse?"

"Gave him a crack with a quirt, and he left."

"Saddle on him."

"No. I left it out there."

The marshal shook his head. "Can't see you got any legal complaint," he said with relief. "Where was this?"

"On a road in the woods, by a creek. Two days' walk from here."

The marshal got to his feet. "You don't even know what jurisdiction it was in. They knocked you around; well, that could happen. Man gets in a fight—could happen to anybody."

Foster said dryly, "Thanks a lot."

The marshal stopped him as he reached the door. "There's a reward for Liberty Valance."

"I still haven't got a gun," Foster said. "Does he come here often?"

"Nope. Nothing he'd want in Twotrees. Hard man to find." The marshal looked Foster up and down. "He won't come after you here." It was as if he had added, Sonny! "Beat you up once, he won't come again for that."

And I, Foster realized, am not man enough to go after him.

"Fact is," the marshal added, "I can't think of any bait that would bring him in. Pretty quiet here. Yes sir." He put his thumbs in his galluses and looked out the window, taking credit for the quietness.

Bait, Foster thought. He went out thinking about it. For the first time in a couple of years he had an ambition—not a laudable one, but something to aim at. He was going to be the bait for Liberty Valance and, as far as he could be, the trap as well.

At the Elite Cafe he stood meekly in the doorway, hat in hand, like a man who expects and deserves to be refused anything he might ask for. Clearing his throat, he asked, "Could I work for a meal?"

The girl who was filling sugar bowls looked up and pitied him. "Why, I should think so. Mr. Anderson!" She was the girl who had walked away with Barricune, scolding him.

The proprietor came from the kitchen, and Ranse Foster repeated his question, cringing, but with a suggestion of a sneer.

"Go around back and split some wood," Anderson answered, turning back to the kitchen.

"He could just as well eat first," the waitress suggested. "I'll dish up some stew to begin with."

Ranse ate fast, as if he expected the plate to be snatched away. He knew the girl glanced at him several times, and he hated her for it. He had not counted on anyone's pitying him in his new role of sneering humility, but he knew he might as well get used to it.

When she brought his pie, she said, "If you was looking for a job . . ."

He forced himself to look at her suspiciously. "Yes?"

"You could try the Prairie Belle. I heard they needed a swamper."

Bert Barricune, riding out to the river camp for his bedroll, hardly knew the man he met there. Ranse Foster was haughty, condescending, and cringing all at once. He spoke with a faint sneer, and stood as if he expected to be kicked.

"I assumed you'd be back for your belongings," he said. "I realized that you would change your mind."

Barricune, strapping up his bedroll, looked blank. "Never changed it," he disagreed. "Doing just what I planned. I never give you my bedroll."

"Of course not, of course not," the new Ranse Foster agreed with sneering humility. "It's yours. You have every right to reclaim it."

Barricune looked at him narrowly and hoisted the bedroll to sling it up behind his saddle. "I should have left you for the buzzards," he remarked.

Foster agreed, with a smile that should have got him a fist in the teeth. "Thank you, my friend," he said with no gratitude. "Thank you for all your kindness, which I have done nothing to deserve and shall do nothing to repay."

Barricune rode off, scowling, with the memory of his good deed irritating him like lice. The new Foster followed, far behind, on foot.

Sometimes in later life Ranse Foster thought of the several men he had been through the years. He did not admire any of them very much. He was by no means ashamed of the man he finally became, except that he owed too much to other people. One man he had been when he was young, a serious student, gullible and quick-tempered. Another man had been reckless and without an aim; he went West, with two thousand dollars of his own, after a quarrel with the executor of his father's estate. That man did not last long. Liberty Valance had whipped him with a quirt and kicked him into unconsciousness, for no reason except that Liberty, meeting him and knowing him for a tenderfoot, was able to do so. That man died on the prairie. After that, there was the man who set out to be the bait that would bring Liberty Valance into Twotrees.

Ranse Foster had never hated anyone before he met Liberty Valance, but Liberty was not the last man he learned to hate. He hated the man he himself had been while he waited to meet Liberty again. The swamper's job at the Prairie Belle was not disgraceful until Ranse Foster made it so. When he swept floors, he was so obviously contemptuous of the work and of himself for doing it that other men saw him as contemptible. He watched the customers with a curled lip as if they were beneath him. But when a poker player threw a white chip on the floor, the swamper looked at him with half-veiled hatred—and picked up the chip. They talked about him at the Prairie Belle, because he could not be ignored.

At the end of the first month, he bought a Colt .45 from a drunken cowboy who needed money worse than he needed two guns. After that, Ranse went without part of his sleep in order to walk out, seven mornings a week, to where his first camp had been and practice target shooting. And the second time he overslept from exhaustion, Joe Mosten of the Prairie Belle fired him.

"Here's your pay,' Joe growled, and dropped the money on the floor.

A week passed before he got another job. He ate his meals frugally in the Elite Cafe and let himself be seen stealing scraps off plates that other diners had left. Lillian, the older of the two waitresses, yelled her disgust, but Hallie, who was young, pitied him.

"Come to the back door when it's dark," she murmured, "and I'll give you a bite. There's plenty to spare."

The second evening he went to the back door, Bert Barricune was there ahead of him. He said gently, "Hallie is my girl."

"No offense intended," Foster answered. "The young lady offered me food, and I have come to get it."

"A dog eats where it can," young Barricune drawled.

Ranse's muscles tensed and rage mounted in his throat, but he caught himself in time and shrugged. Bert said something then that scared him: "If you wanted to get talked about, it's working fine. They're talking clean over in Dunbar."

"What they do or say in Dunbar," Foster answered, "is nothing to me."

"It's where Liberty Valance hangs out," the other man said casually. "In case you care."

Ranse almost confided then, but instead said stiffly, "I do not quite appreciate your strange interest in my affairs."

Barricune pushed back his hat and scratched his head. "I don't understand it myself. But leave my girl alone."

"As charming as Miss Hallie may be," Ranse told him, "I am interested only in keeping my stomach filled."

"Then why don't you work for a living? The clerk at Dowitts' quit this afternoon."

Jake Dowitt hired him as a clerk because nobody else wanted the job.

"Read and write, do you?" Dowitt asked. "Work with figures?" Foster drew himself up. "Sir, whatever may be said against me, I believe I may lay claim to being a scholar. That much I claim, if nothing more. I have read law."

"Maybe the job ain't good enough for you," Dowitt suggested. Foster became humble again. "Any job is good enough for me. I will also sweep the floor."

"You will also keep up the fire in the stove," Dowitt told him. "Seven in the morning till nine at night. Got a place to live?"

"I sleep in the livery stable in return for keeping it shoveled out."

Dowitt had intended to house his clerk in a small room over the store, but he changed his mind. "Got a shed out back you can bunk in," he offered. "You'll have to clean it out first. Used to keep chickens there."

"There is one thing," Foster said. "I want two half days off a week." Dowitt looked over the top of his spectacles. "Now what would you do with time off? Never mind. You can have it—for less pay. I give you a discount on what you buy in the store."

The only purchase Foster made consisted of four boxes of cartridges a week.

In the store, he weighed salt pork as if it were low stuff but himself still lower, humbly measured lengths of dress goods for the women customers. He added vanity to his other unpleasantnesses and let customers discover him combing his hair admiringly before a small mirror. He let himself be seen reading a small black book, which aroused curiosity.

It was while he worked at the store that he started Twotrees' first school. Hallie was responsible for that. Handing him a plate heaped higher than other customers got at the cafe, she said gently, "You're a learned man, they say, Mr. Foster."

With Hallie he could no longer sneer or pretend humility, for

Hallie was herself humble, as well as gentle and kind. He protected himself from her by not speaking unless he had to.

He answered, "I have had advantages, Miss Hallie, before fate brought me here."

"That book you read," she asked wistfully, "what's it about?"

"It was written by a man named Plato," Ranse told her stiffly. "It was written in Greek."

She brought him a cup of coffee, hesitated for a moment, and then asked, "You can read and write American, too, can't you?"

"English, Miss Hallie," he corrected. "English is our mother tongue. I am quite familiar with English."

She put her red hands on the cafe counter. "Mr. Foster," she whispered, "will you teach me to read?"

He was too startled to think of an answer she could not defeat.

"Bert wouldn't like it," he said. "You're a grown woman besides. It wouldn't look right for you to be learning to read now."

She shook her head. "I can't learn any younger." She sighed. "I always wanted to know how to read and write." She walked away toward the kitchen, and Ranse Foster was struck with an emotion he knew he could not afford. He was swept with pity. He called her back.

"Miss Hallie. Not you alone—people would talk about you. But if you brought Bert—"

"Bert can already read some. He don't care about it. But there's some kids in town." Her face was so lighted that Ranse looked away.

He still tried to escape. "Won't you be ashamed, learning with children?"

"Why, I'll be proud to learn any way at all," she said.

He had three little girls, two restless little boys, and Hallie in Twotrees' first school sessions—one hour each afternoon, in Dowitt's storeroom. Dowitt did not dock his pay for the time spent, but he puzzled a great deal. So did the children's parents. The children themselves were puzzled at some of the things he read aloud, but they were patient. After all, lessons lasted only an hour.

"When you are older, you will understand this," he promised, not looking at Hallie, and then he read Shakespeare's sonnet that begins:

No longer mourn for me when I am dead
Than you shall hear the surly sullen bell

and ends:

Do not so much as my poor name rehearse,
But let your love even with my life decay,
Lest the wise world should look into your moan
And mock you with me after I am gone.

Hallie understood the warning, he knew. He read another sonnet, too:

When in disgrace with Fortune and men's eyes,
I all alone beweep my outcast state,

and carefully did not look up at her as he finished it:

For thy sweet love remembered such wealth brings
That then I scorn to change my state with kings.

Her earnestness in learning was distasteful to him—the anxious way she grasped a pencil and formed letters, the little gasp with which she always began to read aloud. Twice he made her cry, but she never missed a lesson.

He wished he had a teacher for his own learning, but he could not trust anyone, and so he did his lessons alone. Bert Barricune caught him at it on one of those free afternoons when Foster, on a horse from the livery stable, had ridden miles out of town to a secluded spot.

Ranse Foster had an empty gun in his hand when Barricune stepped out from behind a sandstone column and remarked, "I've seen better."

Foster whirled, and Barricune added, "I could have been somebody else—and your gun's empty."

"When I see somebody else, it won't be," Foster promised.

"If you'd asked me," Barricune mused, "I could've helped you. But you didn't want no helping. A man shouldn't be ashamed to ask somebody that knows better than him." His gun was suddenly in his hand, and five shots cracked their echoes around the skull-white sandstone pillars. Half an inch above each of five cards that Ranse had tacked to a dead tree, at the level of a man's waist, a splintered hole appeared in the wood. "Didn't want to spoil your targets," Barricune explained.

"I'm not ashamed to ask you," Foster told him angrily, "since you know so much. I shoot straight but slow. I'm asking you now."

Barricune, reloading his gun, shook his head. "It's kind of late for that. I come out to tell you that Liberty Valance is in town. He's interested in the dude that anybody can kick around—this here tenderfoot that boasts how he can read Greek."

"Well," said Foster softly. "Well, so the time has come."

"Don't figure you're riding into town with me," Bert warned.

"You're coming in all by yourself."

Ranse rode into town with his gun belt buckled on. Always before, he had carried it wrapped in a slicker. In town, he allowed himself the luxury of one last vanity. He went to the barbershop, neither sneering nor cringing, and said sharply, "Cut my hair. Short."

The barber was nervous, but he worked understandably fast.

"Thought you was partial to that long wavy hair of yourn," he remarked.

"I don't know why you thought so," Foster said coldly.

Out in the street again, he realized that he did not know how to go about the job. He did not know where Liberty Valance was, and he was determined not to be caught like a rat. He intended to look for Liberty.

Joe Mosten's right-hand man was lounging at the door of the Prairie Belle. He moved over to bar the way.

"Not in there, Foster," he said gently. It was the first time in months that Ranse Foster had heard another man address him respectfully. His presence was recognized—as a menace to the fixtures of the Prairie Belle.

When I die, sometime today, he thought, they won't say I was a coward. They may say I was a damn fool, but I won't care by that time.

"Where is he?" Ranse asked.

"I couldn't tell you that," the man said apologetically. "I'm young and healthy, and where he is is none of my business. Joe'd be obliged if you stay out of the bar, that's all."

Ranse looked across toward Dowitt's store. The padlock was on the door. He glanced north, toward the marshal's office.

"That's closed, too," the saloon man told him courteously. "Marshal was called out of town an hour ago."

Ranse threw back his head and laughed. The sound echoed back from the false-fronted buildings across the street. There was nobody walking in the street; there were not even any horses tied to the hitching racks.

"Send Liberty word," he ordered in the tone of one who has a right to command. "Tell him the tenderfoot wants to see him again."

The saloon man cleared his throat. "Guess it won't be necessary. That's him coming down at the end of the street, wouldn't you say?" Ranse looked, knowing the saloon man was watching him curiously.

"I'd say it is," he agreed. "Yes, I'd say that was Liberty Valance."

"I'll be going inside now," the other man remarked apologetically. "Well, take care of yourself." He was gone without a sound.

This is the classic situation, Ranse realized. Two enemies walking to meet each other along the dusty, waiting street of a western town. What reasons other men have had, I will never know. There are so many things I have never learned! And now there is no time left.

He was an actor who knew the end of the scene but had forgotten the lines and never knew the cue for them. One of us ought to say something, he realized. I should have planned this all out in advance. But all I ever saw was the end of it.

Liberty Valance, burly and broad-shouldered, walked stiff-legged, with his elbows bent.

When he is close enough for me to see whether he is smiling, Ranse Foster thought, somebody's got to speak.

He looked into his own mind and realized, This man is afraid, this Ransome Foster. But nobody else knows it. He walks and is afraid, but he is no coward. Let them remember that. Let Hallie remember that.

Liberty Valance gave the cue. "Looking for me?" he called between his teeth. He was grinning.

Ranse was almost grateful to him; it was as if Liberty had said, The time is now!

"I owe you something," Ranse answered. "I want to pay my debt."

Liberty's hand flashed with his own. The gun in Foster's hand exploded, and so did the whole world.

Two shots to my one, he thought—his last thought for a while.

He looked up at a strange, unsteady ceiling and a face that wavered like a reflection in water. The bed beneath him swung even after he closed his eyes. Far away someone said, "Shove some more cloth in the wound. It slows the bleeding."

He knew with certain agony where the wound was—in his right shoulder. When they touched it, he heard himself cry out.

The face that wavered above him was a new one, Bert Barricune's.

"He's dead," Barricune said.

Foster answered from far away, "I am not."

Barricune said, "I didn't mean you."

Ranse turned his head away from the pain, and the face that had shivered above him before was Hallie's, white and big-eyed. She put a hesitant hand on his, and he was annoyed to see that hers was trembling.

"Are you shaking?" he asked, "because there's blood on my hands?"

"No," she answered. "It's because they might have been getting cold."

He was aware then that other people were in the room; they stirred and moved aside as the doctor entered.

"Maybe you're gonna keep that arm," the doctor told him at last. "But it's never gonna be much use to you."

The trial was held three weeks after the shooting, in the hotel room where Ranse lay in bed. The charge was disturbing the peace; he pleaded guilty and was fined ten dollars.

When the others had gone, he told Bert Barricune, "There was a reward, I heard. That would pay the doctor and the hotel."

"You ain't going to collect it," Bert informed him. "It'd make you too big for your britches." Barricune sat looking at him for a moment and then remarked, "You didn't kill Liberty."

Foster frowned. "They buried him."

"Liberty fired once. You fired once and missed. I fired once, and I don't generally miss. I ain't going to collect the reward, neither. Hallie don't hold with violence."

Foster said thoughtfully, "That was all I had to be proud of."

"You faced him," Barricune said. "You went to meet him. If you got to be proud of something, you can remember that. It's a fact you ain't got much else."

Ranse looked at him with narrowed eyes. "Bert, are you a friend of mine?"

Bert smiled without humor. "You know I ain't. I picked you up off the prairie, but I'd do that for the lowest scum that crawls. I wisht I hadn't."

"Then why—"

Bert looked at the toe of his boot. "Hallie likes you. I'm a friend of Hallie's. That's all I ever will be, long as you're around."

Ranse said, "Then I shot Liberty Valance." That was the nearest he ever dared come to saying "Thank you." And that was when Bert Barricune started being his conscience, his Nemesis, his lifelong enemy and the man who made him great.

"Would she be happy living back East?" Foster asked. "There's money waiting for me there if I go back."

Bert answered, "What do you think?" He stood up and stretched. "You got quite a problem, ain't you? You could solve it easy by just going back alone. There ain't much a man can do here with a crippled arm."

He went out and shut the door behind him.

There is always a way out, Foster thought, if a man wants to take it. Bert had been his way out when he met Liberty on the street of Twotrees. To go home was the way out of this.

I learned to live without pride, he told himself. I could learn to forget about Hallie.

When she came, between the dinner dishes and setting the tables for supper at the cafe, he told her.

She did not cry. Sitting in the chair beside his bed, she winced and jerked one hand in protest when he said, "As soon as I can travel, I'll be going back where I came from."

She did not argue. She said only, "I wish you good luck, Ransome. Bert and me, we'll look after you long as you stay. And remember you after you're gone."

"How will you remember me?" he demanded harshly. As his student she had been humble, but as a woman she had her pride. "Don't ask that," she said, and got up from the chair.

"Hallie, Hallie," he pleaded, "how can I stay? How can I earn a living?"

She said indignantly, as if someone else had insulted him, "Ranse Foster, I just guess you could do anything you wanted to."

"Hallie," he said gently, "sit down."

He never really wanted to be outstanding. He had two aims in life: to make Hallie happy and to keep Bert Barricune out of trouble. He defended Bert on charges ranging from drunkenness to stealing cattle, and Bert served time twice.

Ranse Foster did not want to run for judge, but Bert remarked, "I think Hallie would kind of like it if you was His Honor." Hallie was pleased but not surprised when he was elected. Ranse was surprised but not pleased.

He was not eager to run for the legislature—that was after the territory became a state—but there was Bert Barricune in the background, never urging, never advising, but watching with half-closed, bloodshot eyes. Bert Barricune, who never amounted to anything, but never intruded, was a living, silent reminder of three debts: a hat full of water under the cottonwoods, gunfire in a dusty street, and Hallie, quietly sewing beside a lamp in the parlor. And the Fosters had four sons.

All the things the opposition said about Ranse Foster when he ran for the state legislature were true, except one. He had been a lowly swamper in a frontier saloon; he had been a dead beat, accepting handouts at the alley entrance of a cafe; he had been despicable and despised. But the accusation that lost him the election was false. He had not killed Liberty Valance. He never served in the state legislature.

When there was talk of his running for governor, he refused. Handy Strong, who knew politics, tried to persuade him.

"That shooting, we'll get around that. 'The Honorable Ransome Foster walked down a street in broad daylight to meet an enemy of society. He shot him down in a fair fight, of necessity, the way you'd shoot a mad dog—but Liberty Valance could shoot back, and he did. Ranse Foster carries the mark of that encounter today in a crippled right arm. He is still paying the price for protecting law-abiding citizens. And he was the first teacher west of Rosy Buttes. He served without pay.' You've come a long way, Ranse, and you're going further."

"A long way," Foster agreed, "for a man who never wanted to go anywhere. I don't want to be governor."

When Handy had gone, Bert Barricune sagged in, unwashed, unshaven. He sat down stiffly. At the age of fifty, he was an old man, an unwanted relic of the frontier that was gone, a legacy to more civilized times that had no place for him. He filled his pipe deliberately. After a while he remarked, "The other side is gonna say you ain't fitten to be governor. Because your wife ain't fancy enough. They're gonna say Hallie didn't even learn to read till she was growed up."

Ranse was on his feet, white with fury. "Then I'm going to win this election if it kills me."

"I don't reckon it'll kill you," Bert drawled. "Liberty Valance couldn't."

"I could have got rid of the weight of that affair long ago," Ranse reminded him, "by telling the truth."

"You could yet," Bert answered. "Why don't you?"

Ranse said bitterly, "Because I owe you too much . . . I don't think Hallie wants to be the governor's lady. She's shy."

"Hallie don't never want nothing for herself. She wants things for you. The way I feel, I wouldn't mourn at your funeral. But what Hallie wants, I'm gonna try to see she gets."

"So am I," Ranse promised grimly.

"Then I don't mind telling you," Bert admitted, "that it was me reminded the opposition to dig up that matter of how she couldn't read."

As the Senator and his wife rode home after old Bert Barricune's barren funeral, Hallie sighed. "Bert never had much of anything. I guess he never wanted much."

He wanted you to be happy, Ranse Foster thought, and he did the best he knew how.

"I wonder where those prickly-pear blossoms came from," he mused.

Hallie glanced up at him, smiling. "From me," she said.

EVELYN CAMERON

Evelyn Cameron was one of the first ranch women to work as a photo-journalist. Because she wrote and photographed with the intent to publish, she became a keen observer and carefully recorded details. Her work, including "The 'Cowgirl' in Montana," invariably was inspired by her involvement on the Montana ranch where she lived and worked.

The "Cowgirl" in Montana

THE COWBOY is a household word all the world over. The "cowgirl" to British ears suggests little, except perhaps, a dairymaid. Nevertheless, for some twenty years past there have been cowgirls on Western ranches who are the feminine counterparts of cowboys—riding in similar saddles, on similar horses, for the purpose of similar duties, which they do, in fact, efficiently perform. The abolition of the side-saddle was naturally the first step towards the creation of the cowgirl, and the credit of this essential innovation in Montana has generously been adjudged to the present writer. When I first came to Montana, twenty-five years ago the few women to be found there, or in Northern Wyoming, rode on side-saddles with very broad seats, covered with a piece of carpet, or buckskin in the better class saddles. Did some adventurous spirit wish to try her hand at "bronco busting," she must needs borrow the trousers and cow-saddle of a male relative, for side-saddles are of little use in the West except on "plumb gentle" horses, as I shall proceed to explain. It was my unfortunate experience that nearly all the horses I wished to ride were terrified of a woman in a riding habit, and when their fears were sufficiently subdued to admit of my approach near enough to mount, they declined to allow me to do so. Even when I was assisted to the saddle by several men, the horse "threw a fit" as I raised my leg to put it over the pommel, and, of course, I had the same trouble in dismounting. It was clear that to be perfectly independent I must ride old "dead heads" which were not at all to my taste. I therefore determined to ride astride. Following the advice of the ranch manager, I sent to a well known Chicago firm for what he called a California riding costume, which cost me one hundred dollars. With this divided skirt I found it a simple operation to mount into a cow-saddle. The horn is grasped in the right hand, and, no matter what the horse may do, the rider will swing into place. At the same time, the left hand can hold down the horse's head by the check strap of the bridle, which will prevent the animal from jumping away. Although my costume was so full as to look like an ordinary walking dress when the wearer was on foot, it created a small sensation. So great at first was the prejudice against any divided garment in Montana that a warning was given me to abstain from riding on the streets of Miles City lest I might be arrested! After riding into town forty-eight miles from the ranch, I was much amused at the laughing and giggling girls who stood staring at my costume as I walked about.

EULALIA BOURNE

"Sister" Bourne, as she is better known, says she was born in a dugout in Texas, she learned to read by staring at the labels on coffee cans and she took her teacher's exam at the age of fourteen. After that she taught for forty-three years while ranching in Pepper Sauce Canyon and the Galiuro Mountains of Arizona. She also said she was just "an old gal who likes kids and cows." When she died no one knew just exactly how old she was, but the best guess is ninety. She always maintained that her age was nobody's business. She was a live wire and her writing tells of a zest for life. She was inducted into the National Cowgirls Hall of Fame in Texas in 1996.

Please Excuse the Pants

JANUARY NIGHTS ARE COLD even in southern Arizona. Dashing along a Tucson street on the way to a drug store, I was comfortably wrapped, not modishly dressed. The Sunshine Climate Club would have hated me. On top of intimate garments I wore a two-piece red ski undersuit. Over that I had on a pair of Levi's, a man's cashmere shirt, a short woolen coat and a heavy GI pile-lined jacket much too large, belted around me in deep folds. My head was tied up in a red bandana and crowned with a snug-fitting western hat. Woolen socks and stout cowboy boots protected my feet. From a shoulder strap hung an overloaded leather bag.

When I turned the corner at a narrow side street, my swinging purse banged into a well-dressed fellow emerging from a cocktail lounge. Neither of us stopped. I gasped apologetically. He balanced himself, half-turned in stride, and snarled: "Why don't you go back East!"

Me, of all people.

I was still laughing to myself as I drove out of town continuing my hundred-mile night journey. (If a storm threatened, I drove down Sunday night, instead of early Monday morning.) Thinking over the incident to tell friends, all of a sudden it came to me that it wasn't so funny. How did they really feel about the way I dressed? Away from the range, my appearance must often embarrass my associates. Hoodlum calls of "Hi-yo-Silver" and "Yip-pee-E" I could take without notice and feel only the slight annoyance that goes with any encounter with passing rudeness. But well-dressed friends and companions might actually be ashamed to be seen in company of one so unconventionally garbed.

Faye, for instance. I thought: "As we walk down the street, she in her neat print dress, her bare head stylishly coiffed, and I in Levi's, boots, and Stetson, how does she feel when she meets friends and has to say: 'This is our teacher'?"

I spent the remainder of my journey driving back to school mentally drawing up a brief.

It was consolation to recollect that independent characters who dress for their personal comfort and convenience, rather than for the approval of the public, have been shocking the populace since the human race lost hirsute hides and simian appendages. I thought of the scandal caused by the "bloomer" girls. Farther back, the man who first divided his nether garment into twin cylinders to fit his bifurcated anatomy must have been lonely among the robed and toga-ed. But who likes to be lonely? One must have a good reason to risk being shunned. I appreciated with regret the fortitude and charity it took to be friends with a nonconformist like me, a woman in Levi's.

Actually the man I bumped had a right to be indignant at my bulk and awkwardness; but his judgment was hasty. It was downright poor. Whatever I am, the West produced me. And I was not trying to make a spectacle of myself. I had nothing but business on my mind. With trade as my purpose I was not dressed to pass inspection by style-conscious bystanders. I was dressed for a long night ride in an unheated pickup. Nevertheless, there I was under the bright lights, sticking out like a finger-splint, jostling evening strollers and shocking one into ill-founded criticism.

Whether you dress to be comfortable or to be attractive depends on how busy you are, where you work, and the chronological point of life to which you have attained. In early youth, I confess, I tried to look like other girls. To be in style I bared my calves and clavicles during the years I studied and taught in the city. For a glamorous decade I tried to keep up with the vogue: skimpy skin, cobwebby hose, uncovered head. And I paid for this effort to put on style by constant illness during spells of bad weather. Then I moved into the country, and learned to be comfortable—and the heck with fashion.

It was a blessing to find relief from the respiratory ailments—ear ache, sore throat, congested nose and sinuses, tonsilitis and bronchitis that had plagued me since childhood. I learned that adequate clothing protected my health, for I discovered—with the help of an astute young doctor, that I was subject to an allergy to cold—the temperature cold, opposite of heat. Whoever heard of such a thing? True it is, though, and it condemns me socially to a grasshopper existence—bright and gay only in fair weather. In the heat of Arizona summers I can gussie up in skirts and other feminine frills. If the occasion demands, I can cut off my jeans below the pockets and tan my legs as other women do. But even in summer I must avoid drafts, damp clothes, and high-voltage cooling systems. Comes frost. *Br-r-r!* My pants and boots. Real winter sets in. *Br-r-r-r,* fortissimo! My long-handles and pile-lined jacket. For worse than hurt vanity, embarrassed friends, and an outraged Mrs. Grundy is an aching head and the creeping upward curse of cold, cold feet.

When I voided my teaching contract with the city by getting married, it was my good luck that the county school superintendent had a better opinion of conjugal status than her city counterpart. The latter, and the school board he influenced, never seemed to realize when marriage was banned for women teachers (men teachers of course were allowed to wed), that babies are what keep up tax-supported schools. This is not said in bitterness, for he did me a favor by his decree. Eventually it sent me to Redington, an environment made to order for persons such as I. There, while mentoring my "little cow-punchers," I found physical comfort by shielding my body against the climate. The great open country was alive with horses and cowboys, and pupils with extra mounts who wanted teacher to help "round up the pasture." Having to be ready at dismissal bell, I dared to teach the three R's while dressed in boots, Levi's and shirts with plenty of pockets. A side effect was the exorcising of my demons of affliction. No runny nose. No loss of voice. And with reasonable caution no migraine headaches. I had found my niche. I have never left it, patterning my life to the all-weather uniform of boots, sombrero, and what goes between.

It was never my purpose to start a fashion or even a fad when I made local history by wearing pants into the schoolroom. But for succeeding years, and in each different school, as soon as I put aside pretty dresses and came to school in Levi's, the girls in my classes followed suit. I don't remember that anything was ever said about it, but when frosty mornings arrived every leg in the room was covered with heavy dark-blue jeans. Apparently the mothers accepted the idea as good. And it certainly saved laundering, always a problem in a community such as Sierrita where there was a constant water shortage. It not only helped keep the girls warm but it gave them more freedom in such activity as playing baseball.

Every departure from the ordinary must be accompanied by complications and sacrifices. Some of my school patrons frowned on having a teacher who dressed "like a man" until they got used to me. I dreaded shocking the school superintendent whose once-a-year visits were never scheduled so that none knew at what moment she might pop in. The late winter day she came I'm sure she was startled by my appearance (for which I made no apology or explanation), but my marvelous little cowpunchers put on such a good performance for her that she approved us all and said nothing about my overclad feet and legs. Later she met an itinerant maker of movie shorts and sent him out to make a newsreel of our little school and its projects. And she herself came again, this time for an overnight visit, and brought with her a woman feature writer for the Tucson morning paper. As we three sat before the open fire in my snug little teacherage, I entertained them—off the record, I thought—with accounts of road troubles I'd had on account of river floods, gully washouts, car breakdowns at night, and being stuck to the axles in mud.

To my chagrin, the Sunday paper, which eventually found its way (by the trice-weekly mail car coming down from Benson) over the mountains, contained a half-page yarn about the great pioneering work I was doing in the wilderness of the San Pedro River Valley. I was ashamed to show my face to the mothers, the true pioneers in the district. My closest neighbor and dear friend (mother of five—the youngest she'd had by herself during an isolating flood while her husband was away on the roundup) remarked, as I sneaked into her kitchen where she was ironing with sad irons by a kerosene lamp and getting supper for eight over a wood fire while minding the babies:

"Don't we live in a terrible place and ain't you wonderful!"

The biggest problem of a trousered female teacher is a trip to the city. At teachers' meetings I conformed and suffered the consequences—such as a flat tire on the road; to change it I had to take off my skirt and hose. On Friday afternoon visits to the county library in the superintendent's office, there simply wasn't time to change into a dress. Looking straight ahead in a purposeful manner, I strode in, lugging a heavy box of books, and busied myself at the shelves selecting replenishments, speaking only to those with the courage to greet me first.

One afternoon years ago the assistant superintendent confronted me thusly: "Do you know you are breaking the law?"

Laughingly she showed me a volume of city ordinances, among them an old blue law making it illegal for a woman to appear on the streets of Tucson dressed in men's clothing. Laughing myself, I showed her that I happened on this occasion to be wearing women's denim riders one of the "daughters" had given me. Ordinarily I never use them because they have no hip pockets into which I can slip the metal case containing my reading glasses.

After a while, as with most eccentrics, people got used to me and I was kindly tolerated. Once there was a combined meeting of city and county teachers that I didn't know about ahead of time. Fortunately coats were long in those days. I buttoned mine, rolled my pants up above my knees, and sincerely hoped when I was greeted by my former principal that he didn't know I was not "dressed."

When the Cowboy became the head of my household there were other complications. He objected to my pants if worn anywhere off the ranch. That was long before capri pants and stretch pants and he certainly had precedent on his side. In usual circumstances, even yet, the ranks of women connected with the cattle business who wear pants in public are very thin indeed. Mary Kidder Rak, in her book *Cowman's Wife,* explains that ranch women are delighted at any chance to break the monotony by dressing up and looking feminine. True enough. They do not have my affliction. Besides, they are representing their husbands. A cowman, whatever he may think about others' frontier pants and cowgal rigging, wants his wife to have on the prettiest dress in town, and most of them can afford the best.

Man's authority to dictate—even legislate—what women wear extends back to Adam who doubtless designed Eve's girdle of figleaves. There are good reasons for this. What woman does not like to give her man pleasure at the sight of her?

Before marriage, the man of the outfit said: "You look nice in any old rag." After marriage he said: "Why don't you look like other women?"

There were three great big reasons. Money was the first. We were trying to exist as well as build up the place—watering holes, fences, saddlehorses, bulls, materials and supplies—on approximately $2400 a year. My health was the second. Even a short trip in the unheated rattle-trap car sans pants and boots, and I was sick. My habit of feeling at-the-ready only in work clothes was the third. This habit developed because emergencies are the rule once you get out of sight of civilization. The car lights went out one night and I walked two miles up the canyon bed with nothing between me and the scratching, crawling sand and a possibly-lurking rattlesnake, but high-heeled white sandals. One moonlight night I lost half of my load of hay on a quick turn and ruined my best hose heaving it back on the little truck. The blue dress capped the climax.

I had been on a business trip to the land department and was arrayed in my sheer blue dress that made my eyes look blue. It was sprigged with figures in two shades of darker blue and had bows and a belt of the darkest blue. My big hat of fine soft straw was trimmed with velvet ribbons of the same three lovely shades. I even wore gloves—dark blue to match my pumps. Returning late that afternoon, I ran into a crisis at Mesquite Corral, two miles down the canyon from headquarters. The Cowboy had been working cattle alone all day, an exasperating job if ever there was one, and was now locked in battle with a big steer he had tied down and was attempting to dehorn by trimming off a corner of each side of the victim's skull with a little saw he carried tied to his saddle. Fool-like, I stopped the car, shed my gloves, and went over to see if I could maybe hold a rope or hand him something. His sweaty face was red with passion. His shirt was red with blood.

"Get on his neck!" he cried without a glance at me.

"But my dress," I faltered.

"Get on his neck, damn it!" he shouted.

I got on his neck, damn it. A fountain of blood splattered the sheer blue dress that made my eyes look blue. In the scuffle my pretty hat with the blue ribbons was knocked off my head and landed in a splash of soft green manure.

The slow bitter turning of the years brought changes. To him—the right to identify himself with a woman who looks smart in that special meaning of the word: "stylish, spruce, showy, up-to-date." To me—the independence to dress as my purse, my person, and my work direct and no sham pretenses involved.

Once a year I am right in style. That is during February in Tucson's pre-rodeo days when all on the streets are required to wear cowboy rigging or suffer durance vile at the hands of the vigilante committee (Junior Chamber of Commerce).

One Saturday morning I happened to pass two teenagers loitering in front of a movie theater apparently killing time while waiting for it to open its doors, by remarking about the girls and women dressed in rodeo style who happened to pass by. Evidently I didn't rate much. As I came abreast I heard the older boy say thoughtfully, "No, but I'll bet she has a horse!"

THE CANADIAN NORTH-WEST

MARY E. INDERWICK

In 1883 Mary Ella Lees traveled from her Perth, Ontario, home to live with her brother near Pincher Creek. On the train, she met Charles Inderwick, a young rancher also from Pincher Creek, and the next year they were married. A delightful letter to a relative in 1884 tells of life in the Canadian West. Excerpts of her letter follow.

A Lady and Her Ranch

I HAVE BEEN LIVING HERE SIX MONTHS and have never written you, but you have not written me, and I thought your honeymoon had swept me from your memory till I got your idiotic post card—idiotic but how gladly welcomed!

Dear, This is the only life! I have any number of troubles, in fact too numerous to mention, but I forget them all in this joyous air with the grand protecting mountains always standing round the western horizon. They seem the very spirit of the old hymn "Abide with me"—"Oh Thou that changest not"—and they are the dearest most constant of friends, and Alice let me tell you that in this small corner of this mighty North-West one wonders sometimes if one has any friends or if it is everyone for himself and the devil take the hindmost. However, I shall come to the bothersome humans later, and shall tell you lots of lovely things first.

We are on a cattle ranche which is very large and well watered, having several creeks running through it, as well as its two boundaries, the West and Middle forks of the Old Man River. The other boundary is the mountains so we are in the foothills, no plains here but the most glorious ranges of hills and rolling prairie. They all seem so near that one starts to ride to a certain landmark but finds oneself still no nearer at the end of an hour. I saw the white roofs of the houses of

Pincher Creek the other day though we were 22 miles away. Think of the delights of this clear air, then let the housekeeper in you think of the appetites which this air gives men (and women though we don't count much in *this* way here) and the huge meals that must be forthcoming at regular intervals every day.

We have a cow camp—a shack for the cowboys—and they have their own cook so we only get an occasional one for meals if he happens to be riding nearer the house than the camp. They are a nice lot of men; I love their attempts to help me appear civilized. Though they ride in flannel shirts they never come to the table in shirt sleeves. They have a black alpaca coat hanging in the shack attached to the house and each one struggles into it to live up to the new regime which began with a bride at the ranche. This is done so enthusiastically and with such good will that I have no qualms of conscience that I am a nuisance. Not like a young Englishman who came out to stay with us and came to dinner in a flannel shirt with no collar and no tie, and when I hinted to him that I expected a coat, he bought a buckskin one trimmed with blue flannel and wore it. I spoke of this to Charlie and he said it was that he had always had to dress for dinner and now he wanted a change, and liked to play tough, but when he had been roughing it a while he would appreciate anyone trying to live in a civilized way.

The cowboys anyway back me in my attempts and indeed back me in all my schemes because I ride well. I verily believe if I did not ride they would have nothing to do with me. As it is, they are rather proud of me, and, oh Alice, I do believe I could still take pleasure in riding if I were a deaf mute, and you know what a trial that would be to a red haired girl like me. If you could only feel the rocking motion of a good lope through the grass and hear the creak of the saddle, and see the horses fresh look after a long ride at this pace, especially my own beauty, Joy. When John, my cook, breaks my best cut glass dish I fly to the stables and have my Joy saddled and ride till I know that cut glass is nothing to make or mar one's lovely day.

Then there are the exciting rides when I go with Charlie to drive a bunch of cattle to another part of the range. The other day we were out and I was to drive some cattle through a coulee while Charlie rode over the hill to bring some others. The coulee was a narrow little pass between two high hills and all the cattle went through except three old bulls. They stood pawing and growling and looking at the horses in a way that would have appalled me had I been on the highest hill on foot. But having Joy under me, I cared for nothing, so I tried to ride up to them, waving my quirt—a plaited leather whip the cowboys always use. It hangs over the wrist by a leather loop and it makes a very convenient whip. I use it on the range but I have a lovely crop for Pincher Creek and church.

To return to my bulls. They looked as though they were going to have a free fight and Joy was determined not to take part. He swerved and turned and would not face them. I thought if we rode up they would move on and I wanted to get through, but Joy thought differently, evidently, for he behaved in such a determined way. The bulls by this time were making horrid noises and lashing their tails and horns, casting threatening looks on me struggling with an obstinate horse. Just in the midst of this Charlie came riding down the hill, calling to me to go back. He had to fire two or three shots over their heads before they moved on out of that wretched narrow coulee. It makes me shudder to think of it, for Charlie said if Joy had gone up to them they would have gored him and where would I have been? We won't pursue that question.

I hardly ever blunder into such difficulties and generally can drive a few cattle all right. They do look lovely on the sunny slopes, all looking so happy and strong and handsome. I have my mind full of the finest pictures and if I could transfer them to canvas my fame would be made forever.

There are other days and rides. This is when I go out with Charlie to bring in some horses and if they are bronchos we simply follow, Joy and I. Joy would scorn to take any easy cut so we go over the steep sides of hills at a break neck pace where a false step would end in disaster; but Joy never makes it, nor does Captain, Charlie's horse. We gradually head off these flying horses and bring them nearer and nearer the corrals 'til we at last get them safely inside. And, oh, then for a cup of tea, if it is afternoon and a quiet hour in my sunny sitting room; I in my small rocking chair, Charlie smoking in his long easy chair, and both so happy and contented.

Often I ride alone and then I see such wonderful things. I come suddenly on a small pond with ducks, a pond I must have been the discoverer of, as no one knew of it and all wanted to see it. But I have absolutely no bump of locality and I never could find it again. Once an animal which I believe to have been a mountain lion disclosed itself to view in among some small hillocks, but it looked so surly that we lost no time in getting out of sight. Another day a big grey wolf stood and looked sternly at me. I levelled my crop at him but he only added scorn to his appearance and stood his ground. He was out on an open plain and not near me. . . .

I sometime and very often long for a woman to come and live near me. I have made all sorts of offers to a few of the men who are near us in the way of helping them to get their shacks done up if only they will go east and marry some really nice girls. But they are all so far from being in love with anyone and so charming that they answer me, "The only really nice girl we know is married", with the most cheerful grins at me, that it ends in laughter as many things do here. . . .

I love the freedom of my life here and I try to make everyone about me share a bit in my happiness, so I have plenty of friends. If you were to look into our sitting room almost any evening, you would see a game of whist going on, while one long lank man grinds music through an organette and sings to its accompaniment whenever he can. while I sew or play cribbage with an odd man.

There are times when a snow storm has come and spread a cruel depth of snow over the long grass and the cowboys ride late and early, driving starving cattle to the nearest hay stack, or at any rate driving them from the thickets near a stream where they go for shelter but remain to die. Cows differ from horses in this way; a horse will paw and uncover the grass but a cow has no such instinct. She eats only such stray stuff as may stand out from the snow. This pall of snow throws a shadow over our days for as long as it lasts—10 days, even two weeks—and every ear is listening for the happy sound of the first murmuring of a chinook.

One night we were sitting just as I have told you, and suddenly someone said "the chinook!" We were all outside in a second; there was a low roar in the mountains and in twenty minutes the wind had struck the house. We went in and made coffee and were a much more joyful party than an hour before. That night one end of our roof was carried off, but I was in another part of our rambling house and sleeping like the enchanted princess, I did not hear anything but was content to know that the long looked for wind was reducing the hated snow to great peale of water, and freeing the grass and saving our precious cattle from starvation. It is a wonderful wind. In twelve hours the snow is gone, and in twenty-four the country has dried again. It seems a warm wind, but I have been nearly chilled to death driving in it.

Dearest, I have tried to give you some idea of my life in this unique corner of the Great Lone Land. I hope I have not tired you. I expect in return a full account of your new life, which is so very different from mine. though not happier. My life may seem rough and bare, but there is something to compensate one for every hardship and trial. You must come to see me, though, for it is the spirit of the West that charms one, and I can't convey it to you, try as I may. It is a shy wild spirit and will not leave its native mountains and rolling prairies and, though I try to get it into my letters, I can't. I must warn you that if it once charms you, it becomes an obsession and one grows very lonely away from it. No Westerner who has felt its fascination ever is really content again in the conventional East.

SUSAN ALLISON

In 1860, when she was fifteen years old, Susan Moir moved from England to the intimidating wilderness of Fort Hope in British Columbia. There she eventually met rancher John Allison. They were married in 1868. They raised fourteen children on ranches in the Similkameen and Okanagan valleys, where she had the distinction of being the first white woman. Her memoirs are filled with adventures, including a honeymoon trip over a primitive trail from Hope to Princeton and a trip through a forest fire. In 1931 the Vancouver Sunday Province *published her memoirs. In 1976 they were republished in book form as* A Pioneer Gentlewoman in British Columbia: The Recollections of Susan Allison.

A Pioneer Gentlewoman

THEN BEGAN MY CAMPING DAYS and the wild, free life I ever loved till age and infirmity put an end to it.

On the journey out we rode the two Kates, Cream and Grey. My husband sent the three packboys on ahead to fix camp. (This was over the Hope–Similkameen Trail.) As the three boys will often appear in these memoirs, I may as well pause and introduce them—Cockshist was cargodore, that is, he looked after the packs and cargo generally, storing it under shelter when removed from the horses and assigning each horse its load. Johnny Suzanne was packer. Cockshist assisted in the actual packing but Johnny had to round up the horses, mend saddles, see that the ropes were dry. Yacumtecum or Tuc-tac as he was then called was bell-boy and cook. He led the leading packhorse with the bell when the train started and cooked meals when in camp. We left town just at dusk and in a little over an hour reached the Lake House where we found the tents up and a blazing log fire and Yacumtecum cooking. In the tent a canvas was spread over the floor and a bed made of "mountain feathers," Spruce branches, and a buffalo robe. A wash basin [was] mounted on the box. Outside, there was the most delicious smell of grouse cooking. I went to the creek and washed and did up my hair in the darkness and when I regained the camp Tuc-tac had spread a canvas in front of the fire with fried trout, grouse, bacon and bannock. That [was] washed down with tin cups of delicious tasting tea. We sat and talked till late, the Indian boys sitting with us and telling us stories of the place. Here, Yacumtecum said, one of the Big Men (giants) lived and had been often seen. Cockshist said they also lived on the Okanagan. This led to talking of the creature now called the "Ogopogo." The Indians did not say "Ogopogo." They looked on it as a superhuman entity and seemed to fear it, though none of our boys had seen it nor did they want to. When we were all sleepy we retired for the night but were up with daylight in the morning in order to get the packs over the Skagit Bluff in the daylight. Tuc-tac had the same savory meal ready for us and we were soon on the second day. About noon we stopped at the Cedars for a hurried bite then on up the zigzag to the Skagit. Here we met a coloured man, a fine strong fellow. He stopped and spoke to my husband, who said that he was Richardson who was then removing some slides off the Skagit Bluff. Mr. Richardson assured us there was not even a stone left on the Bluff and added that we would still see some of the flowers for which the Skagit was famous though the best blooms were over. Then we proceeded on our respective ways. Mr. Richardson was right, the Skagit Flat was lovely. The rhododendrons were lovely still though not at their best. I think by the general colouring that there had been a touch of frost. The packboys paused to tighten their packs before we got to the Bluff. Mr. Allison told me to follow the packhorses closely and he would keep behind me in case of accident. We crossed without mishap. We kept slowly on till we came to Powder Flat, now rechristened by the pioneers of the "Nineties" as Cayoosh Flat. We called it Powder Flat from the circumstance that one time [when] my husband and his partner were packing out the camp caught fire and there was a rush to throw the blasting powder into the creek. There was gunpowder, too, but it was in cans and not much danger. It did not even get wet in the creek. As I said the place is now named Cayoosh Flat and the mountain back of it is called Spencer Mountain. Then it had the Hudson's Bay Company name and was called after one of their Chief Factors.

Well, that was my second camp. It was no time before the boys had the tents up and everything comfortable, but the mosquitoes were simply unbearable. They beat against the tent like a hailstorm and as for eating supper, we could not do it without swallowing as much mosquitoes as food. It was worse even than Panama, except one could bathe the bites in clean cold water. I was glad when we started the next morning and got out of that miserable place. That day we reached the "Nine Mile," took off the packs and had a grouse lunch. One of the boys went a little off and got a deer. Then we went on again and were at the Similkameen ford by six. We forded the river and in a few minutes were home.

My husband had just finishes a new log house—large and comfortable. There was a store attached and Indians came from miles with skins and furs. It was rather a costly affair to build in those days as all lumber had to be cut with a whipsaw and cost seven cents per foot. A man named Fitzgerald did all the sawing for Allison and Hayes. Mr. Allison had the whole building double-floored, sealed and partitioned with lumber—it was expensive. This was by no means the first house in Princeton which, by the way, was two miles from the present city. My husband and his partner had built as soon as Governor Douglas had located the townsite. Also Captain Marsden [Marston], a miner, a man named Young and several others had small cabins on the river bank. In fact there had been a nucleus of a thrifty little town but Cariboo and Rock Creek proved a powerful magnet to draw everyone away. My husband and Mr. Hayes stayed as they had just purchased eighty Durham Shorthorns from a man across the line who was anxious to get out of the cattle business. Mr. Hayes had a good supper ready for us the day I first saw Princeton, though he did not approve my dressing for dinner, a habit I was drilled in as a child and has always stuck with me to some extent. As I did not object to his coming to table in shirt sleeves I did not see why he objected to my habits, but I think he half forgave me when he found I could milk cows and was not afraid to go into a corral full of cattle.

As it was getting near snow-fly when the Hope Mountain was closed and all travel stopped with horses or cattle, my husband could only spend two weeks at home, most of the time seeing to the horses and rounding up the cattle for another trip with beef for the Westminster market, so I was virtually alone. I had a visit from an Indian woman, a niece of Quinisco, the "Bear Hunter" and Chief of the Chu-chu-ewa Tribe. She was dressed for the occasion, of course, in mid-Victorian style, a Balmoral petticoat, red and gray, a man's stiff starched white shirt as a blouse, stiff high collar, earrings an inch long, and brass bracelets! I did not know my visitor seemed to think she ought to sit upright in her chair and fix her eyes on the opposite wall. I think "Cla-hi-ya" was the only word she spoke. I was not used to Indians then and knew very little Chinook. I felt very glad when her visit was over. I know now that I should have offered her a cigar and a cup of tea.

I amused myself the best way I could during the ten days my husband was away. The first thing I did was to hang white curtains in the dining-room windows. Mr. Hayes said they made the room dark, he also did not like a tablecloth and said oilcloth was good enough. I thought he was unreasonable at the time and for as long as I had someone to wash for me, but when I had a lot of children and had to do my own washing I agreed with him oilcloth was good enough.

When I looked around my bedroom I thought it would look better with a toilet table. There was a plain wooden table about three feet long and two wide standing under one of the windows. I thought that would do, so hunted amongst my belongings and found some pink stuff with which I covered the table and over the pink gathered a white muslin skirt and threw a white dimity toilet cover over. This, with a fairly good mirror, made a beautiful toilet table. I also made a large pin-cushion of pink and white and as the room was already nicely papered I hung my pictures on the wall. When my husband returned he was delighted with the changes I had effected.

Then began a busy time. It was now the first of November and the cattle and horses had to be driven to their winter quarters. My husband and his partner had about five hundred head of cattle to move that winter and a big bunch of horses, I don't know how many, I had not yet been introduced to them all. It took three or four busy days to gather them all and start them down the Canyon. Some of them would come back but the older ones just hit the trail and quietly grazed down the river and on to Okanagan, where their winter range was. It was a long journey in those days—but later, instead of going by Penticton and the lake, my husband cut a much shorter trail for his own use by Trout Creek. Of course, it was rough but answered his purpose.

When the bustle had subsided my husband set to work to make us comfortable for the winter, sawing logs that lay on the flat near the house for winter firewood. Then he hunted up what planks were left from house building and old tea boxes from which to make a desk, bureau, rocking chair and other articles of furniture we couldn't bring out. My sister had given me her old piano (the first one to enter B.C.) *[sic]* but as it could not then be packed over the Hope trail I left it with my mother. So we made the most of the few things we could get.

As my husband had business in Westminster that August I thought I would take the trip with him. The baby was now a month old and I got one of the women to make me a birchbark basket to pack him in. It was a very comfortable little nest and my husband said he would carry it himself. As we needed only take one pack horse with a tent and food for three days we thought we could make the journey without help. We were told that there were fires on the road when we started. My husband thought the fires might not be bad though the air was full of smoke. When we made the "Nine Miles" it grew unpleasantly thick. As we neared Powder Camp we found the trees were blazing on both sides of us. My husband handed me the baby to carry and went on leading the pack horse. Poor pony he did not like the fire and had to be dragged along the road. My husband wanted to turn back but I, not knowing what was ahead, said "go on" and we pushed on until it became clearer. Near Skagit we met a man on horseback who stopped to speak to us. He said "turn back while you can, no one can get through that fire, the Skagit is boiling." But as the smoke and fire behind us looked far worse, we told him we would try it, and that he had better hurry if he wanted to get through. So we parted. He had not exaggerated. When we got to the Skagit we found the timber on both sides of the creek (which here is smaller) on fire. The rocks were red hot and the water was boiling or at any rate it seemed like it. We dared not stop but hurried on thinking to get out of it. When we reached the Cedars Pony and the other two horses had to be blinded. The whole forest seemed to be on fire [and] the heat was almost unbearable. The smoke was suffocating and we kept a blanket wrapped around little Edgar's basket. To add to our misery a huge cedar crashed across the trail. I held the three horses and baby while my husband tore the bark from some of the cedars lying near and made a bridge on to the top of the cedar, over one side and down on the other, then led Nelly and Pony over this bridge with the third horse. The bridge caught fire and his leg was badly burned, but we did get over, and a little farther we got beyond the fire. We were afraid to camp but too exhausted to go farther that night. We left our dangerous camp early next morning and reached Lake House where we camped and took our ease and rested till next day.

My mother was getting quite alarmed about us when we arrived at the old parsonage. There was no one able to get through to the Similkameen for days.

Hope seemed the same as usual, if anything quieter. I visited my mother for a month or six weeks during which time the trail had been cut out and fallen timbers cut away. The Indian boys brought in our pack train and as the freight had arrived by boat from Westminster we started back home again.

MARY DALEY

When young single women ventured to the North-West in the 1880s, it wasn't long before they were wooed and wed by one of the region's many bachelors. Just two years after her arrival at Fort Macleod in 1887 Mary Daley was married to James Daley, a former member of the North-West Mounted Police. They moved to a ranch west of Leavings (now Granum), and five generations later their descendants still live on the ranch. Mary Daley told part of her story in a letter in 1938. Nearly sixty years later her great-great-granddaughter Doris Daley wrote "From Mary's Window," which was inspired by Mary Daley's letter.

A Letter From Mary

Dear Friends and Neighbours,
It is now over 41 years since I left my small home town of Wiarton, beautifully situated on the banks of Colpoys Bay, Bruce County, Ontario, to accompany my aunt who was going west to join her husband at Fort Macleod.

I still have a dim recollection of my girlish apprehensions of that miserable rainy morning in October, 1887, about two years after the Riel Rebellion. We drove 20 miles to Owen Sound to take the CPR for Lethbridge. The stark trees and brown shorn fields were a mirror image of my own despondency. From Dunmore Junction we travelled to Lethbridge on what was then known as the Turkey Trail, or the narrow-guage. From Lethbridge we journeyed to six miles west of Fort Macleod with a horse and rig.

At times I was very homesick. Winter so near and deep rivers to ford were all the prevented me from starting out to walk back home.

"Skies so blue it makes you wonder,
If it's heaven shining through.
Earth so smiling way out yonder,
Sun so bright it dazzles you.
Birds a-singing, flowers a-flinging
All their fragrance on the breeze.
Dancing shadows, green still meadows
Don't you mope—you've still got these!"

Two years later I changed my name and location. Not a neighbour nearer than six miles. There were very few white women to cheer up the newcomer or sympathize with during those wretched spells of lonesomeness.

I can never forget one exciting incident, when having occasion to ride to where my husband was haying back in the hills. On the way I suddenly became aware of an Indian on his pony close by me. Fortunately I rode a young horse full of pep and go. In a flash I clicked and flicked him with the reins. Away we flew on the wings of the wind, with a real red Indian after us! Sorrel Mike, sensing danger, just flew along with the hounding Indian close behind, quirting his piebald pony mercilessly.

Luckily it was a three mile race and we gradually drew away, leaving our pursuer far behind. He followed on until he saw the camp, then turned and went his way. I still galloped on to the camp, blown, winded and near-collapsing. In my breathless and excited condition I explained as best I could the reason of my haste and alarm. My husband said, "Why did you run? The poor fellow only wanted to see who you were and where you were going." "Maybe he did," I retorted, "But as I did not like his looks or understand his lingo, I did not stop to listen." Many a good dinner of oats Mike got after that ride!

Had I known the Indian and his ways then as I did later, I would not have ran from him. Friendly Indians and their wives would often call to see us. I was soon accustomed to their ways and presence. They would show their visiting card, signed by the agent, as a passport, granting the bearer leave of absence from the reserve. The same card would be repeatedly shown by Many Tail Feathers, Howling Wolf, Weasel Eagle Bear, and others. Many a campfire joke they must have enjoyed at my expense.

Their visits, however, were breaks in the routine for me, though sometimes a nuisance.

The patrolling Red Coat, on his Rounds, was always a welcome visitor, bringing news from the outside world and local items of interest. There were no churches, schools or a post office nearer than Macleod, 18 miles away. When my son became of school age, he had to go to Macleod to live with a town family. I would have been very lonesome without him, but about that time his small sister arrived from Eaton's. She was the proud possessor of a good pair of lungs and insisted on being cared for.

Wolves and coyotes often made nights hideous with their eerie howlings and unearthly lamentations.

In the momentous year of 1892 the railroad from Calgary to Fort Macleod was completed. About the year 1900 the settlers started to come to Alberta. The prehistoric days of the ranches were numbered.

DORIS DALEY

Doris Daley grew up on a ranch established by her great-great-grandfather in southern Alberta more than one hundred years ago. She started creating rhymes at age eight and hasn't stopped since then. She presently resides in Calgary and attends cowboy poetry gatherings across Western Canada. Her poems are published in a chapbook, The Daley Grind. *She signs her books with a terse message: "Ride easy and look for the rhymes along the trail." The following poem was written in response to her great-great-grandmother's diaries.*

From Mary's Window

It's here, from my window, with the moonlight glowing
That night settles in with that wild wind blowing.

That old relentless wind makes my lonely heart moan,
And Jim's away and so I face another night alone.

Sometimes I get so homesick I wonder why I stay . . .
Neighbours few and far between, the Fort so far away.

At times like this it's hard to keep my doubts and fears away,
Still, I know beyond the night will come a bright new day.

And the warm sun will dance on the crocus-covered slopes.
The sage-scented breeze will be full of new hopes.

Jim riding home, my heart-strings humming,
A ranch to build! And a new baby coming.

So here I'll make my stand and together James and I
Will stay the course, we'll build a life beneath this big blue sky.

And maybe someday when our babies are all grown
They'll settle in these hills, raise families of their own.

And the green, grassy slopes will be their home through the years,
The hills will guard their dreams and the wind will dry their tears.

So I rise above the hardships and I leave behind the sorrows.
They vanish in the promise of a thousand new tomorrows.

With enough rain and the warm Chinooks, we'll make it work
somehow,
And pray the grass is tall and sweet a hundred years from now.

So it's here from my window where the moonlight spills
That I thank the Good Creator for this life, this place, these hills.

CATHERINE NEIL

When Catherine Neil boarded a ship in Scotland bound for Canada in 1905, she had no idea of the hardships she would endure on a sheep ranch near Grassy Lake, Alberta. There was no way she would know that the winter of 1906–07 would be the worst in prairie history, and there was no way to know that its toll on her sheep ranch would be heartbreaking. Despite such trials, she lived her life with courage and kindness. In later years she wrote with stark honesty.

A Sheep Herder's Bride

THE WINTER OF 1906 AND 1907 was the hardest I ever experienced. We had very little hay up that year, as the stock running wild on the prairie had destroyed a lot of our stacks.

The winter started early and we were quite unprepared for it. By the beginning of December we were feeding the sheep. We bought a stack of hay from a Dr. Tuller, north of Burdett, and had two of the settlers south of Grassy Lake, Ed Johnson and Charlie Attwood, haul it for us as they had a bob-sleigh and good horses. Many a night we listened for the sound of the bells of the horses returning, and then let the sheep out to feed, only to find that the sleigh had upset or the horses were played out. The wind blew from a different direction almost every day, so that new trails had to be made every morning.

The sheep began to suffer so much from hunger that they started eating the wool off each other's backs as they stood in the corral. It was a terrible sight each morning to see dozens of sheep bare and bleeding, and if any sheep had died during the night there was no wool left on the side turned up.

We cut out the sheep each morning, and those with the wool eaten off were put in little pens where they could get shelter from the cold and wind, and where we could feed them. We had to make sacks into coats for some of them or they would not have had any chance to survive.

Towards the end of January they were dying at the rate of 20 and 25 a day and we could not keep pace with skinning them. We ordered feed from Lethbridge, but it did not come till April, when a thousand sheep were already dead.

One day my husband was skinning some of the dead sheep when a blizzard came up. He just had time to get a coat and a lantern and make for the band. My brother-in-law was herding them, but the snow was drifting so badly that it was impossible to see in front of you, and it would have been hard work trying to hold the band alone.

After some time, we heard a bump at the door, and then it opened and a man tottered in, covered with snow and hardly recognizable. He was our neighbour, Frank Clark, who had been bringing us some oats for feed when he got lost in the blizzard. His horses had been going round and round till they went into the coulee and came to a stop at our door. He was badly frozen as he had not dressed for a blizzard; the sun had been shining when he left home only three miles away. We did all we could for him, and after a rest he felt better, but not foolhardy enough to go out in it again.

The wind did not die down till ten o'clock that night, and Frank went home to a very frightened wife. She had about given him up for lost.

The sheep came trailing in too, and my sister-in-law and I were happy when we heard their bells and knew our men were safe. They had been able to hold the sheep against the banks of the coulee and the lantern had kept their hands warm.

We had been without mail for weeks, so Jim decided he would go to Grassy Lake to get some. He told us not to worry if he did not get home that night as the trails were so heavy with snow it would be hard going, and he would have to give his horse a rest.

He left Grassy Lake late in the afternoon and rode alongside the railway track till he got to a mile from Burdett, then he started south to the Donaldson farm. They had dug-out for a house at that time, and with snow everywhere it was hard to locate. Jim walked about for a long time and then started calling, "Hello, Hello," but no one answered. He began to think he was really lost on the prairie and as a light snow was falling again, he did not know which way to go. He got off the horse and had only walked a few steps when he disappeared into the snow. The noise he made then got the family awake, and after one of the men got out through the skylight on the roof, he helped Jim out of the hole. He had fallen into the entrance to the house; it had filled up with snow, so they used the skylight on the roof to get out and in. They soon got Jim some supper and after talking for some time they all went to bed again. Jim felt he had really something to be thankful for that night, as he had a narrow escape from being lost.

The first chinook came on Feb. 6th, 1907, and we went to our own home to get some coal, having moved early in January to my brother-in-law's place. Our house was surrounded by cattle, many of them dead, and not a pane of glass was left in any of the windows. The curtains were eaten and the tassels off the blinds, and everything that the cattle could reach. I had left some dish cloths and soap on the little kitchen dresser, but these too had disappeared.

We boarded up the windows while the water dripping from the roof soaked us. By morning there was hard frost again, but as we drove back that night to my brother-in-law's the water was splashing all over our little sleigh.

I got a real taste of winter and frostbite that year. One day it was a cold 30 degrees below zero with a strong wind blowing from the south–east. We tried to put the sheep out against it in the morning, but were beat, and we had to put them back in the corral. My husband went for hay to a stack a mile away, but before going he told me to watch that the sheep did not get out of the corral and down to where the weak sheep were.

I was busy washing for the baby when my sister-in-law called out that the sheep had broken the gate of the corral and were out. I did not think of drying my hands or putting a wrap on me. One thought was uppermost: if these sheep got down to the stack they would trample the weak sheep to death. I called the dogs and we fought for nearly an hour before we got the sheep inside the corral again; it was only after my sister-in-law had carried a handful of hay through the corral that the sheep followed. She had brought me a coat and cap, but my hands and face were badly frozen. I felt as if I had a pot on my head for many days afterwards; believe me, I always dried my hands before going out again.

After the first chinook, the prairie was in a much worse condition than it had been before. Even the cattle could not break through the ice for feed and were dying all over the range. It was a common sight to see a long line of cattle going south one day and back north the next as the wind changed. Some of the cattle went mad from hunger and had to be shot. One steer got into our band of sheep and it did not matter how far the men drove him in the morning, he was back by night again, and as he ran through the sheep he broke the legs of several of them.

We came on eight head of cattle one day, backed up against a snowbank in a buffalo wallow and snowed in. We had quite a time digging them out, but if we wouldn't have, they would have stayed there till they had starved or frozen.

Each morning after tucking in my baby to keep her warm, my sister-in-law and I each carried a bundle of hay on our backs and threw it out by the handful, so that the sheep would follow, while the men went ahead with a snow plough, trying to cut the snow down to the grass. Many times the horses would walk on the top of the snow and never crack the ice left by the February chinook and at other times they would fall through and come up with bleeding legs.

As we used the stables for the weak sheep, the horses had to stand tied to the hayrack all night, where the sheep ate the hair off their tails as far up as they could reach. It certainly gave the horses an odd appearance.

The chinook came for a second time on March 25th, 1907, and by nightfall the coulees were running, so we decided to make for our own home again. I bundled up my belongings and made ready while my husband hitched up. When he came for me he said I could drive the wagon, while he would go on horseback, driving the horses and cow.

I did not know much about driving so I let the lines go slack and allowed them to go round the end of the wagon tongue. As I headed for the end of a dam, or rather what had been a dam, the water was coming down like a river and I had no idea where to cross. I had visions of us all being thrown in the stream so I gave a scream and the horses stopped. My husband heard me, came to my rescue, and piloted me across. After that, he gave me a lesson on holding the lines tighter so that they would not get round the tongue.

When I got home I found it surrounded by dead cattle, and some had to be taken away before I could enter the house. The water was coming down the coulee with such force that it was carrying dead cattle with it. I was able to stand on the top of the hill above the house and count 58 dead cattle.

Some of the cattle ranchers lost very heavily. In one blizzard alone 400 head of cattle went over the bank at Cherry Coulee, north of Burdett, and piled up dead at the bottom. The section house at Grassy Lake was covered with brands cut from cattle killed on the track and one house north of Grassy Lake had the cellar filled with dead cattle. They had gone inside for shelter and had fallen through the floor; rather than pulling them out, the owner moved the house.

When lambing came, our sheep were in such poor condition that the lambing was a failure. It was a common sight to see a herder catch a sheep and almost strip her hare with his hands. They were shedding wool so badly. The ewes didn't want their lambs and the lambs were too weak to rustle, so added to all the other work was the suckling of most of the lambs if we wanted to save them.

After the hard winter there were still the dead sheep to get rid of. Some Indians under Chief Yellow Face came along again and seeing a chance of making some money, they offered to skin them. As the carcasses thawed out, they skinned or pulled the wool, pegged the skins neatly on the ground to dry, and spread out the wool. Everyone helped, and when all was finished, the chief told us what each had done and he or she was paid accordingly. After they were all paid, the chief saw where they could make a little more money, so he told us, "Sun come out, sheep smell very bad, missus get sick. We take all away for ten dollars." Judging from the smell one dead sheep can make, we were glad to pay. They took them away several miles east and piled them up in a coulee, and when the first homesteaders came in and saw the bones, they thought it was where a massacre of Indians had taken place.

After such a heavy loss as we had during that winter of 1906–07, it was like beginning all over again; our slogan was, save and buy sheep. It did not seem much of a hardship to do without things, as we always looked forward to a time when we could visit our old homes in Scotland, and we knew that it would take a lot of money.

AUGUSTA HOFFMAN

Many ranch women who left memoirs came from the British Isles, but many others came from the United States. In 1905 Augusta Hoffman moved with her family from North Dakota to Wood Mountain, Saskatchewan, where her family established a small ranch. She did not attend school, and because her parents spoke German, she learned to read and write on her own. In her story she tells of two younger sisters perishing in a prairie storm. The creek where their remains were found is known as Lost Child Creek.

Lost Child Creek

AT THE AGE OF THIRTEEN I took over the job of mowing and raking the hay. As I got some ahead Esther and I hauled in and stacked 18 loads of hay all on our own. Mother would help us unload while Walter was away getting in a week's work. Dad would come home on Saturday night and sharpen the mower knives while I turned the grindstone.

That year I made my first dollar and no one will ever know the wonderful feeling it gave me. There was a sports day at Wood Mountain and I was offered a horse to ride in the ladies race. Sure, I took it and came in second. The prize was a cut glass pickle dish that meant nothing to me, but Inspector Richard's wife came up to me and put a dollar bill in my hand. I could hardly wait to get home and get the Eaton's catalogue. I was going to spend it all on a ring, and I did just that, much against my Dad's wishes; a dollar was just too much money to spend on something like that. I rode in the races again the next year but had an unbroken horse, couldn't control it and someone had to run me down and stop the horse.

About this time Mother went out for a walk up the creek a mile and a heavy fog came on quickly so she sat herself under a willow tree and was not going to move till daylight. Once again; out went the lantern but the fog was too dense to see anything, then the cow with the bell on took a notion to get on her feet and Mother heard the bell and followed the creek home.

January 1907 we had a new baby at our house (Hilda, Mrs. Mitchell – Winfield, B.C.). There was no nurse or doctor, and Mother was terribly sick. In all her pain she asked us children to pray for her as that was all we could do. Mother was 40 years of age at that time. Late that night the baby was born. She was all right and in time Mother was able to be up again.

We had a lot of snow again that winter and come spring the creeks just roared and were away out of their beds with so much water running down from the hills. May of that year will never be forgotten, as one of the worst sorrows of my life took place then. I was the one that did all the riding to look after the horses and cattle. That spring Dad, Esther and I left for Glasgow, Montana, as the folks just had to have coffee and tobacco from there, and that would take us seven or eight days. On our last day when we were about fourteen miles from home we woke up to find a cold rain falling. After going five or six miles we met Walter on horseback. He told us Ruth and Nellie had gone the evening before to get the horses and didn't come back. He had been out all night looking for them but the wind had gotten so strong and the rain had turned to sleet. One of the horses wore a bell but you could neither hear nor see anything. We hurried home as fast as the team could make it. Mother was in a terrible state as she couldn't leave the baby. The first thing was to feed the horses, then tell the Police. They went down east and let those people know and the few people who were there turned out to search. I had to stay with the baby as Mother just had to go along. It turned colder by the hour and turned to snow but they searched all day and most of the night. After three days, it began to clear but we knew they couldn't be found alive. The search continued for a week and no trace was found even of the horses. An old Indian started a story that they were kidnapped and for a big sum of money he could tell us where they were, but we knew Indians too well to believe that. After a week's time Dad and Walter took a tent, food and a wagon and camped down on one of the Poplar Creeks about 8 miles from home and were going to do every coulee on foot. They found the team of horses but not the two yearlings. However, they kept on looking till every foot of ground was covered. Not until eight years later were the remains found, two miles beyond where the folks gave up looking. Mother picked up every little bone and thanked God for letting her have even that much. She took them and buried them in the end of the garden. As I write this in 1960 I can let the tear drops fall, but as always God gave us the strength to go on.

MONICA HOPKINS

Monica Hopkins was a letter writer from a Canadian ranch. She came from England with her new husband Billie in 1909. Her enthusiasm, her sense of humor, her quiet dignity and thoughtfulness enabled her to adjust to the frontier with its endless challenges and surprises. Her writing style takes the reader into the past with ease. In this typed version of her original handwritten letter, written in 1910, Monicca Hopkins delves into almost every aspect of frontier life.

Log Cabin and We Two

"Enmore"
Priddis
June, 1910

Dearest Gill

I think it was raining when I started my last letter to you and it is still doing so. Of course it has not been raining all the time, we have had some fine days in between, but we certainly have had a terrible lot of wet weather, far worse than I ever remember at home at this time of the year. And then Canadians have the nerve to talk about our English climate as if it never did stop raining over there! They try to tell me that this is "an exceptionally wet spring." I try to look as if I believe it because I'm a very polite person, but I dont doubt that we shall get this every year, Billie says not, he also joins the chorus that it "most unusual"—We shall see!

We have had many "two meal" days, we enjoy them, when they occur occasionally, but too many are boring. I have caught up with my correspondance and now everyone—including you, owes me letters, such a nice feeling! it is over a week now since we had any letters—and no one has been up to the mine on account of the creeks being so high, so we are practically isolated; there is one way that we can get to Priddis without crossing the creeks, but it is a long way round. Just a cow path which runs up and down two quite steep hillsides, with a wretched little muddy creek at the bottom, and with so much rain that will be quite deep & a rider would be very apt to mire his horse, also the trail is between poplar and jack pine all the way and would be soaked by the time he reached Priddis, so unless there is a real emergancy we shall just have to wait until the creeks go down and console ourselves with the thought of all the letters that are piling up for us at the post office. Billie and I have been "boating" lately, I think I told you that Billie has an old punt that we use for a bath during the summer; it had been put in a shed for the winter, but one afternoon Billie decided that he would get it out and see if it needed any repairs—it did'nt, so he took it down to the creek. The water is almost up to the top of the banks and simply racing along, we pushed the old tub in and climbed aboard and away we went! It was a mad ride! Billie had a paddle that he meant to steer with, but he did'nt get much chance to use it, for the current was so strong, we simply raced along, and were over a mile away from the house before we could get near enough to the bank to hang on to some willows. The water was a little smoother there and we paddled to one of the creek crossings, where there is an opening in the bank and got ashore, we pulled the punt up and started to walk home. We met Helene and Joe who had followed after us to rescue us if necessary! though how they were going to do it, I'm not quite sure—Billie and Joe fetched the punt back in the waggon—we had fortunately landed on the "Enmore" side of the creek and not the Priddis side–and Billie and I went down again—Joe and Helene refusing to come—I thought if Billie was going to be drowned I might as well be drouned too—ah me! <u>What</u> devotion!! Anyway it was good fun and beats the Water Shute at Earl's Court hollow! The next day, Billie took a neighbour who had dropped in to see us out in the punt, & just as they started Harry got frightened and jumped overboard, he was up to his neck in water and nearly did get drowned, Joe dashed in and dragged him out; but it was quite a struggle to get up on the bank. Billie in the meantime was alone in the punt. Fortunately he got into an eddy in one of the curves of the creek & held on to the bushes until Joe arrived with the wagon.

The barometer is steadily climbing so we are hopeful that the weather will really clear up. Joe, Billie and the other men who have horses on the range are anxious to start on the "round up." I'm very thrilled at the thought of it. It seems to be the culmination of all the years work, everything that has been done has been with an eye to the "gathering" of the horses.

I'm at present very vague about the whole affair, but later on hope to be able to tell you more about it. As far as I can make out, most of the money that we are to live on, will come from the results of the Round up; if not this year—at some future date, but I must confess that, I fear, it will be some time before we are the millioneres, that Uncle Rex, seemed to think we should be in about five years. He figured it out that if Billie had thirty mares this year; then next year he should have thirty colts and also thirty for the next two years, by that time the first colts should have colts—so that would be 60 colts—and from them we would be doubling every year, my mind boggles at the thought of what we should have in ten years—certainly the range would not hold our bunch, let alone all the other people's horses. Such things as deaths, mares having no colts, and the fact that there are also "Boy" colts never entered his optometic mind! Billie says that a good average of colts from 30 mares would be twenty four. Evidently, it is far more risky to raise a colt, than it is a baby, so much can happen to them, they can, and do—get drouned in creeks, mired in mud holes—illness, accidents, or they simply disappear. I think we shall be lucky if we can just pay our way and not expect to have a large banking account, but it is a glorious life, and even if we dont make our fortunes we are getting a great deal of joy & fun out of living. We are able to do <u>what</u> we like, <u>when</u> we like, and <u>how</u> we like, and not many of you poor people who live in cities can say that!

I have a new pet! A baby coyote—Joe presented him to me about a week ago. Joe had dug out a den and killed all the cubs except this one and for some reason he spared this shivering snappy little creature and brought him home for me. "Kazan," as I call him is a funny little fellow, at first he was petrified at everything, if he was picked up he went absolutely stiff and for the first day would'nt eat a thing—though he must have been very hungry, for he quite empty, no little tummy like a puppy has. I have a little puppy too, just about the same age as Kazan—about a month old. Far too young to leave her mother really, but Mr. Burns who gave her to me, said the mother had no milk and he had no cow—so "Poppy" has become another inmate of our home. Billie has adopted her, but it is I who gets up in the middle of the night and warms her milk over a lamp—that is I did—now we have put the two babies outside in a small kennel together and they sleep there. I was a little afraid to do it at first, but Billie said they were too small to hurt each other and would be company, so I put them outside. Poppy tight as a little drum with milk and porridge—poor little Kazan, hungry, cold and frightened—shut the trap door on them and hoped for the best. Next morning I went out as soon as I was dressed rather wondering what I would find; Poppy came out at once, but poor Kazan was huddled in a corner. I yanked him out, snarling and struggling away for all he was worth, and carried him into the kitchen and gave him his breakfast; at first he would'nt eat but when he saw Poppy gobbling away he ventured nearer and finally started to eat too, now he enjoys his meals, but the sound of a door opening or a footstep sends him scurriing under the stove. At first I had a small strap around his neck and a piece of rope for a leash and took him out on that, for I knew that if he started to run I should never catch him again and he would'nt live a day on his own, now he runs about alone always making for the stove if the kitchen door is open—and if he finds it shut he has a hidey hole in the woodpile that he crawls into.

The hounds are so funny, when they first saw him, they sniffed him all over, but never offered to hurt him, though they would have killed an adult in a twinkling. I suppose it's because he is a baby, but they wont have anything to do with him, they just walk stiff-legged away if he ventures near them—but he does'nt bother them much, he and Poppy are great pals, and I see a cheerful time ahead of me keeping things away from them. Kazan has teeth like needles, he's a scrawny little begger at present—thin as a rake—a sharp little nose and a tail that has very little hair on it at present–when he is full grown he should have a lovely brush.

It has stopped raining & the sun is shining, hurrah! Billie has suggested an early supper and then a walk up to see how the garden is. Goodbye for the present.

It cleared up in the evening Billie and I went up to the garden, and found everything looking well and not washed out as Billie feared they would be—and when I was up yesterday the growth was simply marvelous the hot weather has simply made everything spring up. I see that I shall soon be taught the mysteries of "thinning out." The hot weather has also brought out the mosquitoes, and Helene and I are having rather a bad time with the little miseries and scratching is the order of the day–but at least I do have peace—that is more or less—from the little brutes at night. Billie has his mosquito net that he had when he was in Argentine and we have it over our bed so we are fairly well protected, though occasionally a stray mosquito gets in and when Billie hears its "ping," he rises up with a roar like a lion disturbed at its "kill" and crawls madly about the bed making frantic grabs in the direction he thinks the insect is! Between the two of them I'm in danger of being trampled to death, so generally scramble from under the netting and light the lamp and watch the proceedings from the outside, Billie hurling himself after the poor little creature, until he finally corners it and squashes it between his palms. Should there be any blood in the corpse, he triumphantly yells "I knew the little brute bit me," never giving me the credit for having supplied the blood! Once more peace will reign and I'll return to my side of the bed, hoping no more ravishing beasts will get in to disturb us. Billie says the mosquitoes will probably last most of the summer, but that this is the worst time for them, later on it's just the odd one that will bother us, which is cheerful hearing anyway.

Helene and I are much looking forward to Millarville Races, which is evidently the chief social event of the year out here, we have heard so much about them that we are quite thrilled at the thought of going, but as it is a twelve mile drive we shall only go if it is fine, our conveyances out here are open to the elements. I once asked Billy why they did'nt have brougharms out here and drive in comfort, he simply hooted at the idea, but I dont see why they dont, at least one of us would ride in comfort and that one would be me!

Billie has been riding now for over a week and it looks as if it will be quite a time before they have all the horses gathered.

In your last letter you asked me what I meant when I talked about the Range. Well, it means all the many thousands of acres of land that lie to the North, South and West of us—though chiefly to the West—and that so far no one has taken up. Although we have a section, 640 acres of our own, this land would'nt begin to carry our bunch of horses all the year round. A certain amount of our land is kept for hay and green feed—then there is a pasture for the work and saddle horses, two or three cows and odd calves and a steer or two; and so except for about six weeks in the summer when all the mares are gathered for the breeding season, they and all the yearling two and three year olds, are all turned on the range to travel and wander where ever they wish. Of course what few neighbours we have also run their horses on the range which is free to everyone.

When Billie first came and had the range near here pretty well to himself, he used to be able to gather his horses alone for they rarely scattered very far, but now there are more horses on the range, they join up into different bunches and wander much further afield—so that it is almost impossible for one man to gather his own. For this reason five or six of our immediate neighbours have instituted a round up each year on their own. They meet each day at some given spot, which depends, of course, on what part of the country is to be covered that day.

As our place lies pretty well to the South and the Harris' lies to the North of what we call "our range," and as we both have pretty good corrals—most of the corraling is done either here or on the Harris' place, which means that both of us have to have a good substantial meal ready every day they are riding, as we never know at which place the corralling will be done. As Billie usually leaves here about eight o'clock and after does'nt get back until well after two o'clock, you can imagine what appetites they bring with them.

Both Stella Harris and I have very much the same meal ready—cold meat, bacon and eggs—pies with crackers and cheese, nothing to spoil if they do not turn up here & everything will do for the next day.

Helene and I are thoroughly enjoying the novelty of it all—if the corralling is being done here, we can usually get a glimps of the bunch of horses, with riders behind, and on the flanks, as they come around the shoulder of the big hill to the West, then for a minute or so we loose sight of them until they appear at the head of the coulee heading down to our gate. There they have to stop, often they try to break away but seldom succeed; tho it has happened and a whole day's riding is wasted, but as a rule one of the riders comes ahead slowly and gets around the bunch and opens wide the gate: then the horses seem to know they are beaten and will head for the corral gates without much trouble where they are safely shut in. The men loosen the cinches on their saddles and lead their horses into the stable for a rest and feed and come up to the house, where Helene and I are racing around putting the finishing touches to the meal. We have put the washing utensils on a table outside and get great amusement watching them at their ablutions, each one dips his head in the basin, splashes violently then blindly gropes for the towel and comes to the table still slightly dripping—and so hungry and glad for a scalding hot cup of tea or coffee. After they have had a smoke and talked over the ride, they all return to the corrals and Helene and I generally go along with them to watch them cut out the horses. Our own mares are generally turned into a small pasture—some of the mares have colts at foot, such darlings—wobbling along close up to the sides of their mothers, all though usually the older mares if their colts are only a day or two old will drop out of the bunch when they start to return and are left behind and very often come along afterwards and hang round the gate waiting to be let in.

When everyone has cut his horses into various corrals to hold them, the rest of the bunch, geldings, yearlings and two year old mares are all turned out again on to the range. I do hope you are not too bored over all this rigmarole, but you asked for it, when you told me that you wanted me to tell you all about my new life—and you certainly are hearing all about it!

I was very pleased when I found that both my mares have colts, one from a mare that Joe gave me for a wedding present–and the other from the mare that Billie gave me to start my "bunch"—now, counting "Snake" I have five horses and I hope that Uncle Rex's way of reckoning will hold good with my bunch! Billie says I shall soon have to apply for a brand of my own. Both my colts are fillies, is'nt that lucky?

We have a "chore boy," though 'man' would be really more correct, as I imagine he must be in his thirties. Billie with an eye to the approaching haying, when any one who can wield a hay fork is much appreciated, heard that "Crazy Jenks" was on the lookout for a job and "engaged" him right away. This year Joe will be busy at the mine and not able to help as much as usual and Billie, even with the little help that Helene and I hope to be able to give, will need at least one more man, and every one is so busy with their own haying that it is hard to get help—so "Jenks" is another inmate of our house! Jenks is well known in these parts, though it was the first time that I had heard of him when Billie announced his intention of getting him for haying. His descriptive name, or rather nick name, put me off a little and now that he is actually here I see how very suitable it is, for crazy he certainly is in some ways, though in others, especially if he has anything to gain, he can be very wise!

Jenks is one of those unfortunate youths who have been sent to Canada because his people are ashamed of him and want him out of the way. They are, I should imagine, of the lower middle class—railway clerk or something—and they asked some people they once knew who used to live near Calgary to take him; and these people not knowing what he was like consented to have him. At first "Jenks" was all right, but later on they found it impossible to do much with him, and when they left Alberta, they also left Jenks behind and since then he has been going from pillar to post, never staying very long any where. Generally he is "fired," but occasionally "Jenks" gives notice, he always gives one months notice, and we are told that nothing will keep him one day longer. It may be 40° below or a flood, or it may be very awkward for "Jenks" to leave that day—nothing stops him, come "Hell or High Water" off he goes even if he has no place to go to in view.

This then is the individual I have had dumped on me! "Jenks" at present is very new and on his best behaviour, he is quite a good worker and willing to work just as long as Billie is with him. He is not allowed to drive a team but there are many jobs he can do—and some that he cant, as I found to my cost, when I discovered he had carefully hoed up all the mint that I had so carefully planted in a corner of the garden. "Jenks" had been told to hoe everything up that was between the rows in the vegetable garden and as my mint was not in a row it was a weed as far as "Jenks" was concerned and up it had to come—Darn the idiot!—and we have a lamb that was given to us which was to be offered up in a short time and I had been so looking forward to lamb and mint sauce—again I say "Darn" and I mean a great deal more!

To my mind it seems criminal to send these young lads to the colonies in the hopes of reforming them. It is ridiculous to expect that a boy who is inclined to go wrong in England will turn over a new leaf as soon as he comes to Canada, particularly if he comes to strangers, who are not interested as to whether he goes straight or not, and have no desire to help the boy at all. The people to whom "Jenks" was sent out to, were only interested as to the amount of work they could get out of him, and when they found it was not as much as they had hoped for they were more than anxious to get rid of him and I imagine that Jenks was just as anxious to go. One cant help but feel very sorry for the youth (man, I should say!) but I forsee that it wont be easy for any of us at times!

And now before I end this scrawl, let me tell you the sad sad story of me and my photograph. Last March when we were in Calgary meeting Helene, I slyhed away from Billie and had my picture taken. I kept it a dead secret, not even Helene knew—it was to be a surprise for Billie on his birthday. When the proofs came, I managed to smuggle them into my bedroom, without anyone seeing them and opened them in a fever of excitement. In the first, I had a grin like a Cheshire cat—I discarded that at once, far too frivolous. In the second, I sulked and scowled—but the third! oh my! Eyes gazing heavenward, a sweet sad smile, all it needed was the clasped hands and it would have been the dead spit of "The Souls Awakening"—at least so I thought (and still think!!).

I sent away for six copies, all I could afford, but planned to save up and get many more copies to shower on my friends and relations, to show them the real Monica, not the flippant girl they had known! I have decided now, to save my dollars for a more worthy cause!

On Billie's birthday, the photo, along with a pipe, were on the breakfast table at Billie's plate. Breathlessly I watched him open the parcel and look at the picture. "Good heavens, where did you get this?" he roared. "You look like a sick calf!" Helene after studying it for some time said, "Your hair looks awfully nice." Unappreciative brutes! With absolutely no idea of beauty in their souls. Joe was no kinder, all he said was "that you? You never looked like that in your life." After such unpleasant criticism I have rather hesitated to send you your copy, but it is going with this letter and I shall be waiting anxiously to hear what polite things you can think up to say about it. Yesterday, I received Mothers and Fathers reaction to my portrait—Mother says, "Oh my darling, I cant bear to look at it, you look so sad and ill it makes me want to cry. I have put it away in my drawer under my underwear"!! I ask you! Father is even more forceful, he says, "You look drawn and care worn, healthy enough, but the life evidentually tells!" Boy cannot have seen it yet for there are no comments from him. When I think of all the dollars and dollars I spent on those ungrateful creatures—I could weep! You will be glad to hear that at least the pipe was approved of! but my feelings are badly shattered.

Love to you both

Monica

HIGH RIVER COOK BOOK

Ranch life in High River was well established by 1907 when the Ladies' Aid of the Chalmer's Church in High River compiled recipes for their cookbook. The recipes were originally submitted by ranch women, members of the Ladies' Aid, including the authors of the three recipes selected for this book: Mrs. Riley, Mrs. Pflughaupt, Mrs. Koch and Mrs. Wallace. In the original text, in keeping with custom and perhaps propriety, the women have no first names—just the respectful title of Mrs.

High River Cook Book

PICKLE FOR BEEF OR PORK.—For one hundred pounds take nine pounds salt, three gallons water, three ounces of saltpetre, one quart of molasses, three pounds of brown sugar, one-half pound soda. Boil the above and pour on when cold.

Mrs. Wallace.

SUET PUDDING.—One cup of suet, one cup of brown sugar, one cup of bread crumbs, one cup of raisins, one cup of currants, one cup of figs, one cup of sweet milk, one-half cup of citron peel, four eggs, one teaspoonful of soda, two teaspoonfuls of cream of tartar, enough flour to make a stiff batter. Steam four hours.

Mrs. Riley.

PUDDING SAUCE.—Beat two eggs, one cup of powdered sugar, and a quarter of a cup of butter together for ten minutes. Add the juice of an orange, one tablespoonful of lemon juice, a little grated nutmeg, a teaspoonful of vanilla and one cup of boiling water. Cook over hot water until hot and about the consistency of cream. Use at once.

Mrs. Riley.

MINCEMEAT.—Two pounds of lean beef, one-half pound of chopped suet, eight large apples, chopped very fine, one pound and a half of brown sugar, one pound of raisins, one pound of currants, one-half pound of citron, rind of one lemon (grated), one pint of cider. Mix well and put in a pot and let it get thoroughly heated, and after it is cooled, put in half a pint of brandy and seal it up. This will keep for a year. One teaspoonful of allspice, one teaspoonful of mace, one-half teaspoonful of cloves, one-half teaspoonful of cinnamon (ground).

Mrs. Pflughkaupt and Mrs. Koch, Eden Valley Ranch.

MARY AQUINA ANDERSON

On July 25, 1913, Mary Aquina Price married a young rancher, Leonard Anderson, on Rock Creek, southwest of Wood Mountain, Saskatchewan. Years later she compiled her remembrances of life on the ranch in a self-published memoir: Rock Creek Ramblings.

Wedding on Rock Creek

THE ROSES WERE BLOOMING, the berry bushes were loaded with raspberries and plump burgundy gooseberries. Even the ground was carpeted with strawberries in hidden places. The garden was never better. There were new potatoes, peas, beans, crisp carrots, beets and radishes and greens for the wedding dinner. Young frys were ready for the pan; rich cream, sweet yellow butter, fresh bread, cake and pies were prepared. The table, with all the extension leaves was spread with white linen.

I dressed in the Robin's egg blue gown that I had worn for graduation from public school in Dakota, and wore the matching velvet bonnet.

Guests arrived about noon. It was a "Dakota" do with my parents, Adolph and Gunda Anderson and their baby Marvin, Earl Anderson, Knute Rye, his housekeeper Mrs. Johnson, Ole Larson and the Solvey Solversons with baby Violet. Mrs. Solverson's father, the Rev. Morris performed the wedding ceremony.

I played the piano. Then I stood up and Leonard and I exchanged vows with the Rev. Morris presiding. By 2 o'clock the ceremony was over and everyone was seated, enjoying their dinner.

To the northwest a new school, Sister Butte was built during the summer. The young people we chummed with insisted we should give a wedding dance in the fall. So Leonard asked for the schoolhouse. During the supper hour one fellow who was bit tipsy caused a row, resulting in a fight on the dance floor. Some one took a lariat and tied him up in the coal bin for a while. The dance went merrily on.

Two of our wedding gifts stand out in my memory. Grandma Arnold gave me six silver spoons. They were so much better than pewter. And then one day Leonard rode to the post office and brought back a letter from New York, from my aunt's sister. In the letter was twenty-five dollars. Twenty-five dollars! While Leonard was riding on the horse herd in the mornings, I studied Eaton's catalogue, decided which set of dishes I would order. In the evening while I played the piano Leonard studied a different catalogue. It was Franklin's Veterinary Supplies. He had a herd of about fifty horses, many of them were yearlings and two-year olds in need of castration, so while I dreamed of dishes, he had other dreams. Needless to say, the money was spent on a set of pickle-plated emasculators.

I was, indeed, a rancher's wife.

AGNES COPITHORNE

Agnes Rollefstad's writing was inspired from her poignant childhood memories of an Alberta homestead, as well as the years she spent with Harry Copithorne on a ranch in the Cochrane district. Of her poetry, Agnes wrote, "These are not modern poems. They give up their meanings easily." She could have added "and with grace, joy and honesty." In communities across the western plains there have always been women modestly telling it like it is—Agnes Copithorne represents them well.

The Day I Fell in the Well

"Don't go near the old well,"
my dad warned us.
"The Spring run-off
has filled it with water
and the cover is unsafe."
Never one to take advice
or heed a warning,
I said to my brother Twig,
"Let's go see if there really is
water in that old well."
Ever handy with barnyard language
he called me all kinds of a fool.
"Pooh to you," I said,
"I've jumped on that old thing
a thousand times."
I skipped to the well, Twig following.
Feeling a delicious prickle of daring
I stepped gingerly
atop the weathered boards

of the well cover.
With a sickening crunch
the rotten boards gave way.
Shrieking, I plunged downward
with terrible speed
the sky disappearing above me.
Clawing frantically at the cribbing
my fingers found and hung on to
the flimsy ladder that reached
from top to bottom.
Stomach churning, brain exploding
in numberless stars,
I was frozen with fear
and ice-water to my armpits.
"Get me out, Sweet Jesus," I prayed.
"Get me outta here and
I'll be good the rest of my life."
A promise so empty
it should have brought on
thunder and lightning.
I lunged upwards, rungs splintering
with each frenzied toe-hold.
Finally my fingers found the top
of the cribbing. "Help!" I yelled.
Twig was peering down, mouth
hanging open.
Bracing himself he grabbed my hands
and pulled me out.
Sobbing and dripping I ran to the house
his laughter following me all the way.

Holding Hands

We sit by the fire, holding hands;
hands spotted and dry with age
of which we are not aware.
Our hearts are still young,
making the days worthwhile
the nights peaceful.
The phonograph purchased secondhand
forty years ago still entertains us.
Wilf Carter yodels,
McDonald and Eddy still call
their love songs over the miles.
On starlit nights we rock
on the porch, a great moon watching.
We are still young at heart.
Young enough to play at love
with dry weightless kisses
and gentle embrace.
Still young at heart we hold hands
drawing strength from each other.

ANN CLIFFORD

Ann Clifford and her husband, Raymond, were residents of High River and, beginning in 1931, spent twenty years of their lives on the Bar U Ranch when it was part of the Pat Burns ranching empire. Ann's Story *is the story of those memorable years. The book brings together Ann's outstanding pictorial record of life on the ranch including a series of quiet unassuming vignettes. One of these, "Bar U Store House," written as a grocery list not originally intended for publication, is featured in this anthology.*

Bar U Store House

There was a store house lined with tin. When we got supplies it consisted of the following:

1 ton flour
½ ton sugar
100 lbs coffee beans
50–100 lbs of tea in large cardboard boxes lined with heavy tinfoil
Cases of:
Cornstarch
Pepper
Salt
Royal yeast cakes
Jam
Dried prunes
Dried appricots
Dried apples
Rolled oats
Raisins
Macaroni

Tapiocca
Rice
Brown sugar
Whole big cheese
No canned vegetables

Bar U grew a wonderful garden of potatoes, carrots, turnips, cabbage, onions, beets and sometimes corn. There was a huge root cellar with bins for the different vegetables. Very dark inside. Cabbage and onions hung from the rafters. There was one electric light bulb, but when we had the 32 volt plant you might as well have had a candle.

Mother taught all seven of us girls how to bake, but I had never started from scratch. I learned how to bake bread with those old Royal yeast cakes.

I found that starting about supper time I would soak the yeast cake with a bit of sugar till it was soft and bubbly and add water, salt, shortening and flour. Mix all together in a large bowl and wrap it up and hope it would rise all night.

Later when we moved into the other house with hot and cold running water I would put the mixed dough in a large bowl and place it on a board on top of the hot water tank. Just this little heat did the trick. When you got up the next morning it had risen to the top. You punched it down, put some in pans and had hot buns for breakfast. Cinnamon buns, etc. It was great to have your bread baked before 10 am in the morning.

Everyone seemed to like my pies made of dried fruit; cakes and cookies made from that thick cream.

A COMMON RANGE

The American and Canadian West

ROSE BIBBY

In the past ten years, poet and humorist Rose Bibby of Westlock, Alberta, has become better known across the Canadian West as the Hayshaker's Wife. She has partnered up with her husband on the ranch and recently on stage as well. Her poems are published in a series of tapes and chapbooks including Rosebriar Ranch Ramblings.

Things We Learned From Our Fathers

I can see the flowers bloomin'
　　and the greenin' tree leaves
　　　　I can watch the birds nestin' and the buzzin' bees . . .

I can talk with my neighbour
　　I can smell the fresh cut hay
　　　　I can watch the coyote and the deer at play . . .

Sittin' deep in my saddle on the Ol' Ranch.

I can feel the sun a warmin'
　　See the risin' moon in the sky
　　　　I can watch the fluffy clouds tumble on by . . .

I can smell the welcome rain
　　I can see the soil turn mellow
　　　　I don't punch a clock or envy any fellow . . .

Sittin' deep in my saddle on the Ol' Ranch.

I can see the grain a ripenin'
And the storm clouds churnin'
I can see geese a wingin' and fall colours turnin' . . .

I can check the feed and beddin'
Ride out in the driftin' snow
I can watch the spring calves frolic and grow . . .

Sittin' deep in my saddle on the Ol' Ranch.

Don't take it away
Because here I'm free
Don't take it away
It's where I want to be . . .

Just a hopin' and a prayin' and a plannin' on a stayin'
Deep in my saddle on the Ol' Ranch.

MARJORIE LINTHICUM

Marjorie Linthicum of Glentworth, Saskatchewan, considers herself first of all a rancher. She would not tell anyone she is a writer. Like the majority of working ranch women, she does not have a lot of time for writing. Yet, when Marjorie Linthicum wrote and presented a brief for the Public Hearings on the Proposed Development of a Grasslands National Park *in southern Saskatchewan in 1976, she spoke from the heart on behalf of her family ranch. In 1996 the Linthicum family continues to ranch on land adjacent to the Grasslands National Park.*

A Part of This Land

I HAVE A SPECIAL FEELING FOR THIS LAND. My father and mother came here to ranch in 1911 and it is where I was born, grew up and lived all my life.

I appreciate and respect—first flowers in the spring, the wide star-lit sky and the night winds whistling, the lonely call of the mourning dove and the thread of the long-billed plovers, the howl of coyotes, the waving of the throats of the sage hens, the smoothness of an antelope as it runs a short distance to pause and look back and snort its familiar warning, the screech of the hawks as I come up on a nest of their young, the vastness of the prairie under a blanket of snow, the threat of an approaching snow storm and the shelter of a brush coulee, the sharp thorns of a buffaloberry bush, the skill of red ants as they pack away crumbs from a noon lunch to some small stone.

I know what it's like to ride all day and never encounter another person, to have a faithful horse bring me sixteen miles home through a blinding storm, to drive cattle home in the fall and have them strung out for two or three miles heading for winter pastures, to see bands of wild horses trailed out to packing plants, to sit on a knoll and watch cattle graze on an alkali flat or two mighty bulls battle over a harem of cows, to repair fence all day and pick woodticks off all evening, to sit on the high butte and look south over the prairie for miles and miles, to drive cows and calves to summer pastures and then sit and watch until they mother up, to dream as a young girl of riding south to the Badlands and driving cattle with my dad and then having this dream come true, to trail carloads of grass-fed beef thirty miles to the railway in 35 degree below weather, to see buffalo horns on the prairie and wonder if the buffalo died from a winter storm or an Indian arrow, to have a horse get loose and leave me fifteen miles from home. I am as much a part of this land as the coyotes and the gophers.

ELIZABETH EBERT

Elizabeth Ebert of Lemmon, South Dakota, is the wife of a retired rancher. Through carefully crafted, rhymed and metered verse she tells a gentle story, often with humor, sadness, and always with sincerity. She is presently one of America's best-loved ranch poets. Her poems have been published in several chapbooks including The Pick-up Cowgirl.

An Ordinary Morning

'Twas just an ordinary mornin'
　Somewhere along in May,
When my husband hollered from the yard,
　And then I heard him say,
"I'm goin' to the pasture,
　It'll take an hour or two,
And if you'd like to come along,
　We'll drive out in Old Blue."

Now I don't get to tag along
　Much, as a general rule,
But I'd finished with the chorin'
　And the kids were all in school.
'Twould be just like we were courtin'
　I was happy at the chance,
For you take if where you find it
　When it comes to ranch romance.

Now Old Blue is kind of ancient
　And he's got some scars and dents,

'Cause we use him when we're feedin',
    Checking cows and fixing fence.
But the engine runs like clockwork,
    And the tires are pretty fair,
All except that right front whitewall
    That sometimes loses air.

And there's a chunk of baling wire
    To fasten down the hood,
And a saddle blanket for the seat
    Where the cushion's not too good.
The cab is kind of cluttered up
    With stuff we need, that's true,
There's vet supplies and fencing tools,
    And ropes and rifles too.

Well, we headed for the pasture
    ('Course I opened every gate.)
And we found that little heifer,
    The one that calved so late.
Her bag was near to bustin'
    Milk was dripping' from each teat,
For she'd kick that little feller
    Every time he tried to eat.

So my husband said, "I'll fix her
    And I'll do it slick as soap,
'Cause I've got you here to help me,
    And I brought along my rope.
Now I'll ride Blue on the fender,
    And you steer him from the seat,
And I'll rope that little mama
    And we'll let her baby eat."

Well, I lined up on that heifer,
  And he built himself a loop.
Then she took off at a gallop,
  So I just poured on the soup
And Old Blue was doing thirty
  When we topped that little knoll,
But he had her caught for certain
  —Then I hit that badger hole.

The cow kept right on goin'
  But we made a sudden stop.
My husband landed underneath
  And Old Blue was there on top.
I saw that rope come trailin' past,
  And it cheered me up a mite,
So I jumped right out and grabbed it,
  And I snubbed that critter tight

Around a most convenient rock.
  You should have heard her beller.
Then I went lookin' for the calf,
  And I brought that little feller
And I held him to his mama,
  And it really pleased me some
To see his little belly
  Growin' round, just like a drum.

Made me think about my husband. . . .
  So I went back to Old Blue
To kind of take a look around
  See what I had to do.
Blue was standin' kind of hip-slung,
  'Cause one wheel was up some higher,
But 'twas nothin' that I couldn't fix
  With just some balin' wire.

My husband lay there underneath,
    Said he thought his leg was broke.
But it made me pretty happy
    Just to know he didn't croak,
So I twisted stuff together
    And I stuck Blue in reverse
And I backed out of that badger hole.
    Then I heard my husband curse;

And when I stopped to think of it,
    He was right, without a doubt,
Instead of backin' over him.
    I should have pulled him out.
Well, I got him loaded in Old Blue
    'Mongst all those other things,
Propped his leg up with that blanket
    Though it made me ride the springs.

And we finally limped on into town,
    Not travelin' very fast.
Old Blue, he got new tie rods,
    And my husband got a cast.
Just an ordinary mornin'
    Really nothin' out of line.
By the way, I checked that heifer
    And that calf is doin' fine.

GWEN PETERSEN

With humor, Gwen Petersen deals with the sometimes difficult aspects of country life. From the first line in A Ranch Woman's Manual *to the last line in* The Greenhorn's Guide to the Woolly West, *and in the chapbooks in between, Gwen keeps us laughing. After taking part in the National Cowboy Poetry Gathering in Elko in 1985, Gwen founded the Montana Gathering.*

Branding

Wherein one learns how to deal with tally sheets, vaccine guns and Mountain Oysters.

On branding day (the day when your ranch mark is burned into the hides of all those freshfaced baby calves) you do double duty. Not only do you act as hired hand, but you're also chief cook, hostess, and runner-after of anything anybody has forgotten. Sometimes a day of indescribable hilarity, sometimes laced with small tragedies, branding is always a whole lot of work. As a thinking Ranch Wife, estimate how many neighbours and extra hands are coming to "help", add fifteen, and lay in mountains of provisions, because every country custom says you must feed all those men promptly at 12:00 noon. All food must be home-cooked. Fortunately, some of the neighbor Ranch women feel it is their duty to help out in the kitchen.

While you nestle cases of beer and pop among the rocks at the edge of the creek, the men are furiously busy. Calves are cut away from their mammas, branding fires are started, ropers swing loops. Calves are roped and dragged, bellowing towards waiting cowboys who grab the north and south ends of the poor little things and stretch in both directions. Other cowboys leap to apply the hot iron, castrate the little bulls, notch the ears and gouge the nubbins of horn.

You and the other women not smart enough to stay in the house, are in charge of the vaccinating, the tally sheet, the disinfectant, the scour pills, the blood stopper powder, and keeping track of the dehorning spoons.

The watch word for the Ranch woman wielding any of the branding day implements is "Look Out!" Exude confidence as you approach a calf captured firmly by north and south cowboys. Have the vaccine gun ready. Pinch a bit of skin away from the calf's rib cage just under the foreleg. Thrust the needle in, making sure you don't poke through one side and out the other of the pinch; thereby squirting vaccine in the air. Move quickly and try to keep out of the way of the man with the hot iron who is searing the brand into the calf's hide at the same time you are doing your needlework. The second you've finished, remove the needle and turn nonchalantly away.* While being nonchalant, do not dawdle. Those two cowboys holding the calf will turn loose all at once. Being struck by flying hooves can take the enthusiasm out of the day.

About your person hang a small notebook and pencil. Dangling from the belt on the hipside of your leg is a handy spot. Remember to tie these items on. Merely stuffing a notebook and pencil in your pocket won't do. AT the wrong moment it will fall out and into a fresh juicy pile. Fish it out and use it anyway. AS each critter is vaccinated, it's up to you to tally heifer or bull in your little book.

When you tally the bulls and heifers, you always get mixed up, but NEVER admit it. Always answer promptly and confidently even if you have to make it up.

Once or twice a lull occurs in the feverish activity. The men sag against the corral posts or flop on the ground, beer cans in hand. At this point, race for the house, make sure the big coffee urn is full and functioning, check the roasts, stuff a bushel of potatoes in the oven to bake, mentally count the chairs around the dining room table, and decide some people will have to eat from laps in the living room.

---

*CAUTION: Although nonchalence is the key attitude, alert attention must be the Ranch Woman's prime mover.

Then race back to the corral where the thoughtful husband has saved you one last swallow of warm beer.

At the noon break, pick up the bucket of Mountain Oysters* and dash for the house ahead of the men. While they "wash up", load the food on the table. No matter how starved, the men will politely hang around outside in the yard til you ring the come-and-get-it bell. Once seared, absolutely no sound is heard for the first ten minutes besides the clinking of eating utensils. When the first panic subsides, limited conversation begins to trickle around the table. By dessert, the morning's funny episodes and catastrophes have been repeatedly analyzed and all bachelors have been teased about their girlfriends.

Naturally you and the other women keep the coffee pouring and serving dishes full. Between trips, you get to eat standing up in the kitchen.

---

*Mountain Oysters: Those items separated from bull calves. To be laboriously cleaned, egg-battered, crumbled and deep fried at a later date. Old timers claim they're delicious as well as having certain rejuvenating powers. It is not a good idea to dispute this claim.

GERTRUDE MINOR ROGER

Lady Rancher *is the story of Gertrude Minor Roger's initiation into life on the large Minor cattle ranch, first on the Saskatchewan prairie and then in the Chilcotin region of British Columbia. In the chapter "Planely Speaking," selected for this anthology, Gertrude Minor Roger writes with warmth and humor as she tells of the success, failure, loss and recovery she has experienced while ranching.*

Planely Speaking

WITH A NEW SON and his first solo flight all in one week, John was so elated his feet hardly touched the ground. When he wasn't flying, he was sneaking in the back door of the hospital to see me. He pampered me with flowers, chocolates and special duty nurses.

When it was time for me to leave, John told me he had arranged for Jim Murray to fly us home in Jim's four-seater plane. This announcement just about sent me into a coma.

"Why, that's a crazy idea!" I cried. "What do you want to do, kill us all?"

"It's the safest way to go," he maintained stoutly. "There's nobody up there to crash into."

"There's the Law of Gravity," I told him. "Everything that goes up has to come down."

John spent many hours at the hospital and later, at Aunt Flora's, trying to convince me of the safety of air travel. It didn't make any sense to me. John had been cautious enough to drag me to Medicine Hat two months before the baby was due, and now he wanted to run the risk of killing us all.

As soon as I was up and around, he took me to the airport to see Jim's plane. Jim explained about the elaborate safety precautions and mechanical check-ups involved before a plane took off. He might have saved his breath for I didn't believe a word of it. But I had now been away two months and was anxious to get home with my little son. And I could see that the only way I was going to get there was in this flimsy-looking airplane. Against my better judgment, I agreed.

The single-engined plane stood waiting for us on the runway. It surely didn't look very safe to me, no matter what John said. Somewhere I had read that twin-engined planes were better. What a bad time to start remembering such things, I told myself. As I mounted the step into the machine's back seat, I started praying. Jim Murray insisted that I do up my seat belt. How was this going to help me when one of the wings fell off, I wondered.

Suddenly the engine burst into life and we began to move down the runway—slowly at first, then faster and faster. The engine roar deepened and the ground started to fly past at a dizzy rate. I was sure the whole thing was going to blow up. Before I could yell at them to take me back, we parted with the ground, leaving my stomach far behind. I clung to my baby, closed my eyes and prayed again—oh how I prayed!

During that seemingly endless journey, I stared blankly ahead. John was smiling and looking out the window. Every once in a while, he would point at familiar landmarks.

"See, over there!" he cried, "that's where the Red Deer joins the South Saskatchewan!"

To me, nothing seemed familiar from the air, even when I got up enough courage to look. In moments of supreme daring, I glanced quickly out the window, turning my eyes sideways without moving my head an inch. That was enough for me. Who cared where the two rivers joined. I had no desire to do any aerial sightseeing.

John swung around in his seat and drew the blanket gently from the baby's face so he could look at his son. Little John was sleeping peacefully, smiling a little.

"See, he really likes it!" John beamed. "This kid will be able to fly a plane before he learns to walk!"

"He will *not!*" I snapped. I had agreed to this trip, but that was *it* as far as I was concerned. Shuddering, I wrapped the baby up again and held him tightly. For some reason, I felt very depressed.

Every time the whine of the plane's engine changed pitch, I was certain it was going to quit on us, and every time the machine shook I shivered. At any moment I expected it to come apart in mid-flight. But to my amazement, none of these certainties came to pass.

Soon we were circling over the main ranch. The roar of the motor lessened as we came in to land. I felt a sense of relief as the good earth came up to meet us, not knowing that this is one of the most hazardous moments of flying. Next thing I knew, we were bumping over a grassy field. When the door of the plane was opened, Pop was there to take the baby from me and carry him tenderly into the house. It was then I caught a look on the old man's face I had never seen there before—a mixture of love and tenderness and pride. For the first time, I began to see that Pop Minor was really not such a terrifying person after all.

Although Pop's house at the main ranch had no modern conveniences, it was much better than ours, so we decided to stay there until spring. As far as Pop was concerned, if you got along without something in the pioneer days you could get along without it forever. Any comfort developed since that time was senseless pampering. But John tossed this philosophy out the window the day he brought his son home. Even though lots of newborn babies had survived in the old house with only the heat from three coal and wood stoves, John decided this wasn't good enough for *his* son. While in Medicine Hat he had purchased an oil burner and had it shipped to the ranch with special instructions to his cousin Dode to have the thing working when we arrived home.

"Did you get that oil burner set up?" was his first question as we were walking from the plane to the house.

Dode shook his head. "Pop said he wasn't going to have that son-of-a-bitchin' contraption in his house. He says he's lived here fifty years and raised nine children, and what was good enough for him is good enough for you folks."

"Oh, he did, eh?" said John, and I saw his face beginning to set the way it had when we were arguing about the airplane.

By this time, we had reached the front porch, and there was the oil burner still sitting in the crate it had been shipped in.

John didn't even stop to remove his coat. He grabbed a hammer and began to knock the crate apart. Leaving the wood strewn all over the porch, he and Dode dragged the new burner into the dining room.

Pop stuck his shaggy head out of the lower bedroom.

"You're not setting that son-of-a-bitch up in here!" he bellowed.

John paid no attention. Without saying a word, he strode over to the coal and wood heater in the center of the dining room and methodically began to tear it apart—in spite of the fact it was still hot from the dying embers inside. Pop didn't say anymore, but he showed his displeasure by stomping from the room, whistling that dry little whistle of his.

Smoke billowed from the hot stove as John and Dode finished dismantling it. Soon we were all gasping and choking, but that didn't stop them. A trail of ashes followed them across the floor as they dragged the thing through the door and heaved it out the back. From around a corner, Pop gazed in dismay at the fate of this old friend he had stoked and poked for fifty years.

As always, when John decided to do something he just did it. I thought he might have been a bit more tactful with his father. After all, it is harder to accept change as you grow older.

John just laughed when I suggested this. "Heck, in a few days you won't be able to pry him away from that oil stove."

As it turned out, he knew his father a lot better than I did. Soon Pop was back in the dining room, standing silently behind John and Dode as they wrestled the oil burner into position. Next thing I knew, he was telling them how to fit the pieces of pipe together. When they finally got the stove working, he was the first to warm his hands over it.

Pop stayed awake most of that night for fear this new contraption would blow up. But when morning came and the house was still intact, he emerged smiling from his bedroom. The dining room was warm, he had one less fire to light and one less pailful of ashes to carry out.

In the spring, John decided to dismantle the oil burner so we could take it back to our place with us, but Pop protested.

"I'm getting kind of used to that son-of-a-bitch," he said. "You'd better order another one."

We ordered two—one for ourselves, and another one to heat the other side of Pop's house. The oil burner's arrival signified a new era at the Minor Ranch. We decided to modernize the whole operation. The next step was a more dramatic one. John made up his mind to buy an airplane.

Pop—who by nature opposed any innovation—just about blew his stack. Buying a plane was the craziest thing he had ever heard of. As usual, he said so in no uncertain terms.

"If we'd been meant to ranch that way they never would've invented horses!" he shouted.

John explained how much easier and better this big ranch could be run with an airplane, but the old man would have none of it.

"I've been running this place for fifty years," he snorted, "and I never needed any goddam plane!"

John sighed resignedly. He knew he would have to buy the plane from his own personal savings—the same way he had bought the oil burner. This time, however, he would have to dig up a lot more money. I opposed the purchase of the plane too. My position was that it would be much too dangerous to have him up flying every day of the year, and that we had more important things to spend our money on.

As usual, there was no stopping John once he was certain his idea was sound. I think both Pop and I realized this as soon as John broached the idea. We knew we were fighting a hopeless rearguard action.

The secondhand, single-engined J-3 arrived at the ranch on a clear April day. When John landed, everyone gathered around the machine to inspect it. All except Pop, that is. He stood away from the others, silent and stony-faced. Every line of his body showed his disapproval.

"Come on, Pop." John shouted. "I'll take you up for a ride!"

"The hell you will!" the old man bellowed. "You couldn't get me into that son-of-a-bitchin' thing for a million dollars!" Then he turned and walked briskly toward the house and we heard that tell-tale whistle again.

Most of those first days I went about my work with my eyes half-turned toward that great expanse of prairie sky. When I wasn't working I would be pacing up and down in front of our living room window. And I kept on worrying until John had landed safely. Each time he came in he regaled me with enthusiastic details of how the ranch looked from above and of how fast he could check over the whole operation by plane.

"Man, it gives you a free-and-easy feeling when you're soaring around up there!" he would say.

But he could never get me to agree to go with him, no matter how he tried to sell me on the idea. Flying was "strictly for the birds," and to me this was more than just a popular expression. I was terrified of it.

Finally, about a week after the plane's arrival, I faced up to the problem. I was preparing for another day of pacing and worrying when I suddenly thought to myself, "What's the sense going on like this? If he's going to get killed, I might as well get killed too." Without giving myself time for any further thinking, I told our hired girl to look after the baby, followed John out to the machine and climbed in. He didn't say anything but he looked pleased.

As expected, I did not enjoy the flight, but it was a lot less nerve-wracking than worrying about John from below.

Next day, John was busy warming up the plane when out walked Pop from the front of the house. With determined steps, he headed for the machine and climbed into the back seat—all without saying a single word. They circled slowly over the buildings a couple of times, then headed toward the hills on John's daily check of cattle, windmills and fences. In less than half an hour they were back, having done a job that would take a couple of fence riders all day. Pop was beaming broadly as he climbed from the plane.

"Yes sir," he said, "that's quite an outfit we've got there!"

Strutting over to a group of his men working nearby, he began to brag about all he had seen. You would think the whole idea of getting the plane had been his alone.

"Why, you can even see the goddam brands on those cattle!" he finished, with a look of satisfaction.

By this time, I was beginning to *want* to go up in the plane, but now my opportunities were few and far between. As soon as Pop heard the machine start up, he would run out of the house and jump in. No matter how I tried I could never beat him to it.

The plane became John's constant companion. His flying day began before breakfast, when he would go up just so he could catch the full beauty of the awakening day. As he predicted, the machine proved to be a big timesaver, leaving him time to consider other projects and activities. He flew to where he was working each day, both to save precious time and to have the machine available so he could fly into town for repairs whenever any equipment broke down.

Besides the daily check of the whole operation, John saw he could use the plane to spot cows in trouble during the calving season, to round up the cattle for branding day by chasing them in toward the windmill where the riders picked them up, and to take lunches and messages out to the distant locations where the men were working. More than anything else, the plane pushed the Minor Ranch into the efficiency-oriented twentieth century. In this case, it hadn't taken much pushing, for John was crazy to fly.

One windy August day John was haying near the farm when a black, black cloud appeared over the horizon. Suddenly remembering that the plane was only lightly tied down, John and one of his men jumped into a truck and rushed for the airstrip. But the dust storm was already upon them. As they struggled to turn the little craft into the wind, they were struck with a blast which tossed the machine about thirty feet into the air. The next moment it came crashing back to earth, a total wreck.

"Well," said John later, as he slumped dejectedly into a kitchen chair, "you didn't want me to have a plane, and I haven't got one, so I guess you'll be happy now."

"What happened?"

"The wind smashed it. Picked it up and tossed it on the ground like an angry kid would break a toy."

"I'm sorry," was all I could think to say. And I really meant it, for now that the machine was smashed I realized what a handy thing it was to have around the place.

We knew it was useless to think about buying another. Our total savings had gone into buying that one.

Next morning at five a.m. Pop came roaring through the hills in the old army truck. "JOHN!" he shouted, as he stomped into our kitchen, "You'd better order another one of those goddam flying machines. We need it around here!"

We could hardly believe our ears. John was the first to recover. "I sure will!" he beamed.

Within a few days he was off to Oshawa, Ontario, to pick up a new Piper Super Cub.

Later that year I became ill soon after returning home from the hospital where I had been recovering from a miscarriage. John wanted to rush me back to the doctor right away, but I assured him it was nothing but an attack of flu. Things went on like this for three days, with John trying to convince me to go to the doctor and me insisting there was nothing seriously wrong. Finally, John got so worried he phoned my sister, Evelyn, who is a nurse.

"Never mind what she says," Evelyn told him, "you get her to the doctor as fast as you can. It sounds to me like she's got blood poisoning. Our mother died of that you know."

I remember John carrying me to the plane and strapping me into the back seat. That was the last thing I was to remember for three days. John radioed Medicine Hat to have an ambulance waiting at the airport when we arrived. Had we been an hour later, it would have been too late.

The hospital was the same one where John had spent so much time trying to coax me to take my first flight. As I lay there now, I had plenty of time to consider how fortunate I was to have a husband who was a pilot, and that we had an airplane. Although I had made my case as difficult as possible, the plane had saved my life. My fears about the machine disappeared. It was a vital part of our ranch operation now and I wouldn't have it otherwise.

That was our plane's first ambulance mission—the first of many, many more. During the following winter, roads in our area were blocked for days on end with drifting snow. In the middle of his busy schedule—no matter what the weather was like—John would answer distress calls from people who had to get to the hospital in a big hurry.

I remember three days in particular. In the middle of a howling blizzard, John picked up a woman who was going to have a baby. He flew her into the hospital at Cabri, twenty miles southeast of Abbey, in plenty of time for the birth. Then he headed for home, happy in the knowledge he had helped a neighbor in need.

The second day, he received a frantic call from a father-to-be on a farm near Shackleton, about ten miles due east. When John arrived to pick up the mother, he found the house in a turmoil. It was too late to move the woman, and her husband—clad only in a fur hat and a pair of long-johns—was running around in confusion as he tried to get things ready.

"I've gotta get a kettle—a big kettle," he kept repeating.

In spite of his agitation, the man was able to tell John that a doctor was already on his way from Cabri so the baby could be delivered right here in the house.

John jumped into his plane and flew down the road until he spotted the doctor's car. Landing well ahead of the vehicle, he flagged the doctor down, helped him into the plane and took off for the farm. True to the tradition of the old west, the doctor arrived in the nick of time to save the perspiring father and deliver a bouncing baby girl.

But sometimes even a western tradition can fall by the wayside. The next day was bitterly cold, with the yellow sundogs pacing a pale gold sun across the sky. It was a good day to stay inside and toast your feet beside a roaring fire, and John would have done just that if we hadn't received a distress call from an expectant mother near Lancer, a few miles to the northwest.

When John saw the woman, he was sure it was too late to move her. He was becoming a bit of an expert on the frequency of birth pains by this time. "Are you sure you should be going, ma'am?" he asked.

"Aw, it took me hours to have my other kids," she told him confidently. "Don't give it another thought."

Three thousand feet in the air, and about half the distance to the Cabri hospital, John was forced to think of it again when the woman suddenly yelled, "Hey, I'm going to have the baby!"

Then the windows began to fog up so that John had to open a door to see where he was going. With the 20-below-zero air streaming into the cab of the plane, the mother called desperately: "I'm having it . . . I'm having it!" and she fainted dead away.

John did not panic. There was nothing he could do but keep flying and get the woman to the hospital as quickly as possible. (Laughing about it later, he said it's easy to keep cool when the temperature is 20-below.)

In a few minutes, the exhausted mother regained consciousness.

"The baby's here!" she announced.

"Good!" John shouted over his shoulder. "But for God's sake wrap it up and keep it warm!"

In Cabri, he landed the plane right beside the hospital and charged inside where he encountered two startled nurses.

"I've got a woman in my plane who has just had a baby!" he told them. "You'd better call the doctor and get me some blankets!"

When they still stared at him in disbelief, he repeated it, and added, "I'll need blankets to wrap around her until the doctor comes."

Still in a daze, they produced some blankets, and shoved them toward John. Rushing out to the plane, he wrapped the blankets around the woman and child. Then the doctor ran up, carrying his little black bag. In that 20-below wind, with John passing the instruments, the doctor set calmly to work. When they were finished, they transferred the patients to the hospital. Both mother and child came through that harrowing experience with no ill effects at all.

When John reached home, he swaggered into the house wearing an impish grin.

"Well, Gertie," he chuckled, "this is one time I didn't make it."

"What do you mean?" I asked.

"She had it in the back of the plane."

"Oh, you're kidding!" I laughed, and walked out of the room.

"If you don't believe it," he yelled after me, "come on out and help me clean up the back of the cab!"

I believed it all right when we had to spend the rest of the day chiseling away at the frozen afterbirth. I had come a long way from the little girl who wondered where calves came from each spring.

PEGGY SIMSON CURRY

Peggy Simson Curry became the first Poet Laureate of Wyoming in 1981. Best known for Red Wind . . . of Wyoming, *a poetic interpretation of the Johnson County range wars, she also wrote short stories while she worked as a teacher, introducing many students to creative writing. "A Life of Our Own" is taken from* Landmarked, *a book of short stories.*

A Life of Our Own

JIM JAMISON DIDN'T SEE THE PORCUPINE until he'd almost run over it. He slammed on the brakes and got out, carrying the .22 rifle. It was a young porcupine, and as he drew a bead it turned and looked at him.

"Why are you cryin' at me?" he asked impatiently. "I've got trouble enough now." But he lowered the rifle, for the look in the little eyes reminded him of the hopelessness in Mary's eyes when he'd told her about Sue-Ellen. "Get on with you, Spike," he said, and turned back to the truck.

He drove on down the dirt road. In a few minutes the buildings of the lower ranch came into view, the red roofs bright in the amber sun, the big barren cottonwood trees towering above them. It was here that he had brought Mary as his bride so many years ago, and it was here that their daughter, Sue-Ellen, had come only six months ago with the shiny new wedding ring on her finger.

He and Mary had never had either the money or the time to fix up the ranch house for themselves. They'd talked about it a lot, pretending they had money to spend, and they'd planned every room in detail. But the years had gone by, and the house had stayed the same.

Then Sue-Ellen wrote that she and Roy, her husband, would be coming to stay, and Jim and Mary had moved up to the old house, the original homestead on the property, which was too far gone to permit any daydreaming about it. Jim had hardly noticed the moving; all the available hours had been spent getting the lower ranch house ready for the day Sue-Ellen and her husband would move in. He'd felt a great sense of pleasure and accomplishment when that day finally came: his and Mary's dream had finally come true—for their daughter.

He got out of the car now and walked slowly toward the house, remembering sharply the money he had spent on it. He'd had it remodeled and had put in a gas stove and electric lights. He'd even started a lawn.

His daughter was in the kitchen, packing the last of her cooking utensils. "Sue-Ellen . . ." he began and then paused, not knowing how to go on. Instead of a young woman of twenty he seemed to see the grave face of a little girl with dark pigtails. For a moment he wished with all his heart and soul to return to that time.

"I'm sorry, Pa," she said. There was a stiff set to her lips, and she did not look at him.

She was prettier than Mary, he thought. Mary had been a sturdy little bride with strong capable hands and a way of walking that set the dishes jiggling in the kitchen cupboard. But Sue-Ellen was like a willow growing along the ditchbank in spring, tall and slender and beautiful.

Jim looked down at his big hands and his heavy wrists. How had he fathered a wonder like Sue-Ellen? And then the pain of losing her came up in him and he blurted out, "Your mother and I . . . the hard years with nothin' fancy . . . and then fixin' all this up for you and—"

"I know," she said softly. "But Roy doesn't like the ranch And I—I get lonesome for town, Pa."

"And so you're pullin' out and leavin' me to run this place and the homestead too." He couldn't keep the bitterness from his voice.

"The boys," Sue-Ellen said. "They'll help you."

"A fat chance of that," Jim said sourly. "They get home from that high school in town and what do they do? Mike has to practice the violin. All Joey wants to do is ride the calves." He glanced around, seeing the open, empty cupboards. "You're not leavin' this afternoon?"

There was a long silence. "Yes," Sue-Ellen said finally. "Roy's gone to borrow his father's truck. I've got to finish packing." Then she began to cry. "Don't try to keep us, Pa, she said. "Just leave us alone. We only want to live where we like—"

"And where's that?" Jim shouted. "What's he got to offer you? Where's he gonna work?"

"In a filling station."

"A filling station!" he muttered. He yanked his dust-stained hat lower on his forehead and walked blindly out of the house.

Outside, he stood looking at the land. He'd paid for every acre in sweat and backbreaking labor. And Mary—Mary had worked just as hard. For what? For a daughter who didn't care about the land or the sheep and cattle that grazed on it.

He drove home, remembering how afraid he'd been that he couldn't keep Sue-Ellen here; that was why he'd spent so much money fixing up the house, while he and Mary went on doing without. The old homestead looked shabby in the afternoon light; the log walls were bleached silvery gray by time and weather. When he stopped outside the kitchen door, he heard young Mike's violin. . . . *Like a yowling she-cat,* he thought.

He walked across the back porch and into the kitchen. "Mary," he called. "Where are you?"

Mary was in the front room. She sat with her hands folded, a soft smile on her face as she watched Mike practice the violin. She looked up at Jim, her clear gray eyes shining, and motioned to him not to interrupt. Jim clapped his big hands over his ears and walked out.

He was part way to the corral when he stopped and stared, for his older son was riding the milk cow. "Joey!" Jim cried, running toward the fence. "Get off that cow! You want sour milk for supper?"

"Okay, Pa," the boy said and slid off the cow's back He was short and stockily built, with a fine fuzz showing on his cheeks.

"If you've a mind for exercise you can begin shovelin' out this corral!" Jim leaned against the fence, breathing heavily. Then he looked at his son and added, "Didn't mean to yell at you, Joey. It's just—"

"That's okay," Joey said. "Listen, Pa, can I have a rodeo out here Sunday and invite the class?"

"No!" Jim shouted. "Think I spent my life learnin' to raise steers so a bunch of kids can ride 'em thin?"

Joey frowned. "I already asked the kids, Pa," he said.

"Then tell 'em I won't have it!" Jim said, and turned back to the house.

Inside, the violin was still being worked over by his younger son, but Mary was in the kitchen starting supper. She paused beside him and put her hand on his shoulder. "Jim—" she began, and then stopped. The question in her mind showed in her eyes.

"Sue-Ellen's leavin'," he said. "She'll be finished packin' and gone by now."

Mary's mouth quivered and he wanted to hold her in his arms, to feel her softness against him. In the living room the sounds from the violin stopped. Mary turned and shouted, "Mike, get on with that practicing."

Mike appeared in the kitchen doorway, fair-skinned and blondheaded as Jim had been as a boy. "This stinky deal!" he said, glaring at the violin.

"Music lessons cost money," Mary said. "You practice."

Mike looked over his shoulder at his father. "Is Sue-Ellen pullin' out, Pa?"

"Yes," Jim said shortly. "You better go check the sheep before supper."

"I can't, Pa. I gotta get started on a theme for Miss Murphy. I gotta have it in the mornin'. Ain't that a deal?"

"Isn't," Mary corrected. "Your grammar, Mike." She paused and then said, "Play the waltz for me, honey. I always wanted to be a violinist." Her eyes became soft and dreamy. "There's nothing like music."

"Lord," Jim said when the boy had left, "you don't call *that* music."

"Hush, Jim!" Mary cried. "Let me think of something besides Sue-Ellen."

"I can't," he said dully. He picked up his hat. "I better check the sheep."

He knew Sue-Ellen and Roy were gone when he drove out the gate to the lower ranch. The curtainless windows reflected the red fire of sunset. He drove past, making a mental note to stop and milk the cow on his way back.

As he drove up the long slope toward the fenced pasture he saw the sheep there above him—three hundred purebreds with black faces, drifting slowly toward the flatter land with the blazing sunset behind them. He recalled suddenly the words of an old sheepman he had worked for as a boy: "Sheep don't like to look into the sunset, lad. It's too bright for their eyes. They'll go east with the evening."

He stopped the truck and sat quietly, the words ringing as clear in his mind as the tinkle of the sheep's bells. Beyond the flock, in the higher pastures, he saw his cattle standing dark against the crimson skyline.

Mary had supper waiting when he got home. "It took you a long time," she said.

"Yes," Jim replied. It had taken him years, he thought, but he didn't tell Mary that. Nor was there any need to tell her now that Mike wouldn't ever be a musician or that Joey might never want to carry on the ranches.

When supper was over, he asked the boys to do the dishes. "Mary, we're goin' for a little ride," he said. "I've got something to tell you."

She put on the torn sweater she wore outdoors to feed the chickens, and they got into the truck and drove down the narrow dirt road. When they came to the lower ranch, Jim turned in. "Get out," he said. "Come inside." And he held her small, strong hand tightly as he led her into the kitchen. He turned on the electric light.

"Mary—" he said, and drew a deep breath, "we're movin' back here. I'll sell the other place or hire a man to run it. This is ours and always will be—if it suits you."

She touched the shining gas stove and the new sink He saw a gleam of tears in her eyes. "It's fine, Jim," she said, "only—I wish it could have been for Sue-Ellen. She's young. We're not, not any more."

For a moment a terrible ache was in Jim's throat and then he smiled. "We're still young, Mary," he said. "We just forgot it for a while."

He looked at Mary and realized that it was true. She was still young—and even the torn sweater couldn't take away any of the beauty that was there. He reached out and brushed her hair back gently. "The way I figure it, Mary," he said, "a man can't live his kids' lives. It's hard to learn that, but it's true. And there's something else I want you to think about: A strong man shouldn't be afraid to look into the sunset—by himself, without his kids to lean on."

Then he put his arms around her, holding her hard. "It's only sheep," he said, "that go east with the evening."

JO ANN JONES

Jo Ann Jones is a rancher and rancher's wife, and has always lived in the rural area just north of Calgary. She has worked both on and off the ranch, but her preference is life on the ranch, and now that she is semi-retired she has more time for horses and writing.

Semi-Retired

Can't swing my leg over the saddle too fast
So they don't let me ride the "Hell-Bitch" kind any more
Say my bones are too brittle now an' I couldn't handle a fall
Too slow t'help sort calves on foot in the corral any more
Hold the book do the counting watch the grandkids don't get hurt
          godamn womanjobs
At branding I hand out beer take prairie oysters back for frying
          godamn kidjobs
An' the kids who once did these jobs are runnin' the ranch an' don't ask my permission t'spend or borrow or sell

BUT—when it's hayin' time an' after lunch I'm hot an' tired an' I take some time t'snooze in the shade on the cool green grass—nobody minds.

–when it's twenty below an' a foota new snow I stand at my window an' watch the kids feed cows thaw waterers saddle up – FREEZE – noses finger toes t'bring in that black baldy looks like she might calve early.

–when it's two in the mornin' an' I hear the old half-ton down at the barn I know it's the kids checkin' on the mare gonna foal—I pull up the covers an' go back t'sleep.

–when it's Sunday mornin' an' there's an April snowstorm an' I hear the kids drive in early to feed cows check calves treat scours cuss Alberta weather—I roll over in our soft warm bed an' make love with their mother an' maybe semi-retired ain't so bad.

BETTY THOMSON

Betty Thomson of Rockglen, Saskatchewan, has always been a working partner with her husband and her family on their ranch. She is more apt to be found in the corral than in the kitchen. In her writing, Betty gives significance to small moments, which ranching women everywhere should be able to recognize.

Riding for the Heart Brand

Across the dusty plains
in saddles I can't see
ride three young cowboys
on Fade Away, Too High and Dixie.
They herd their Hereford cattle
branded with hearts on their left hips.

Phantoms bonded to their ponies
ride across my mind.
With leather faces, level eyes
beneath battered Stetsons
they trail cows to summer pasture.
Ponderous hooves
are lost in clouds of grey.

I watch them fade in distance
and taste the bitter dust.
Time has left them on the hill.

I never ride these trails alone.
Friendly spirits circle my campfires

with eyes like fireflies.
Footsteps pace me in the dark.

When my roundup is over
I'll gather in their corral,
drink water from their spring.

Three Wire Fences

We build straight fences
pound posts in sod
string barb wire on them
hammer staples in deep.
Through the shifting seasons
our wires sing in the wind
shiver in bitter cold
shimmer in heat.
Broken strands intertwine
but we fix fence as we go.

LINDA HASSELSTROM

Linda Hasselstrom, rancher and environmentalist, writes from the land. Her poetry and nonfiction have appealed to readers across the United States and Canada. Often her writing takes her away from the ranch, only to bring her back again. She has received several awards in the United States for her writing, including a fellowship from the National Endowment for the Arts in 1984. The selection reproduced below, "Choosing the Boneyard," was originally published in Land Circle *and makes the ranch very much the main focus.*

Choosing the Boneyard

THE COW WAS AT LEAST TWENTY YEARS OLD, maybe more. When I was twenty years old, a junior in college—before I'd met my first husband (seven years) or my second (nine years and counting); before I knew I'd never have children of my own and fell in love with my four stepchildren (by two fathers); before I graduated from college; before any of my writing I still respect had been published; before I learned any of the lessons I've won by pain and love—she had been born.

Her birth night was no doubt a cold one in March. Her mother probably lay in the scant shelter of a low prairie hill that created a little windbreak; if a storm was brewing, she was shut in the corral with the other cows, and had her calf in a sheltered corner. But probably she was in the pasture, where snow sifted into a drift behind each clump of grass. Once the calf slid out, steaming among its birth fluids in the icy air, the cow stood—a little shaky, perhaps—and began licking the new calf vigorously.

Her rough tongue lifted the wet, skinny flanks clear of the frozen ground as she licked, forcing the blood to flow beneath the tender hide. Occasionally the cow raised her head into the wind and sniffed, and listened to the coyotes circling around, afraid to come too near even though the calf and the smells of blood and tissue were tempting.

The cow licked the calf all over, from her pathetically thin tail along her spine and the fresh umbilical wound in her belly to her slick black head and drooping ears. By the time the cow's motherly chore was finished, the calf's ears were almost dry, pink-tinged inside; the calf's eyelashes were separated and beautiful around the white-rimmed black eyes; the soft yellow hoofs had begun to harden as the calf scrabbled to stand up on ground slippery with fluid, grass, ice and fresh snow. While the cow tiredly chewed afterbirth, the calf struggled to stand, collapsing frequently, until at last the cow finished her strength-giving meal and began to murmur encouragement.

Finally the calf was more or less upright, legs spraddled ridiculously, tongue reaching out. She found a teat, and sucked her first milk, the rich, warm colostrum, packed with extra nutrients for her first few days. By morning, when my father came in the warm pickup to check the cattle, the cow lay with her back to the storm, the calf tucked into a hollow by her belly, blinking at him in the dawn light. Coyote tracks in the snow led away, as the coyotes hunted mice and birds, having given up on fresh calf.

But tonight they have her, after waiting twenty, maybe twenty-five years. While I finished college and married, and learned about pain and loss and death and hatred and stepchildren, the coyotes waited. They raised their pups on mice and crickets and gnawed the bones of cattle we hauled to the boneyard in winter, and fat steers that ate too much wet alfalfa and died of bloat. Maybe coyotes prefer beef, but their main strength is their adaptability, and they'll eat anything, including snakes and fruit. Ninety percent of their diet is meat, and most of that was dead before they got there.

The calf born that night was branded and earmarked and vaccinated for disease two months later, in May, and learned her first lessons about pain. She was turned out with her mother to summer grass in June, and grew fat and beautiful, in a young cow's way, until my father brought her to the corrals in September. He put all the young steers in one corral and the young heifers in another, and slowly looked the heifers over. Most he put into the pen with the steers, to be sold. He kept twenty or twenty-five heifers that year because they looked as if they would grow into good cows capable of raising healthy calves and feeding them well. He judged by a number of qualities—straight back, ample udder, good lines, and some indefinable quality that a good rancher instinctively recognizes. (Some modern ranchers have to keep elaborate bloodline records because they don't have the instinct, or don't trust it.) She was one of the ones kept, turned out for the winter to be fed with the grown cows. A female bovine is called a "heifer" and usually kept separate from older cows; she is bred to a bull chosen for his small head, to make birth of her first calf easier. Even then, she may require a rancher's help in birth. After that, she is known as a cow, and is expected to calve without help. During calving season, we observe older cows, but usually don't help with birth unless the calf is too large, or incorrectly positioned in the womb.

She went with other heifers and an Angus bull to a private pasture for the winter, and in the spring, perhaps with my father's help, she bore her first calf in a dark, chilly barn. She went on having calves every spring, raised them through the summer, went back to the pastures in fall when they were weaned. All we ever did for her was provide grass, water, and a little salt in summer, protein-rich cake and hay in winter. In return she gave us between eighteen and twenty-two calves. We took most of them to the sale ring and sold them; some of her daughters stayed here, to become cows and mothers, and support us with their offspring.

In the spring we discussed how old she was; she wore a tag of a type I swore we hadn't used for twenty-five years; my father insisted she couldn't be that old, but I think he knew she was. By July, she was thinner than usual, and her calf had almost given up trying to suck milk from her shrunken bag. But he was fat; though he'd miss the milk she gave, he was doing well on green summer grass. The cow seemed glad to abandon him; she began to limp, and was always a little behind the other cows when we moved them to new pasture, a little slow to move to water.

Afraid she'd suffer, we began slipping her extra feed. One fall day when we'd hauled the horses to the pasture, I decided to take her home in the trailer so she wouldn't have to walk when we took the other cows home. She'd slow the entire herd down, and she might simply be unable to walk that far. I found her on top of a hill, where the breeze kept flies away and provided relief from the heat. When I approached, she didn't shy away, but raised her head and stared at me. I shouted at her to start her down toward the trailer. Then, when she didn't move, I slapped her on the flank. She turned and took a step—and I heard a grating sound from the region of her hips. Slowly, carefully, like an old lady in a walker, she worked her way down the hill. I followed, my hand on her hip, listening to her old bones grate together. She made no sound, and didn't wince as if she were in pain; I heard only that awful grinding.

We pushed and pulled her into the trailer—she didn't fight us, as a healthy cow would have—and brought her home to the corral. My father fed her oats and cake every day for a month, but she grew no fatter, and the grating sound didn't go away.

"I haven't got the heart to shoot her," he said. "Take her to that good fenced bottom with the running water, and turn her loose. If she lives, we'll sell her in the spring. If she dies . . ." He shrugged. "If she doesn't start putting on weight, or if it storms, you'll have to shoot her. Don't let her suffer."

For another three months, through mid-January, we fed her a daily ration of a couple of pounds of cattle cake. She always ate eagerly, shuffling toward us through the belly-deep grass she ate the rest of the time. But when we turned other cows in with her, she avoided them, staying by herself in the shelter of an old barn.

Then one day she was standing where she had never ventured: beside the gate. On the other side was only the field containing the boneyard. George took it as a sign, a cow demonstrating the right to die, and opened the gate.

She shuffled through, hips still grating loudly, and tottered up the slope. The grass is good in the boneyard, fertilized by the bodies and bones of dozens of cows that have died over the years. If they're in the corral, or anywhere near the buildings, we hook a chain to their legs and drag them to the boneyard—far enough away from us so we won't get the smell, and the coyotes can feed without fear.

The cow stared at us a moment, then lowered her head to the tall grass, and began to graze. George placed the pistol near her ear and pulled the trigger. She folded up, dropped, and then her old legs scrambled like a newborn calf's as she tried to flee her fate one more time.

When she was still, we drove away. Six months later, gathering bones, I would notice her pelvis, as full of holes and delicate as lace where age or decay had eaten it away: the source of that grating. The morning after we shot her, only the great pink arch of her ribs rising above the grass showed where the coyotes had fed. They'd waited a long time.

ANNE SLADE

When Anne Slade married rancher Robert Slade and left the city to live on his ranch south of Tompkins, Saskatchewan, she was unsure of what to expect, but Delores Noreen, a ranch hand, stepped in to teach Anne many necessary ranching skills.

Delores

She's a cowpuncher
been workin' here some fifty years,
sweat and swears
outworks the toughest man.
She taught my husband to ride.
First time we rode together
(her on the buckskin she was breakin'
me on the twenty-year-old mare).
I remember her reachin'
for tobacco pouch and papers
and left-handed she rolled that cigarette.
Through blue smoke haze
she hollered,
"Don't hold onto the horn,
scared you're gonna fall?
Go with the mare, don't fight her!"
I, in awe of this woman, obeyed.
Yesterday she rode by,
our youngest son behind.
I heard her holler,
"Don't hold onto the horn,
scared you're gonna fall?"

And even though the words were harsh,
her voice was warm with love.

Making Bread

"Can't be running fifteen miles into town
every time you're short of bread."
she said, as she dumped the potato peelings
and coffee grounds out of the basin and into the slop pail.
She mumbled something about 'city girls,'
while she scubbed the white enamel basin
with the red rim around the edge
and the black chips punctuating every dent.

She got the stack of bread pans from the pantry.
"No, there isn't a recipe, you just mix it till it feels right!
Scald the milk and melt the lard
and cup your hand and fill that hollow twice with salt,
then knead it, that's the secret, the kneading."

She chain smoked, sitting at the end of my kitchen table
her boots propped up on the oak bench
and her nose in another Louis L'Amour.

I sprinkled the oil cloth with flour
and kneaded that dough till my arms ached,
and my shoulders.

"No, it isn't ready yet. I haven't heard it squeak!" she said.
And still I kneaded,
and fifteen loaves of fresh bread
on the kitchen counter later,
I knew that bread making wasn't necessarily
an act of love.

MARY CLEARMAN BLEW

Despite the many colleges and universities where she has taught, Mary Clearman Blew has never been able to leave behind the isolated Montana ranch where she grew up. In her writing she confronts the reader with the difficulties women have experienced on and off the ranch, and she depicts women's struggle to be recognized as independent and caring individuals. The following selection, "Alberta's Story," is part of her book Runaway.

Alberta's Story

SIXTY YEARS IS NOT A LONG TIME, and some of these old sandstone buildings have stood on Main Street ever since I can remember, but the Empire Cafe is the only business in town that is older than I am. As I pause with my hand on the door handle, I am looking straight into my own reflection in the dark glass and, wavering behind me like a bad memory all the more bitter for its lingering ghost of the familiar and well-loved, the outline of the gift shop and bookstore across the street where the old Bijoux Theater and Kale's Veterinary Supply used to be.

Any time I work up my nerve, I can open the door and step off the sunlit pavement onto soft pine flooring hollowed like a friendly palm. I can walk past the display case with its cigars and Life Savers under the rusty linoleum counter just as Father end I did every sale day and, unless Clay has beaten me to it, take one of the tables at the back where the faint rancid odor from the grill mingles and the smell of tobacco and spearmint to reassure me that something, at least, continues. And I might as well make up my mind to open the door as stand out here in the sun where Clay could come along any minute and leave me looking like a fool.

The iron door handle is smooth and warm as a familiar handclasp; more familiar than my own reflection which advances upon me, grinning lumpishly, and disappears as I pull open the door, only to rematerialize out of the tarnished depths of the mirror behind the counter as I walk into the cafe. I avert my eyes too late not to see the dry frizz of hair under the Stetson and the sag of shirt and levis above and below my belt. Sixty years have settled without warning, and quite chapfallen is how I look.

But nobody is in the back except two men in white Dacron shirts drinking coffee and going over the figures jotted on a paper napkin. They hardly glance up as I take my usual seat with my back to the wall. Of course Clay wouldn't be here at this time of day, the sale won't be over for hours. *Unless the crew takes a coffee break. Unless for some reason he isn't working the sale this afternoon.* I catch myself hoping, and I cast around for a distraction. The menu, a typewritten sheet between limp gray plastic leaves, is wedged between the napkin dispenser and the salt and pepper shakers, and I think about ordering something to eat. A chicken-fried steak, perhaps. But it is too early in the afternoon to eat a heavy meal.

Debbie comes over to wipe the stains off the formica tabletop and set down a glass of water. "Are you having coffee, Alberta?"

"Please."

I must have been about nine years old the first time Father brought me in the Empire Cafe and ordered a chicken-fried steak. Had we been to a 4-H meeting? A bull sale?—There weren't many reasons why he would have taken me with him, which is why my memory of those times is so sharp. Mother, of course, never left the ranch, but that was on Margaret's account—at any rate, I wore a pair of brand-new levis, so stiff I could barely bend my knees, and I walked with dignity at Father's side. The cafe struck me with its grave air of men and their commerce, their unhurried comings and goings and pronouncements of the weather. It was town, what lay at the end of thirty miles of ruts leading in from the ranch, and it mattered. Sometimes even now I get a glimmer, a memory of a memory of how it felt to be driving into town, when I gear down the truck at the top of Main Street hill and look down at the familiar store fronts and cottonwood trees.

Debbie brings my coffee. "Are you going to order anything to eat, Alberta?"

"Oh—I don't know—" I think about consulting the menu, decide against it. "I guess just coffee."

Debbie slides her pad into her apron pocket and sits down to keep me company for a minute. "Wow, what a morning we had!" she sighs, lighting a cigarette. "It can stay slow all afternoon for all I care."

"I suppose all the boys came in from the yards for lunch today?"

I had asked it idly, and only when Debbie looks away do I realize how my question sounded to her.

"I guess they got a slew of consignments this morning. The boys were saying they'd be lucky to finish loading cattle and come in for supper by midnight," she says. From the way she keeps her eyes on the match she is putting out, I understand what she is telling me, and I ought to be grateful when I am only flooded with shame that Debbie, young Debbie, would know—

Everybody knows. *—at her age? Alberta got just what she was asking for. After all, he only married her to get his hands on the ranch. She must have known that. And you can't fault him for it. Not really. What could she have done with that ranch on her own? And she was no kind of a wife for him*—oh, I can hear them.

To shut out their echoes, I turn to Debbie. She is the only one of the Knutson girls to grow up with the looks and the calm of her grandmother. At one time I would never have believed it. Debbie, so bashful that her sisters had to drag her into her first 4-H meeting by force, squirming red and unable to answer the judge when he asked her about her yearling. It's hard for country children to get over their shyness, I ought to know—but Debbie, at least, had her sisters to play with, and she went to a real school when the time came. Debbie's grandmother and I—and Margaret, if she had been capable of learning to read—and a few others like Johnny Ware who grew up in the gumbo country before the roads were graveled had only the 4-H meetings and the correspondence courses we studied at home, which probably taught us more about books, at that, than schools do now. Shakespeare we read, and Sir Walter Scott. But there is so much more to learn.

Debbie has learned; she's done just fine. She has been saving her tips and wages from the Empire for three years so she can go away to the state university this fall.

"Have you done your clothes-shopping yet?" I ask her, and her face lights up as she talks of the sweater and slacks she has put on lay-away and the down parka she would have bought—"but it was a hundred and fifty dollars, and I couldn't manage it and the dormitory deposit. All freshmen have to live in the dorm," she explains. Her hands gesture in humorous resignation—she is, after all, a girl who has rented her own room and looked after herself through four years of high school—and I notice how much older her hands look than the rest of her.

"You make me almost ready to go off to college myself," I joke. I mean to joke, at least, but she takes me seriously.

"Oh, Alberta!" Her young face is suffused with sympathy. "I never knew you wanted to go to college. And you never had the chance, always the work on the ranch coming first—"

"No, no! Really, Debbie. I meant to joke. All I ever wanted was the ranch."

But perhaps because she looks so doubtful, my words sound hollow to me even though I know they are true. For who would believe, after all, that the ranch was all I wanted? Clay didn't. *What's your story, Alberta?* he asked me the Wrst week he was on the place. *How come you've hung around?*

"Just seems like it would be so lonely for you out there now." Debbie's eyes plead with me to take it in the spirit it is meant and not as meddling.

"Lonely? I wouldn't know what it means to be lonely," I scoff. Getting lonely wasn't a fashion in my day, or going off to college, either. Not that it necessarily is nowadays, from what I read. Debbie is behind the times, saving her tips for the state university because she is a country girl and she already has come so far—and I hate to think what she may find there—but then I remember the small weather-beaten hands that are so at odds with the smooth brown hair and young face, and I reassure myself that Debbie will do just fine.

A shadow falls off the door, and I look up to see the angle of a stetson silhouetted against the bright sunlight and the line of shoulders that catches at my breath and draws the whole story so plainly across my face that Debbie has to avert her eyes. *—has she no shame, has she no pride? What did she expect, following, that she would find him doing in the granary? A man has a right to expect something better than a bag of bones like Alberta. The truth is, she as good as drove him to it. After all, what kind of a poor excuse for a woman is she?—has anybody ever seen her in a dress? and that house is a mess!—nobody's lifted a hand to clean it since her mother died—*

An instant is enough to set the rumors ringing in my ears and my face hot and cold and then drain me of all but a disappointment as sharp as a bad taste in my mouth as I see that the light has deceived me. It is not Clay coming past the counter, but only Johnny Ware, and of course I am not disappointed but relieved.

"Alberta," says Johnny, unsurprised, for of course he had the advantage of coming in with his back to the light and being able to see who was sitting in the back. Johnny hangs his hat on the back of a chair and eases his bones down, while Debbie runs off for a glass of water and the coffee pot.

Johnny watches her go; "She's the only one of those girls who's anything like her grandmother," he remarks.

"Debbie's getting prettier every day," I agree. But it isn't prettiness that makes me think of Lila. Fifty years ago when I started 4-H, Lila and Johnny were the big kids in the club, and we all depended on Lila even then. Now Lila is gone, and Johnny is so stove-up in the hips that for an instant I could mistake his walk for Clay's although Clay's broken bones come from the rodeo circuit and Johnny's from a lifetime of killing work on the ranch.

Debbie brings more coffee and goes off to clean up after the Dacron-shirt men, while Johnny settles down comfortably to drink his coffee and talk, as he can do for hours, of the weather and the roads and the grass this fall and the number of cattle trucked out of the country north of the river to be consigned at the sale this morning—"this is a big sale, but you won't see the big sales every week like they had six–eight years ago. Not that many cattle in this country any more. The boys all cut back on yearlings—price of feed what it is, they can't afford to raise cattle—" and while he talks, I think of all the sales Father and I worked together, earning money for the ranch, and the sales I worked with Clay after Father's accident.

I'd be working in the yards myself today, riding old Lightning up and down the center alley and hazing calves through the main gate into the sale barn, if it weren't for Clay. Avoiding Clay means staying away from the Wednesday sales, and driving past the Farmers Union without stopping for gas if his truck is parked by the pumps, and being afraid to walk into the Empire. That's the worst part.

No. The worst part is missing the sales, because of the money. Johnny is still talking, explaining something that Sim told him about the number of consignments they need every week to keep the cash flow at the yards high enough to pay overhead. He omits no details, and I can sip coffee and nod as though I am listening to more than every tenth word or so while my thoughts skitter off: *moneymoneymoney.*

Suddenly I wish I could tell Johnny about it. Through the dull flesh that has slipped from the bones of his face into bags and jowls, I can almost but not quite see *Johnny,* Johnny with the clean Ware features and blue eyes. How can I tell him anything? He's an old man, older than I am. What does he know? Years ago when we took the same correspondence course, Johnny and I made a game out of the verse quotations that headed every lesson. Oh, those lessons were full of knowledge about books. Even more than I, Johnny has grown up in a backwater. I am assuring myself that I cannot possibly tell him anything in the same instant that I hear my own voice blurt, "Johnny, I'm broke!"

Interrupted in the middle of a word, Johnny stares at me. His mouth has gone slack, but his face looks as if it could break into pieces, and I think unwillingly of Father's funeral and how Johnny began to cry at the graveside.

"It must get awful lonesome out there," says Johnny, getting the better of the wobble in his voice.

"Who said anything about lonesome? I'm never lonesome, I wouldn't know what it is to be lonesome! What I am is broke!"

Johnny nods. His old man's eyes, faded and inflamed, gaze on me but seem to see something else. "It's a damn fine ranch," he says after a while.

"The ranch is all that counts with me. All the years Father put into it, and I—"

"Best pastureland in the country," says Johnny. "Too damn bad you can't make money running cattle any more."

"Johnny. As long as I could work at the stockyards, I could support the ranch. But—"

All at once I know I can't go on. Bad enough to make a fool of myself in public without having Johnny in tears. Debbie, arriving with the coffee pot, saves us both by pouring our cups full as if nothing in the world out of the ordinary were going on.

"After all Father and I did for him, took him in when he was too crippled up to work anywhere else—" *and then he took up with that bitch*—have I spoken aloud, when I meant to keep all complaints to myself? My fault, my own fault, I know.

Johnny sets his coffee cup down angrily. "No damn reason why you had to quit. Sim would sooner have you working for him than Clay."

"Yes, but Clay wouldn't have quit."

How can I explain that the world has divided into Clay's share and my share? His territory and mine, his friends and mine—and my share keeps shrinking as I let him take more. Like letting Margaret take what was on my plate because she didn't understand the difference—*the truth about Margaret, have you heard what Clay told? That she was really hers and old Albert's and that was why she was never right?—and her mother covered it up*—

Johnny looks as if he can read the rumors written right across my forehead. "You can't make a dime on it, but the land's worth a lot of money."

"I'd never sell it! It was Father's homestead, and now—"

"Still it can't be the same out there with everybody gone," says Johnny.

Against my will I remember how it used to be when the light in the kitchen meant Mother would be getting supper on the table and Margaret grinning out of her chair when Father and I came in from the chores. Margaret was good company. Mother never liked anybody outside the family to see her, but after her death, I used to take Margaret with me whenever I could, and she learned to recognize people and was glad to see them. But I couldn't sell the place. It would be like selling off Father. Johnny ought to know how it is, he's got a ranch of his own.

"Who gets it when you're gone?" Johnny wants to know. "There's only that nephew of your dad's left in the family."

"Junior. He'll get it eventually, I suppose."

Johnny snorts. "That damn fool. That jackass. I wouldn't want to see you do without a thing, Alberta, I wouldn't care what it was, just to see Junior turn around and sell the place after you're gone."

Johnny bangs his cup down loud enough to make a man buying cigarettes at the counter look our way. I don't know what to say. Of course I could sell. I know who'd buy me out in a minute and leave me the buildings and the horse pasture in the bargain.

"Hell, Alberta," says Johnny. "We all depend on you too much to have you giving up on us."

I have to laugh to myself. Coming from Johnny, of all people, when I always have known that a better woman would have handled things better.

A tiny memory surfaces, of going out to catch Lightning after a 4-H club meeting and finding Debbie sobbing behind the barn—

—Honey, what's wrong? To hear her, I would have thought somebody'd died. But no.

—I hate my mother! sobbed Debbie.

—Debbie, honey! People don't hate their mothers. I was thinking that Lila would have known what to say to her.

—I do. Debbie lifted a piteous face. I hate mine. I wanted to go with the boys,

but my mother told me—tearful gulp—she told me I'm too big! She says no girl my age, no decent woman, hangs around the men and does men's work!

—Oh, Debbie—

I am jerked out of the reverie by the opening of the door to the street, and this time no glare of sunlight can blind me to his silhouette. Others are with him, the crew must have taken a break after all—but all I can focus on is that it wasn't disappointment I felt when it turned out to be Johnny walking into the Empire a little while ago, but relief. What I am feeling now leaves no doubt whatever. At least I don't have to worry about that.

"Of all the places in town the son of a bitch could go to drink coffee," somebody—is it Debbie?—hisses. I am half out of my chair, somehow getting the heel of my boot tangled in the absurd wire folderols on the chair leg, knowing I am red-faced and foolish.

Johnny's hand, horny-nailed and embedded with permanent grime, falls on my arm. "What have you got to run off for, Alberta? Sit down."

"But—"

"Sit down and let that son of a bitch walk out if he wants to!"

Johnny looks fed up with me, and I sink back in my chair, more taken aback by him than I am by Clay. The jigsaw fragments of my assumptions, blown apart by Johnny's anger, are filtering down like motes in the sunlight and beginning to reassemble in a new pattern that I could begin to perceive if I were not too frightened. *For of course I am guilty—*

Clay glances over his shoulder, laughs loudly, says something to the man next to him and nudges him. The other man's face turns blank, but my gorge is rising and I must run out or be sick—*keep my stinking carcass where he can't be disgusted—*

"You sit there and listen to me, Alberta. I've been hearing how he tracks you around town and runs you out of places, and it's all a lot of nonsense."

"Alberta," says Debbie, and it is toward her voice that I turn. "Don't you remember what you told me the time you found me crying?"

No, I don't remember telling her anything. What I remember is the stricken little girl and the dead certainty that what they accused me of was true. *Not a real woman, not Alberta. If she amounted to anything, she'd fold up and die like her mother. But not her, no, she stays healthy and goes to work right alongside the men. But she'll get what's coming to her. That rodeo hand, that's what's coming to her. Serves her right.* Is it possible that, for once in my life, instead of sinking willingly after the siren voices into the luxurious bog of self-hatred, I went right on saddling Lightning and said, *Work's work, Debbie! Been doing it all my life! Do you see me crying about what people say?*

Clay is standing there grinning, and the sloping line of his shoulders and the muscles of his neck are more familiar than the freckles and the loose skin I am always surprised to see on my own hands. Three weeks ago I could walk up to Clay and put my hand on his shoulder and feel warm. Now I have to watch that I don't reach out from force of habit, and the very air is divided between us: either his or mine to breathe.

Johnny hasn't budged. His back is turned to Clay, but his eyes don't spare me. Debbie is still standing behind me, so what can I do but sink back into my chair and pick up my coffee cup, which turns out to be empty? And lightning does not strike me dead, and thunder does not cleave the earth under me and let me fall through. All that happens is that Clay straddles a chair at the opposite table and starts to pick his teeth.

Johnny glares at me. "You just sit still a few times, and he'll quit."

The fragments have reassembled; the picture they form is painful, for all my hours of self-pity will buy nothing back, and nothing is going to happen except that Debbie will fill my empty cup. Still, clarity brings a certain relief.

And Johnny is right. It's not the same out at the ranch now. I think: I could keep the buildings and the horse pasture. Go back to work if I feel like it. And I can stop by Western Wear on the way out of town and have them lay back a down parka. She might as well look like the rest of those young kids that look like they're starting on a month's pack trip instead of on their way to class. Why not? I'm rich.

MELA MLEKUSH

Mela Mlekush brings a special sensitivity to her free verse poetry as she writes of a ranch girlhood in the Crazy Mountains of Montana. She has taken part in cowboy poetry gatherings in Montana and Elko. Mela is presently involved with the Poets on the Prairie school project as well as with keeping an eye on the activities of three teenage daughters.

Moonlight Ride

Sweat ran under our T-shirts
horses lathered without effort
that summer night nearly hot as day.
My Seattle cousin and I
swam our horses in clear cold snow melt
thirty miles from the Crazies
camped a quarter mile from home
on a creek bank ripe with mint.
Kim, Comanche, Velvet and I.
Picketed horses lipped grass
and fought buzzing bott flies.
We settled around the fire
with willow sticks, waiting
for the pop sizzle of hot dogs.
Smooth river rock rubbed our bellies
as we drank from mossy pools.
Marshmellow intermissions
Between the bawdy songs
we sang at the top of our lungs
sweetened secrets we would never tell

beyond the circle of firelight.
Beneath the rising moon we stripped.
Barefoot careful we bridled horses,
swung up, heels gripping,
hands let loose bunched mane
gathered in its place
sweat-soft reins.
Bare legs squeezed
mounts to motion
to lope across flats
yipping like coyote pups
over first kill.
Soap-rich lather stung bare thighs,
buttocks balanced on backbone,
leaving
then rejoining flesh
in the cadence of a canter.
Innocence raced
through a hot Montana night,
Kim, Comanche, Velvet and I.

TERESA JORDAN

*Teresa Jordan grew up on a Wyoming ranch until, as a young woman, the ranch was sold. In the following years, she moved from place to place, never able to find another "home" until she settled in Nevada. Through her writing—*Cowgirls: Women of the American West, Riding the White Horse Home, Graining the Mare: Poetry of Ranch Women; The Stories That Shape Us: Contemporary Women Write About the West*—Teresa Jordan has given the West back to women. She returns to Wyoming in "Effie's Garden" and confronts the last inescapable landscape of the West—where dust returns to dust.*

Effie's Garden

In Wyoming, the altitude is high and the air is thin and clear. Even snakes hold their breath without effort. Children grow tall and have chests as broad as pick-ups. They move to cities as soon as they are able; on the coasts they run forever and never break sweat.

Things happen in the clear high air. Men watch their skin grow translucent and their wrinkles carve so deeply they can't grow beards anymore. Women watch their eyes get bluer and bluer until they go blind and they see just what they've always seen: They see the endless sky. They walk on this sky, on the thin blue air. They never need to eat. They are thin, of course, and their arms are incredibly long. Their fingers grow so bony that their wedding rings fall off, and then they can't remember if they married at all, or if they bore children.

Lanky dogs live at this altitude, and they lounge around in ungrassed yards. They chew on old bones of prospectors, and they get thinner as the water runs out. Their urine is yellow before it dries up completely, and the sky is always blue. The only mineral people need is phosphorous and they mine it in their yards.

An old woman digs in her yard, plants rows of seed in hard ground without any water. Her name is Effie and her garden won't grow. The dogs die. Effie watches as their skins shrink back, little by little, like newspaper curling up in a fire and turning to ash, turning to dust. She watches as the bones whiten and the skeletons sink in on themselves. She listens as the cartilage and tendons dissipate, the bones fall with little bell-like clinks. Soon the wind scatters the toe nails and the smallest bones and scapulas. Effie watches the dogs, like the garden, ride away on the wind, grain by grain and particle by particle.

A few weeds grow in the yard, and the old woman sits and watches them die in the thin high air. She thinks how nice weeds might look and cactus, but even the cacti go the way of the bones. Their meaty, fleshy parts get harder and drier and their prickles scatter, making a small raspy sound. The dust turns whiter and whiter and Effie remembers drinking out of a glass. She remembers the feel of water on her lips: she wasn't thin back then, she still needed to eat.

As Effie sits in her garden, she remembers once touching a man. He pressed against her, but she knew what happened to gardens in the thin high air, and she drew away. He lay down then, in the white dry yard. His bones lost the connections of gristle and tendon. They scattered, losing the shape of him, and he blew away particle by particle and dust bit by dust bit. Not even his shadow remained. Sometimes late at night when the winds sound loneliest and the dust quits glowing, Effie can still feel a part of him pressing against her, hard as bone.

Like a horse, Effie never lies down to sleep. She used to lie down but the lightness of her body made no impression on the ground and it scared her. This is what death is like, she had thought, as the wind tugged at their skin. Now she sleeps sitting up. Wind can't touch her if she keeps her distance from the dust. At night, she sees white horses racing. They are just wisps of moonlight, she is sure, and clouds of dust, yet she can hear the sound of their hooves connecting with the hollow earth beneath the ground, she can hear their leader snort. She watches as the horses circle her yard. Some animals, she has heard, rearrange the bones of their dead in a ritual manner, and she thinks that the horses are looking for bones. They are certainly looking for something. Sometimes they seem to be looking for her.

She sleeps upright, and even in dreams she sees horses. She watches them sway in their sleep, and she knows they feed on moonlight rather than grass. The horses are phosphorescent as bone, and they eye her through their inner lids. They know the things she has forgotten: the words to lullabies, the taste of water, the press of a tall man's thigh.

The wind blows and Effie ages. She is eighty years old, a hundred-and-two. She should be growing weaker, joining the piles of bone and the kisses of dust. She can remember less and less, but she still has a flinty strength. She rises sometimes and walks across the yard, pushes on the rickety fence posts and pounds them deeper into the alkali with a rock. She knows she should die but she chooses not to. She no longer needs bone, nothing needs bone up here. Life is a simple matter of wind and rearrangement.

When the dinosaurs return, she will be here, moving around her yard. When great fires sear the forests in the lower part of the world, she will be here, pounding on fence posts. When all the animals climb up steep cliffs to let go of their gristle and bone, she will be here, alive as a sneeze of talcum, vital as a quick cloud of dust.

LINDA HUSSA

Linda Hussa's ranch writing has taken her from a ranch in the Surprise Valley of California to the Library of Congress reading room and to many cowboy poetry gatherings along the way. Poems included here are taken from her first book, Where the Wind Lives.

Sewing Circle

Use the long curving needle
    better for speed and it's sharp.
Start with a slip stitch
    no need to sew blind, simply sew it
    and gentle, be gentle.

Pull soft where the pieces are missing
    time will fill in the rest.
Begin and just sew,
    it's slippery, I know. Quickly,
    work quickly, work fast.

"Old Ned? (Lapper, Spot, Sox, Little Bess)
    Why, he was curled by the fire
    my slippers under his chin
    his running dreams made the children laugh
    never hurt a fly, that one."

My evening by the flashlight's fire
    quilting bloody flaps,
    pushing puckers out into a whole sheep.

Five little town dogs, crazed by sport
    follow a full moon through meadows
    pack of shadows slide along
    where the flock is bedded
    until they woke to a low wail,
    and yip.
    We woke to their pain.

Twenty-seven little sheep, dazed by death
    strewn, whimpering
    —sheep whimper when hurt, like us—
    three floating in the pond, one gutted
    fine white wool dyed a vomitus shade of red.

We sewed them, skinned faces
    jaws flapping, legs waving
    our anger seared by the work.

So, you say it wasn't old Ned (Blackie,
    Irish, Tommy or Princess).
    I stood under the porch light
    and handed over his collar
    —strands of bloody wool in the catch.

The Barren Mare

Filly foal
    not considered
    for a saddle horse.
No mares allowed
    they cause trouble with the geldings.
Brood mare band
    in her third year.

Next spring
    no foal.

One more chance
    'cause she's strong
    good bone
    straight
    good back.

Next spring
    no foal.
Call the killers.

What chance
    does a woman have
    in a world like that?

The Blue Filly

She is just three.
Weaned again.

First time from her dead mother
    small blue head
    in the flank of a still heart.

Second time from a spotted burro
    who let her stand near
    as they swept flies in their head-tail sleep.

Last from the mare band
    that taught her with stinging nips
    to stand back and wait.

She sees him coming.
    Hay poking out in mid-chew
    does she wonder, "What now?"

He speaks her name
    in sound and breath
    she will come to know as her own.

A halter slips over her nose
    and she follows him into the barn
    shivering.

Hobbles hold her
    while the brush sweeps
    firm and soft over her skin.

And when his hand slides down her neck
    I feel it on mine.
    We both relax
    and prepare ourselves for the saddling.

GRETEL EHRLICH

Gretel Ehrlich left filmmaking and the city for the wilds of Wyoming, where the landscape and her involvement in ranch activities helped to create a strong sense of home. Gretel Erhlich continues to write from a western perspective, which is evident in the following selection, "From a Sheepherder's Notebook: Three Days," taken from The Solace of Open Spaces.

From a Sheepherder's Notebook: Three Days

WHEN THE PHONE RANG, it was John: "Maurice just upped and quit and there ain't nobody else around, so you better get packed. I'm taking you out to herd sheep." I walked to his trailerhouse. He smoked impatiently while I gathered my belongings. "Do you know *anything* about herding sheep after all this time?" he asked playfully. "No, not really." I was serious. "Well, it's too late now. You'll just have to figure it out. And there ain't no phones up there either!"

He left me off on a ridge at five in the morning with a mare and a border collie. "Last I saw the sheep, they was headed for them hills," he said, pointing up toward a dry ruffle of badlands. "I'll pull your wagon up ahead about two miles. You'll see it. Just go up that ridge, turn left at the pink rock, then keep agoing. And don't forget to bring the damned sheep."

Morning. Sagesmell, sunsquint, birdsong, cool wind. I have no idea where I am, how to get to the nearest paved road, or how to find the sheep. There are tracks going everywhere so I follow what appear to be the most definite ones. The horse picks a path through sagebrush. I watch the dog. We walk for several miles. Nothing. Then both sets of ears prick up. The dog looks at me imploringly. The sheep are in the draw ahead.

Move them slow or fast? Which crossing at the river? Which pink rock? It's like being a first-time mother, but mother now to two thousand sheep who give me the kind of disdainful look a teenager would his parent and, with my back turned, can get into as much trouble. I control the urge to keep them neatly arranged, bunched up by the dog, and, instead, let them spread out and fill up. Grass being scarce on spring range, they scatter.

Up the valley, I encounter a slalom course of oil rigs and fenced spills I hadn't been warned about. The lambs, predictably mischievous, emerge dripping black. Freed from those obstacles, I ride ahead to find the wagon which, I admit, I'm afraid I'll never see, leaving the sheep on the good faith that they'll stay on their uphill drift toward me.

"Where are my boundaries?" I'd asked John.

"Boundaries?" He looked puzzled for a minute. "Hell, Gretel, it's all the outfit's land, thirty or forty miles in any direction. Take them anywhere they want to go."

On the next ridge I find my wagon. It's a traditional sheepherder's wagon, rounded top, tiny wood cookstove, bed across the back, built-in benches and drawers. The rubber wheels and long tongue make it portable. The camp tender pulls it (now with a pickup, earlier with teams) from camp to camp as the feed is consumed, every two weeks or so. Sheep begin appearing and graze toward me. I picket my horse. The dog runs for shade to lick his sore feet. The view from the dutch doors of the wagon is to the southeast, down the long slit of a valley. If I rode north, I'd be in Montana within the day, and next week I'll begin the fifty-mile trail east to the Big Horns.

Three days before summer solstice; except to cook and sleep I spend every waking hour outside. Tides of weather bring the days and take them away. Every night a bobcat visits, perched at a discreet distance on a rock, facing me. A full moon, helium-filled, cruises through clouds and is lost behind rimrock. No paper cutout, this moon, but ripe and splendid. Then Venus, then the North Star. Time for bed.

Are the sheep bedded down? Should I ride back to check them?

Morning. Blue air comes ringed with coyotes. The ewes wake clearing their communal throats like old men. Lambs shake their flop-eared heads at leaves of grass, negotiating the blade. People have asked in the past, "What do you do out there? Don't you get bored?" The problem seems to be something else. There's too much of everything here. I can't pace myself to it.

Down the valley the sheep move in a frontline phalanx, then turn suddenly in a card-stacked sequential falling, as though they had turned themselves inside out, and resume feeding again in whimsical processions. I think of town, of John's trailerhouse, the clean-bitten lawn, his fanatical obsession with neatness and work, his small talk with hired hands, my eyesore stacks of books and notes covering an empty bed, John smoking in the dark of early morning, drinking coffee, waiting for daylight to stream in.

After eating I return to the sheep, full of queasy fears that they will have vanished and I'll be pulled off the range to face those firing-squad looks of John's as he says, "I knew you'd screw up. Just like you screw up everything." But the sheep are there. I can't stop looking at them. They're there, paralyzing the hillside with thousands of mincing feet, their bodies pressed together as they move, saucerlike, scanning the earth for a landing.

Thunderstorm. Sheep feed far up a ridge I don't want them to go over, so the dog, horse, and I hotfoot it to the top and ambush them, yelling and hooting them back down. Cleverly, the horse uses me as a windbreak when the front moves in. Lightning fades and blooms. As we descend quickly, my rein-holding arm looks to me like a blank stick. I feel numb. Numb in all this vividness. I don't seem to occupy my life fully.

Down in the valley again I send the dog "way around" to turn the sheep, but he takes the law into his own hands and chases a lamb off a cliff. She's wedged upside down in a draw on the other side of the creek. It will take twenty minutes to reach her, and the rest of the sheep have already trailed ahead. This numbness is a wrist twisting inside my throat. A lone pine tree whistles, its needles are novocaine.

"In nature there are neither rewards nor punishments; there are only consequences." I can't remember who said that. I ride on.

One dead. Will she be reborn? And as what? The dog that nips lambs' heels into butchering chutes? I look back. The "dead" lamb convulses into action and scrambles up the ledge to find his mother.

Twin terrors: to be awake; to be asleep.

All day clouds hang over the Beartooth Mountains. Looking for a place out of the wind, I follow a dry streambed to a sheltered inlet. In front of me, there's something sticking straight up. It's the shell of a dead frog propped up against a rock with its legs crossed at the ankles. A cartoonist's idea of a frog relaxing, but this one's skin is paper-thin, mouth opened as if to scream. I lean close. "It's too late, you're already dead!"

Because I forgot to bring hand cream or a hat, sun targets in on me like frostbite. The dog, horse, and I move through sagebrush in unison, a fortress against wind. Sheep ticks ride my peeling skin. The dog pees, then baptizes himself at the water hole—full immersion—lapping at spitting rain. Afterward, he rolls in dust and reappears with sage twigs and rabbit brush strung up in his coat, as though in disguise—a Shakespearian dog. Above me, oil wells are ridge-top jewelry adorning the skyline with ludicrous sexual pumps. Hump, hump go the wells. Hump, hump go the drones who gather that black soup, insatiable.

We walk the fuselage of the valley. A rattlesnake passes going the other way; plenty of warning but so close to my feet I hop the rest of the day. I come upon the tin-bright litter of a former sheep camp: Spam cans flattened to the ground, their keys sticking up as if ready to open my grave.

Sun is in and out after the storm. In a long gully, the lambs gambol, charging in small brigades up one side, then the other. Ewes look on bored. When the lamb-fun peters out, the whole band comes apart in a generous spread the way sheep ranchers like them. Here and there lambs, almost as big as their mothers, kneel with a contagiously enthusiastic wiggle, bumping the bag with a goatlike butt to take a long draw of milk.

Night. Nighthawks whir. Meadowlarks throw their heads back in one ecstatic song after another. In the wagon I find a piece of broken mirror big enough to see my face: blood drizzles from cracked lips, gnats have eaten away at my ears.

To herd sheep is to discover a new human gear somewhere between second and reverse—a slow, steady trot of keenness with no speed. There is no flab in these days. But the constant movement of sheep from water hole to water hole, from camp to camp, becomes a form of longing. But for what?

The ten other herders who work for this ranch begin to trail their sheep toward summer range in the Big Horns. They're ahead of me, though I can't see them for the curve of the earth. One-armed Red, Grady, and Ed; Bob, who always bakes a pie when he sees me riding toward his camp; Fred, wearer of rags; "Amorous Albert"; Rudy, Bertha, and Ed; and, finally, Doug, who travels circuslike with a menagerie of goats, roosters, colts, and dogs and keeps warm in the winter by sleeping with one of the nannies. A peaceful army, of which I am the tail end, moving in ragtag unison across the prairie.

A day goes by. Every shiver of grass counts. The shallows and dapples in air that give grass life are like water. The bobcat returns nightly. During easy jags of sleep the dog's dream-paws chase coyotes. I ride to the sheep. Empty sky, an absolute blue. Empty heart. Sunburned face blotches brown. Another layer of skin to peel, to meet myself again in the mirror. A plane passes overhead—probably the government trapper. I'm waving hello, but he speeds away.

Now it's tomorrow. I can hear John's truck, the stock racks speak before I can actually see him, and it's a long time shortening the distance between us.

"Hello."

"Hello."

He turns away because something tender he doesn't want me to see registers in his face.

"I'm moving you up on the bench. Take the sheep right out the tail end of this valley, then take them to water. It's where the tree is.

I'll set your wagon by that road."

"What road?" I ask timidly.

Then he does look at me. He's trying to suppress a smile but speaks impatiently.

"You can see to hell and back up there, Gretel."

I ride to the sheep, but the heat of the day has already come on sizzling. It's too late to get them moving; they shade up defiantly, their heads knitted together into a wool umbrella. From the ridge there's whooping and yelling and rocks being thrown. It's John trying to get the sheep moving again. In a dust blizzard we squeeze them up the road, over a sharp lip onto the bench.

Here, there's wide-open country. A view. Sheep string out excitedly. I can see a hundred miles in every direction. When I catch up with John I get off my horse. We stand facing each other, then embrace quickly. He holds me close, then pulls away briskly and scuffles the sandy dirt with his boot.

"I've got to get back to town. Need anything?"

"Naw . . . I'm fine. Maybe a hat . . ."

He turns and walks his long-legged walk across the benchland. In the distance, at the pickup, an empty beer can falls on the ground when he gets in. I can hear his radio as he bumps toward town. Dust rises like an evening gown behind his truck. It flies free for a moment then returns, leisurely, to the habitual road—that bruised string which leads to and from my heart.

DORIS BIRCHAM

Doris Bircham wears many hats on the family ranch south of Piapot, and most of them are western. With the changing seasons, she moves from cattle drives to calving barns and from sales rings to brandings. She is probably better known as a "cowboy" poet as she has performed across the Canadian West. At the Festival of the Cowboy in Calgary in 1997, she was the recipient of the Bully award for her contribution to cowboy poetry. Each fall Doris rounds the poets up for a big gathering at Maple Creek, Saskatchewan. While her rhyming poetry is full of humor and entertainment, her free verse poetry often contains more serious thoughts on ranch life. Examples of each type of poem are represented in the following two selections.

Somebody

Four men and I walk down to the corral
    on a raw March afternoon.
We wear tall boots 'cause down at one end
    there's a bit of stale lagoon.

These are calves coming yearlings we start to sort;
    we separate heifers from steers,
and something I notice while working away
    is the fact that my name disappears.

I become SOMEBODY, the gopher kind–
    Sombody, do this and do that.
The vaccine gun's back up at the house
    and while there you can pick up my hat.

My popularity seems to increase.

Somebody, see that calf over there;
the muck's pretty deep so watch your step
and she's snaky so handle with care.

We move to the back of another pen,
push steers up a steep slippery rise.
Four duck under a tree and before you can spit
they race past two of the guys.

But is it their fault? Good heavens, no!
My son turns and glances at me.
This never would have happened, you know,
if *Somebody'*d stood under that tree.

We finally get them in the top corral
and our energy's just a bit drained,
but *Somebody* has a new job to do.
Make sure that far gate is chained.

Each of us grabs a short chokecherry stick.
No one can afford to be lax,
but *Somebody* makes a mistake at the gate;
a red baldie slips in with the blacks.

Next I get some double instructions.
Hold that calf! No way, let it through!
And of course amidst all the kerfuffle
Somebody should have known which to do.

Then there comes a round of discussion
'bout a heifer with a touch of foot rot
and whether that last pair of steers
fits in with the light end or not.

I come up with a few good ideas

and my expertise is for free.
I say, Cut out that white-footed steer,
but not one soul listens to me.

We finish and walk up towards the house
and there comes a quick end to this poem
when I say, Now you guys can make coffee,
'cause *Somebody* hasn't been home.

Foreclosure

it's just dirt, she said,
that's what I thought when I came to this farm
before I saw the field my husband's grandfather
ploughed with a team of oxen, before I walked
inside teepee rings in the east pasture and drank
from a spring bubbling up from the ground   before
I watched Canada geese come back and nest year after year
along the creek bank and I heard frogs
in our pasture slough announce spring's arrival
and I planted trees

before I learned to ride with my face to the wind
when I hadn't yet smelled new mown alfalfa or seen heads
heavy with wheat bow beneath the sun

it was before I learned about stillborn calves
before I helped feed cattle in a blizzard
and stayed up all night with a heifer
then watched her mother up with a newborn calf

when I'd experienced more seed times than harvests
and watched swaths lay for six weeks
rotting in the rain

and after I'd helped trail cattle to their summer pasture
year after year   gradually I knew
this is not just dirt, this is our land

all this happened long before our children
picked crocuses on the hillside behind our barn
long before we couldn't find the words to tell them
we have to leave

SHARON BUTALA

Sharon Butala came to a southwestern Saskatchewan ranch from the city and exchanged her life as a university professor for life on the land. Ranching traditions and the nuances of life on a ranch often left her unsettled, but as she bonded with the natural environment, Sharon also began to understand the ranching community. Coming to terms with this life has been the theme of much of Sharon's writing as she probes difficult human relationships. Her books have twice been short-listed for the Governor General's Literary Awards in Canada. The story "Breaking Horses" is taken from one of her earlier books Queen of the Headaches.

Breaking Horses

EDNA WATCHES THE HORSEBREAKER cross the yard with her husband. Stan is tall and lean, almost thin, and he walks as if he thinks the barn may possibly be on fire, but is too polite to run. The horsebreaker, Chuck, is average height but stockier, in no hurry. They are both wearing chaps and spurs and heavy parkas. The wind is up. A November blizzard is blowing in from the west, but already Edna can see that it will be a dry blizzard blowing more dirt than snow. Anyway, she knows it won't stop anything, not the calf-weaning, not the horsebreaking, not the eternal slope of the hills to the west that block her view of nothing, not the watchful tension of Stan's face.

I am forty this year, Edna reminds herself as she watches the horsebreaker and her husband cross the corral.

All day the horsebreaker has crossed and recrossed in front of the kitchen window, his big back moving up and down in a cautious rhythm. His face is shadowed by the fur of the parka's hood. His hands are hidden in leather mitts; chaps hide his legs. She has seen him pass in front of her view six, ten, a million times, and now evening has crept up on them again.

After the dishes are done she sits in the living room in front of the TV. Stan is asleep in his chair. The horsebreaker is lying on his back on the floor. He begins to do sit-ups. Between sit-ups he talks to her.

"She left me," he says as he rises, "for an Indian." He drops back down again quickly. The muscles of his abdomen unfold. "An Indian!" He rises halfway, grimacing, and holds for a second. "Took the kids," grunting as though he wanted to say more. Edna pulls her legs in to the chair. The horsebreaker speeds up. He is like a clock, up and down, up and down, a crazed clock with unnatural speed: tickety-tock, tickety-tock. "Fifty," he says, and stops. He swivels on his bottom to look at her. "I was in Calgary," he says. "Drunk. I didn't care. I was driving downtown and I couldn't decide where to go, see? Made a U-turn doing fifty right on the main street. I just didn't care." He stands up and begins to do knee bends balancing on one foot. After a while he does them balancing on the other foot. Edna watches him. She thinks how perfect his body is. His shirt is open and she can see the curly black hair that grows on his chest. It is wet with sweat. It crosses her mind that her kids are grown up and gone, that nobody can take them away.

"I didn't make enough money to suit her," he says, panting as he bobs up and down. Stan has wakened.

"She was no good, a bitch," he says. "You're better of without her."

"But my kids," the horsebreaker gasps.

"You're just rid of grief ten years sooner," her husband says. This makes Edna angry, but she doesn't say anything. The small room has begun to take on a dampness, a faint, salty odour from Chuck's exertions. She would like to see his rage played out. She would like to see him smile. She would like the horsebreaker to look at her with his bright blue eyes. She rubs her palms nervously on her thighs. She can feel the heat in her cheeks and hopes she isn't blushing. No, she thinks, she would never do that.

Chuck finishes his exercises, goes outside to the toilet. When he comes in a moment later, he says, "Well, time for bed," although it is only nine o'clock. He goes and washes and soon the house smells of liniment. All night Edna smells it as she weaves in and out of dreams.

Edna puts on her ragged yellow jacket that she wears to do barn chores or to ride with Stan. She ties a blue scarf under her chin and goes outside. She crosses the yard and goes to sit on the corral. Inside the corral Stan and the horsebreaker are just about to untie the gelding that lies on his side on the frozen ground, all four feet trussed. They put a halter on him and loop a rope around his neck. They put a rope through the halter and then the horsebreaker goes in and carefully unties the ropes around his feet, leaping back out of the horse's way. For a long moment the horse doesn't move. It is as if he doesn't realize that he has been untied. Then he rocks to his feet, whinnies, and tries to run. Stan and the horsebreaker both hold onto the rope that ends around his neck. They dig their heels into the ground and lean back. The gelding drags them slowly. When he stops to rear they quickly loop the rope around the snubbing post several times and the horsebreaker runs and jumps onto his saddle horse which has been standing quietly by the barn. The gelding pulls on the rope and when he can't free himself this way, rears, twisting his neck. Edna can see the whites of his eyes as they roll back in fear. He rears again and again until finally, he falls. The horsebreaker takes the rope from Stan, who has unwound it from the snubbing post, and wraps it around his saddle horn. The horse is still lying on its side, its four legs stretched straight out, its ribs heaving up and down. Stan goes over to it and hits it on the flank with his rope. The horse rolls to its knees and thrusts itself upright with its powerful back legs. It tries to run, and is brought up short by the rope. Chuck's horse digs in, then backs up slowly, trying to keep the rope taut, jerking the gelding into a turn. Stan, keeping a careful eye on the two horses, walks over to where Edna sits on the corral, and says, "He'll be on him by tomorrow."

The gelding is black with one white spot on his face and a flick of white on one pastern. His mane and tail are black too. His coat is beginning to lengthen and he has a shaggy look about him. Edna remembers when he was slicked off for summer and shone like coal. He is following behind Chuck's horse now, only balking now and then, or twisting his neck. Stan walks behind with his rope ready to hit him on the rump if the horse balks or rears.

Edna shivers. She climbs down off the corral and goes back to the kitchen.

There is a letter from Merrilee, their oldest daughter, in the mail. Billy, their oldest son, works on the oil rigs in Alberta; Larry rides on a government lease south of them; Lucy, married at sixteen, lives in a town a hundred miles away with her mechanic husband and their three children. Only Merrilee writes. Merrilee is a model in Calgary.

Stan holds his face expressionless while he reads the letter. Then he tosses it onto the table and makes a sound, perhaps a grunt, or maybe a snort. He goes outside. Edna picks up the letter and reads it.

"Dear Mom and Dad," Merrilee writes. "I am thinking of moving to Vancouver. There are more opportunities for models there, and I am getting tired of Calgary. I managed to lose another two pounds last week, Mom. I have stopped going out with Hans. Last night I went to a really fancy new restaurant. The waiters and waitresses were all dressed in togas. You would have loved it, Mom. I think I'll leave for Vancouver at the end of the month. I'll try to get home before I go, but don't expect me. Love, Merrilee."

After Edna has read it, she puts the letter down and walks to the sink where she begins to wash the dishes. She is crying. While she waits for the tears to stop, she continues to wash the dishes. The horsebreaker, who has been with them a week now, comes in for a drink of water and sees that she is crying. He hesitates in mid-step, then looking at her as though he is seeing her for the first time, asks, "Is something the matter?"

"No," Edna says, and then laughs at the silliness of this. He looks puzzled for a moment, but he grins back at her as though her behaviour is not unexpected. He pats her back awkwardly as he goes by to the door. When his hand is on the doorknob, he looks at her again.

She notices how perfect his jawline is, a clean masculine line, but with a delicate quality. After a long moment, he opens the door and goes outside.

"She should be married," Stan says to her in a low voice. "You keep encouraging her."

"I wanted something better for her. That's all," Edna answers. She turns away, but he pulls her back toward him, one hand on her bare shoulder where the strap of her nightgown has slipped down. They stare at one another.

"I'm afraid of what she does," he says, letting his hand drop to his side.

"She's a model," Edna insists. "Models get paid well. They go out with lots of men. Merrilee is beautiful," she adds. Stan lies down on their bed and stares at the ceiling.

"Maybe," he says. Edna lies down on her side of the bed.

"Look at Lucy," Edna says after a while. They lie side by side not speaking. Edna says to the ceiling, "I meant for Merrilee to get an education. You know that."

"Two months in nursing and she quits to go to modelling school. I blame you," he says. "You filled her with ideas how nothing around here was good enough for her." He turns over so that his back is to her. She wants to say, "But what's wrong with modelling? What's wrong with it? At least she isn't stuck on some god-forsaken ranch somewhere. At least she doesn't have three kids at nineteen, like Lucy, like me." But instead, she turns her back on Stan and tries to sleep.

Edna sees that it is past ten and nobody has come for morning coffee. She takes it off the stove and fills the thermos. Through the window she can see the horsebreaker riding at a lope in big figure eights. She watches for a moment, and then impulsively she jerks her jacket off the hook, puts it on, and takes the thermos outside. She stands just to one side of the invisible figure eight he is making. He glances away from the horse long enough to take in the thermos.

"I'll ride him to the corral," he calls to her. She follows them over to the corral where the horsebreaker hobbles the gelding. As he comes toward her, she sees the sweat trickling down beside his ears from his hair. He takes the filled thermos cap from her. He is panting slightly, and takes a deep breath before he sips the hot coffee.

"Bronc riding's hard work," Edna says sympathetically. He grins.

"You can't wear the bastard out," he says. "I'll get him though. Soon be tame as a pussycat."

The horsebreaker has been with them three weeks. Stan has taken two broke horses to a horse sale in Lethbridge. It is midnight. The horse-breaker, lying beside her, suddenly bunches his muscles and in one quick movement, turns on his side and gathers her in his arms again.

"I love you," he says into her hair.

"You don't even know me. You just met me."

"What do you stay with him for? Come with me."

"I'm five years older than you are," Edna replies. She is staring at the opposite wall, noticing that the brown stain on the wallpaper near the ceiling is getting bigger. The horsebreaker takes her by the shoulders and pushes her onto her back and kneels above her.

"I'm crazy about you," he whispers, staring into her eyes. His own eyes are like flowers, Edna thinks, cornflowers. There is no depth behind them. He puts his face down into the hollow of her neck and takes her skin gently in his teeth. She is afraid he will leave a mark. He holds her so tightly she can hardly breathe.

"I love you, I love you," he says to her fiercely. "Come with me."

"Maybe," Edna answers, looking at the darkness at the edge of the lamp's glow.

Edna is washing dishes. The horsebreaker has gone into town to a movie. It is unusual for Stan to come and sit in the kitchen while she does the supper dishes. He is usually asleep in his chair in front of the TV set by now.

"He's got nothing," Stan says.

"Who?" Edna asks. Stan stares at her till she drops her eyes.

"He can't stick to anything, he'll never amount to anything."

"His father didn't leave him a ranch," she says.

"I'm going to throw him out. He's been here a month. The work's done."

Don't be silly, Stan," Edna says, turning around. "He's nothing to me. I'm not interested in him." She turns back to her dishes.

"I don't like the way he looks at you when he thinks I'm not looking. I wouldn't trust him not to make a pass at you when I'm not around." Edna bangs the frying pan into the dishwater.

"You wouldn't give a damn," she says. "I'm just something you own, like those horses out there." Stan gets up and goes out of the kitchen.

At breakfast, Stan has told her that the black gelding is still too jumpy, "too goosey," he says. She goes out to watch him work with the horse, knowing what she will see, but unable to stop herself from going. The horse is saddled and standing in the corral. Stan takes another rope, ties it to the side of the saddle and then loops it around the horse's right rear leg. He pulls it tight from the front. The horse tries to free his leg, but Stan is close at his side making the loop into a sling from the side of the saddle around the horse's leg. He loops the rope twice and then secures the end with a couple of half-hitches to the saddle. The horse becomes helpless. He can barely walk on three legs. Then Stan bends carefully at the horse's front legs and hobbles him. Now the horse tries to move and finds himself with only one good leg. He backs into a corner of the corral, supporting his rump against the fence, and stands. His front legs begin to shake from the effort of standing in such an unnatural position. Stan takes another rope, secures it to the saddle horn, then throws the loose middle section over the horse's back. Then he walks behind the horse and pulls the rope across his rump. He goes up to the horse and shakes the saddle vigorously. The horse starts to buck and begins to fall. Quickly Stan pulls on the rope and holds him upright. Again he tries to buck, springing upward on his front legs and trying to throw his back legs out. He starts to fall again. Stan pulls him upright again. Then, snorting, the horse kneels on his front legs and lowers his head to the ground. Stan rubs his back and his flank roughly. The horse leaps upward in a fluid jump that straightens his front legs. Stan walks around him talking to him, patting him, rubbing his head, shaking the saddle, throwing the rope over him. After ten minutes of this, the horse is standing quietly, not flinching at every sound and movement. Stan loosens the ropes, mounts him and rides out of the corral. Edna goes back to the kitchen.

Stan begins to ride all day now too. He tells the horsebreaker not to start another horse, to ride the greenbroke one he worked on first. He himself, Stan says, will ride the big black gelding. So now Edna watches Stan on the black horse ride back and forth in front of her kitchen window all day long. It is much colder now and there is a thin covering of snow on the ground that doesn't melt during the day. At supper the horsebreaker says, "I'll be heading south soon. Winter's coming." Edna doesn't look up from her plate, but her hands are moist and she can feel a flush rising in her cheeks. Stan says heartily, "Be sorry to see you go." He and the horsebreaker talk to one another about Chuck's departure. He says he'll leave Friday. It is Wednesday evening now.

Early Thursday afternoon the horsebreaker corners her in his bedroom where she is making his bed. Stan has just driven off to get the mail, and the horsebreaker has hurried in, only bothering to take off his overshoes. He flips his parka hood down and holds her by both arms.

"I'm leaving for Montana. Come with me." His eyes gleam like a coyote's. She thinks, he likes the excitement. He likes the danger. He is so strong that when he pulls her toward him and kisses her, she doesn't even try to resist. She sees herself driving off beside him in his maroon pickup, sees the ranch growing smaller and smaller behind her, sees the road widening, becoming blacktop, leading into a city, its skyscrapers rising mistily toward the morning sun. She imagines the horsebreaker sitting beside her, his heavy thigh touching hers. She begins to kiss him back, raises her arms and puts them around his neck.

"It would be easy," she says, not to him.

"Come," he whispers. "I can't live without you." They hear the purr of Stan's truck driving into the yard. She pulls away and turns to finish making the bed. The horsebreaker hurries into the kitchen where he turns on the tap and takes a glass down from the shelf. In a moment, Stan comes into the house, sets the mail on the table. The horsebreaker wipes his mouth, flips up his parka hood, and goes back outside without speaking. Edna finishes and comes back into the kitchen where she sits down at the table across from Stan, who is reading the mail. He lifts his head and studies her, then he goes back to his reading. She looks at Stan a long time, thinking how it used to be when they were first married.

On Friday morning Stan is out at the barn while Chuck is in his bedroom packing. Edna goes to the bedroom door and says to him, "I'm not going with you." He lets his duffel bag fall back on the bed, shirts spilling out of it.

"Please," he says, crossing to her, trying to hold her. "I love you, I can't do without you. Please."

He means to overwhelm her with his passion. It makes her angry. She pulls back and hisses, "Can't either of you leave me alone? I'm not a horse that you keep at and keep at until you win." She is furious. Chuck would have slipped to his knees by now if she hadn't jerked away. Suddenly the outer door opens and Stan comes in. Chuck turns back to his packing. Stan stares at Edna as she crosses the room, but she is so angry with both of them that she doesn't falter, and Stan doesn't speak. The horsebreaker takes his duffel bag and walks out without a word. From the sink Edna can see him loading his saddle into his truck. He gets in and drives away.

"Good riddance," Stan says, with more relief than anger in his voice. He puts his arm around her, but she pulls away and faces him.

"What?" he asks.

"I'm leaving tomorrow."

He drops his arm and stares at her.

"Alone," she says. She can see his thoughts as they cross his face.

He is trying to make sense of this. Finally, he asks, "When will you be back?" She is silent for a moment. She hadn't thought of coming back, but now she realizes that this is a possibility.

"I don't know."

"Good," Stan says, as though everything is now explained. "A holiday. Go visit Merrilee. You should have gone a long time ago." He doesn't mention her departure again that day. Edna is too baffled by his response, too uncertain of herself to want to talk about this.

In the morning he gives her a cheque for several hundred dollars. Then he says, "Tell Merrilee . . . good luck." He hands Edna a second cheque and tells her to give it to Merrilee to help pay for moving. "I'll drive you to the bus," he says. "You can use Merrilee's car in the city. Maybe you should go to Vancouver with her. Help her get settled."

He helps her onto the bus, neither of them speaking in front of the ranchers who lounge, gossiping, against their half-tons, or the truckers checking their rigs.

"Phone me," Stan says, holding his hat on against the wind, and turns away. She watches him walk to his truck, climb in, and back out without looking at her again. She knows he is afraid to look at her.

Edna sits behind the tinted window glass holding her purse tightly with both hands. It seems thick and clumsy to her, heavy with the weight of the two cheques. As the bus pulls out with a pneumatic sigh, her tears stop as if the source has suddenly dried up. She sits holding her purse, feeling the tight cool tracks that mark her cheeks where her tears had been.

She sits for a long time, for hours, on the bus, watching the passengers sway as if they are one person. It will take more than you and a horsebreaker, she thinks. She sets her purse down on the empty seat beside her and stretches slowly. The bus rolls on west, into the sunset, toward the distant mountains.

KATIE KIDWELL

Katie Kidwell, also known as the "The Cariboo Song Rider," moved with her family to 100 Mile House in British Columbia at the age of nine. Music, horses, cattle and family have been her preoccupations. She has attended cowboy poetry gatherings on both sides of the border, entertaining the crowds with her singing and guitar playing. Less is known of her poetry, including the selections following, which present a wry humor.

Cow-Less

Tonight they waited
By the mangers,
                Just over a bit
So they would see me;
So I would see them
When I drove into the yard.

I didn't have to check
My watch.
They knew;
I knew
It was feeding time.

Even the milk cow
Was there.
It isn't often she shows herself
With the beef cows.
They used to push her around.
But tonight she remembers;

I remember
When I milked her in the hay shed.
When the beef cows were on the other side
of the fence . . .

They must have broken the fence.
I must check the fence.

I wish;
They wish
They were still here.

Let Life

Let life
Lift your chin
Stir your heart
Dance your limbs.
Let life
Take its course . . .

You hold the reins;
You ride the horse.

DORIS DALEY

Doris Daley, introduced earlier as the great-great-granddaughter of Mary Daley, has written many poems: some serious, some humorous. Unlike "From Mary's Window," the following selection, "Bossy's Profits" (also from her chapbook The Daley Grind*), represents a more lighthearted approach to writing about ranch life.*

Bossy's Profits

There's no particular rhyme scheme to this one that I can figure out. It reads like a stumble-footed-horse rides; you'll just have to hang on and hope for the best. Or better yet, let's call it Experimental Literary Open Verse.

So, about the poem. My capital assets consist of a good set of pots and pans, my grandma's butter tart recipe, and four cows. Like all cattle barons, therefore, I must decide each fall what to do with all the money I make in the beef business. I'm sure many of you can identify.

This year, I've decided to put all the money I make from ranching
to good use.
Oh no, not I;
I'll not fritter all the glitter that Bossy can produce.
A money machine she is, and no loan is too big to spook her.
Oh it's grand to be a cattle baron counting filthy lucre.

Now if you're from Wall Street you may say, "Invest! Invest!
Stocks, bonds, Louisiana shrimp ponds and all the rest!"

Or how about some champagne wishes and caviar dreams?
We all know ranchers can take conspicuous consumption to

lofty new extremes:

Alligator boots
Porter Wagner suits
Imported designer water
Or a diamond-studded fly swatter!

Oh Bossy, folks have such good advice.
And wouldn't it be nice
If there was a device
To turn beef into economic paradise?

But for now, dear cow, all that I ask is that you don't forsake me.
Don't be dry, and with all the money that you make me
I don't think I'll go too wild:
No dinners with Mr. Rothschild.

No bathtubs full of almond roca
Or investment meetings with Iacoca.
This year, Bossy, I think I'll call it quits
On skiing trips to St. Mortiz,
And just spend all the money that you bring
On one big blow-out
    at Burger King.

MARILYN HALVORSON

Marilyn Halvorson runs the cattle ranch she grew up on near Sundre, Alberta. Cowboys Don't Cry *is the best known of her award-winning novels about western life. This selection taken from her journal and later published as the novel* To Everything A Season, *tells of certain extraordinary moments on the ranch.*

To Everything A Season

September 23

IT COMES AROUND EVERY FALL. Cow-moving day. Time to bring the herd home from summer pasture on the north quarter. This year it's on the most beautiful fall day you could ever imagine. The total opposite of last year—as sour a day as could be found in your worst nightmares. Ice-cold rain, mud and slop, in the middle of a run of such evil days. And I with my wrist in a cast. A cast doesn't do well in the pouring rain, so, all things considered, I decided that riding after the cattle that day just wasn't worth it. Instead, I resorted to two bales of hay in the back of the half-ton. It worked, with a little help from some friends. But it didn't work perfectly. The first time I got the whole herd out onto the road a car came along at the strategic moment to spook them all back in again!

But that was then. This is now. By nine o'clock it is warming up and the cows have spread out from their usual fall early-morning vigil at the pasture gate. Some have even crossed to the far side of the soft-bottomed creek. That isn't good. Taking a horse through that bottomless mud is not something I want to try.

Now, cows, the first question is, are you feeling cooperative today or are you going to make this hard for all of us? We're in luck. As I ride into the pasture, heads go up. Bawling starts. The message goes out. "Hey girls, she's finally here. Time to go for winter vacation." Strings of cattle line out toward the gate.

The three calves that have been blissfully grazing in the neighbor's pasture skitter back under the fence and come tearing over to their mothers. Now the bunch of cattle across the creek stare, bawl, finally come jolting, stiff-legged, down the hill, and wade slowly through the creek. Except for two head. The village idiots. They stand on the hill on the other side and gawk, too dim to comprehend what every other critter has already figured out.

The rest of the cattle line up at the gate while those two gawk some more. The others begin to fidget. I begin to fidget. I ride up and down the creek bank, trying to get the idiots' attention, spook them, do anything to get some action—anything except wallow through that muddy crossing. The idiots take two steps. They gawk. Then something spooks the bunch at the gate. Half of them start moving farther back into the pasture. Back toward the thick willow brush. Oh no you don't! Definitely not the willow brush. We've done the willow brush before. Last time that happened, I was riding a young half-broke Angel horse. By the time that she, I and the cows saw the light of day again, she was a well-broke and thoroughly seasoned cowhorse. Chasing cows by sound in willows too high to see over and too thick to ride through is very educational for all concerned.

The movement of the back-turning renegades catches the attention of the idiots. At last they begin to move toward the creek. I ride to cut off the willow-seekers, urging my horse to hurry but mindful of the gopher holes that pepper the ground beneath her. Funny, I could avoid those gopher holes at a dead gallop when I was fifteen!

The rebels turn, the idiots catch up. We all head for the gate. I wave to my accomplice to open the gate. It's a stiff one. For a minute she wrestles with it. Come on, lady, pull!

The gate's open. The cows stream out onto the road in one compact, calm herd. No straggling calf panics and heads back for the boonies. No deranged mama decides to take her calf and play bunch-quitter at the last second. No confused cow decides to run along the inside of the fence instead of going out. This is almost too good to be true!

Once on the road, it's easy. One neighbor catches up in her truck just before our corner. We pass the time of day. She's in no hurry. Now a car is coming from the west, but we're in luck. The last cow sweeps around the corner and onto our sideroad just in time.

Up the long, slow hill. A minute's visit with Jim Haug, my nearest neighbor who has ambled down to stand in his gateway as the herd goes by.

Then, we're home. I stand in the road, holding Angel and counting as the red and white bodies flow in through the gate. As usual, I count wrong. Two counts later it works out right. I am careful not to count again!

I check my watch. An hour and fifteen minutes have passed since I rode away from the barn. Not bad for riding two miles, gathering the cattle and bringing them two miles back.

Either luck or skill rode with us today. I refuse to speculate on which it was.

February 15

After a day of liveable temperatures (up to 20°F yesterday), we're back in deep winter. Light snow and a cold east wind all day. That meant mega-chores this afternoon. Then, as I finished feeding, I discovered that #88, a three-year-old due to have her second calf, wasn't eating but wandering around looking grumpy and unsettled. I stuffed her into the barn without much difficulty. Three hours later I came out for my pre-dark check and peeked into the barn. Sure enough, #88 had doubled! Now I had one big, solid cow and one little, wet bundle standing beside her. It was a good thing I had got her in. It will hit -20°F, still with snow and wind, tonight.

Before bed, I make one final check. In the barn, the new baby is lying stretched out on his side. Has he sucked? Is he getting chilled and weak? I walk over and start prodding him a little to see if he can get up. The next thing I know, #88, normally the mildest of cows, has her head down and is making a fairly earnest attempt to knock me over. Fortunately, the calf is between her and me so her reluctance to step on it, combined with the mighty roar I instinctively come out with when attacked, discourages her from giving me more than a little push. I go inside the stall gate and try reaching out from there to prod the calf. Then #88 gives the gate a good slam. I capitulate.

Either the calf is well or he isn't. One way or the other, his mother will have to deal with it herself. She is very definitely *in charge.*

April 21

Cowboy time again. The day for vaccinating, castrating and dehorning calves. A lot of people brand the spring calves now, too, but I don't. Mainly because my dad never thought it was necessary and his system worked.

As a kid, I loved this job. Bringing in the cattle, cutting out the calves, roping and wrestling them made me feel like a big-time cowgirl, straight out of the Old West. Now, I guess I've gone soft, or grown up. It's a dirty job that makes me feel mean and cruel, but it's a necessary one. All the Walkers come to help, and the work goes quickly and smoothly. By evening the cattle are back in the field, the calves recovering in a warm sun and gentle breeze.

Copper did his first cow-work today, bringing the cattle out of the field. Not particularly demanding work, but he paid attention and cooperated. I switched to Angel for separating the cows and calves in the corral. She's an excellent corral horse because she doesn't get excited in tight places, though sometimes she should get *more* excited and move a little faster.

June 24

As I write this at ten-fifteen P.M., the big spruces outside my bedroom window are just shading from green to black and an apricot-gold sunset glows between their branches.

Today was the Sundre Rodeo. I wonder how old I was when I went to my first Sundre Rodeo. I can't remember but I'm sure my dad and I went to at least twenty together. It was always a special time for me. I guess that I can identify with the song title "My Heroes Have Always Been Cowboys." The rodeo always made me feel close to a great, western tradition.

The earliest ones I can remember were in a little makeshift arena at the bottom of Snake Hill. The grand finale I will always remember came at dusk when a wagon train pulled into the arena, circled and unhitched. Then, suddenly, on the brow of the big hill, a line of riders appeared. "Indians"! With spine-chilling whoops they charged down the steep side of the hill, shooting into the air. (Were they shooting blanks? Who cares. Nobody got killed.)

A couple of circuits around the arena and then one of them touches a torch to the paper canvas of one of the wagons and it bursts into flames.

The flames die down and night falls. The rodeo ends for another year.

Great stuff, when you're a kid. Now, I'm sure it couldn't happen. Someone would cry "racism" and a protest would break out. Rightly so, maybe, but I think those were more innocent times. No one was making a statement that Indians were savages. Nobody was making a statement at all. It was just fun.

I probably drank some of my first coffee at the rodeo. Strong, black and hot from a cardboard cup as we shivered after a sudden downpour.

I remember another downpour at the rodeo, years later when the grounds had been moved to the far end of town and I was old enough to be racing Goldie, my one-in-a-million-bought-for-one-hundred-and-sixty-dollars horse in the stock horse race. I was out warming her up when the rain hit and I remember my round-braided rawhide reins, soaking wet, stretchy and slippery, making it almost impossible to hold back the excited horse until the starting gun. There was a lot of motivation to win that day. Only the front-runner finished with a clean face!

The grounds have moved again, back almost to the first site. The rodeo is professional now. The Gary Logan Professional Rodeo, named in honor of a local cowboy who died with three others in a plane crash in California a few years back. I sit in the stands and watch this year. The performance runs smoothly. High-class riders, good stock, a huge metal grandstand. The Sundre Rodeo has come a long way.

But I miss the wagon train, I miss the thrill of that grown-up coffee. I miss the adrenalin high of racing around a dirt track on a horse that loved to win. And I miss my dad.

TERRI MASON

The only source for Terri Mason's sometimes wildly hilarious and almost always humorous poetry is first-hand experience. It has been said "She has a good memory, 'cause she can remember things that never happened." She has been a guider and a logger. Poems included here are from her book Livin' On Cowboy's Wages.

What I'd Do in Paris . . .

If ol' Rusty and me
were sent cross the sea
to the capital city of France

I'd recite cowboy prose
from the land of Wild Rose
in this city of sweet romance

I'd have something to say
on the Champs Elysees
'bout ropin' & ridin' the range

and if they're rude to me
I'll get even – you see
I'll spit snoose in their sidewalk cafe's . . .

Lesson # 1

We worked and scrimped and saved for years
to buy our chunk of land
The life of a small time rancher
we wanted to try our hand

To show thanks to the Lord
I promised to board
and protect the life of our first cow

Never send her to auction
or grind her into burgers
old age and dignity I'd allow

I vowed she'd live out her days in gentle peace
and die gracefully of old age
and that's just what she did
two days after
she set foot on our place.

JUDY ALSAGAR

A British Columbia transplant originally from Saskatchewan, Judy Alsagar, along with her family, bought one of the largest ranches in the world—the Gang Ranch—which stretches a mere seventy-five miles through mountain wilderness. Eventually and tragically, the family lost the ranch. Judy Alsagar tells that story in her book The Gang Ranch: The Real Story. *In amongst the heartaches and the misadventures, Judy presents the land and everyday life on the ranch.*

Home Ranch Cattle Drive: Fall 1981

WE SETTLED INTO THE RUSH OF FALL WORK: haying, cattle movements, roundups, and last-minute branding. A couple hundred head of cattle needed to be moved to Williams Meadow from their "dumping out" spot at Home Ranch. The cowboy crew was further out in the back-country with the main herd so other "movers" were needed. I hastily volunteered my services thinking a day out in the glories of the autumn splendor would do my spirit good.

I never have been one for organized religion; I have never felt, like others obviously have, that God was inside that building called the Church. But put me out in the wilderness where everything you see is a miracle, and I become the most religious person around. I can feel Him everywhere there. I was on a continuous "high" out in the bush.

Dan Patten was presiding over this particular drive. In high spirits, we all headed to the corrals at Home Ranch early in the morning and selected and saddled a ranch horse. Although a late fall chill was in the air, and the morning frost had not yet melted from the slippery rails of the corral and the white crystal-tinged grasses all around, it promised to be a clear, glorious day.

As I sat quietly on the horse waiting for the next step, I looked around at the rest of the "crew" who were in various stages of mounting their horses, adjusting cinches, tying jackets and water canteens behind saddles, applying sunscreen and bug repellant. We were mostly women and children this time, along with Raymond Rosette and Dan Patten. I thought comically to myself that I would sure have a hard time getting hired on as a professional cowboy today. In my mind's eye, I saw the real cowboys with their meticulous white shirts, vests, big belt buckles, distinctive cowboy hats, oilskin slickers, and real silver spurs jangling on the heels of expensive snakeskin, slant-heeled cowboy boots. I glanced down at my corduroy shirt. I had discovered on that bug-infested Graveyard trip that mosquitoes and blackflies did not bite through the ribbing of corduroy. They landed on the raised part of the cloth, and if they did bite, it didn't get down to the skin. Today I wore my comfortable old running shoes—again, not exactly stylish for a cowgirl but my cowboy boots had never been the same since the "monsoon" trip with Howard and Denis. Still, I wasn't as bad as Oren. I remembered, with a smile to myself, the rainy, then snowy cattle drive that Oren had taken part in, and how I had laughed to see him trotting by on his horse Tall Timber with his spurs fastened to the heels of his rubber boots.

Everyone was mounted, and Dan was pointing out directions for different riders to take gathering up the widely spread cattle. We finally got them concentrated into the semblance of a herd, with riders placed strategically on the outer edges. We heard the age-old "Head 'em out" call from somewhere up front and began to move them out, up the side hills surrounding Home Ranch.

I was riding "drag," which meant stuck at the back in the dust, pushing along mothers with small calves and the old tired cows that would soon be wanting to stall at every puddle of water or a batch of grass. I didn't mind; it was a beautiful day and I had lots of heavy-duty thinking to do.

For most of the day, we trailed along. True to form, the old cows became tired, and the mothers held back, refusing to move along if their calves hadn't caught up. Gradually, the herd split more-or-less into two herds: the faster group, with Raymond Rosette as "lead man," and the slower ones at the back. Half the riders followed the faster group. We continued to follow happily along the trail, and eventually the faster bunch got so far ahead of us that we lost sight of them. Even their dust settled and disappeared. Soon the faster group came to the cutoff trail in the bush that branched off to our destination, Williams Meadow cow camp. Turning their herd to the right, they quickly got swallowed up on the tree-lined path to Williams Meadow.

When the lead riders at the front of our "slow" bunch came to the cutoff corner, they didn't notice that this was where the first bunch had branched off. They rode right on past the cutoff path, leading our herd with them.

The afternoon went by in a relentless, mindless haze of pushing the slow-moving group. I had cut myself a long, whip switch from a passing willow tree to coax the balky ones along. I kept expecting to break through the bush into the openness of Williams Meadow at any minute. There wasn't a lot of daylight left.

Suddenly, through the dust, I caught sight of Dan's arms waving frantically way up at the front of our strung-out group. He was yelling and gesturing toward us; I couldn't hear a thing over the bawling of the cattle, but it seemed, from the flinging motions of his arms, that he wanted us to turn back. He, himself, was trying to turn the lead cows around!

I left my station at the back and trotted up to where he and the other front riders were pushing the cows back and trying to stop the fleeing animals from going forward around them. The tired cows had obviously smelled the lush meadow grass of the huge clearing I could see up ahead and were bound and determined to get to it.

"What's wrong?" I yelled, over the commotion.

Dan, turning his horse in half-circles, was desperately trying to turn the herd and not winning the battle.

"We're back at Home Ranch! Turn them around," he hollered back at me.

I couldn't believe my ears, but there was no time to ponder on it, or even laugh about it. If we didn't get the lead cows turned around, the whole works would be gone after them. All the riders were now at the front, and finally we managed to get the resisting herd heading back in the direction we had just come from. Some went floundering off into the bush, but a few riders could gather them up once things were under control again.

As we pushed them hard back up the trail, a few kept trying to break away and get back to that open area. I looked behind at the huge clearing through the trees and could hardly stifle a giggle. Sure enough, it was Home Ranch Valley. We had missed the turnoff, gone in a great huge circle, and come back down into Home Ranch again. Following along in my contented, thought-filled daze, I hadn't even noticed when we bypassed the turnoff.

Eventually the front riders came to the cutoff trail and, after some persuasion as it was uphill, the lead cows began the arduous climb up through the trees toward Williams Meadow. We followed, up over the top, through the darkening bush until at long last we started coming down again, straggling into Williams Meadow cow camp just as it was getting dark. The cows were tired and the small calves that followed doggedly behind no longer held their tails up in the air. All of them quickened their pace, though, when they spotted the rest of the herd milling about on the meadow.

A grinning Raymond Rosette and his crew were relaxing at the cabin, well-rested and fed. By now, Raymond had pretty well figured out what took us so long and was chortling away, his well-worn cowboy boots propped up on the windowsill, hands clasped behind his head, ready for a good round of merriment.

After our horses were taken care of, and we had a chance to tromp into the cabin and relax for a while, pull out a few cracked, coffee-ground-riddled cups, and pour ourselves some life-saving and potent "cow camp brew," the humor of it all began to hit us. Many jokes were told and retold about the "great greenhorn cattle drive," when we ended up in the same valley we started in!

SARAH TRUSLER

There is a quietness in Sarah Trusler's poetry, a certain serenity that reins the reader in. The poems are like riding at dawn or at dusk. Horses race through her poems; she has been a horsewoman: roping, riding and shoeing horses most of her life. Some of her poems, such as "Figure Eights," were included in Ten Years Gatherings: Montana Poems and Stories.

Figure Eights

This poem kinda tells the story—just as it happened

Today, in the summer's morning quiet
you surprised me.
You drifted by on your dun colt,
easing into a lope, figure-eighting silver sagebrush,
stopping and backing
patting and praising,
a reining pattern on the banks of Sunday Creek.

The dun colt's tail swished lightly at flies;
his ears searched the cottonwoods
at each pause.
I would have called out a greeting to you,
but I hesitated.
You turned and loped toward home,
a brown-red rocker melting into the trees.

From the veil of green, metal cracking metal,
a steel post shatters slumbering sandstone

as you begin the work
your father sent you to do.
I retreat to the meditations of my heart
having been touched
but regretfully not touching.

I hope you don't mind, Jess,
that I watched you.

PAM HOUSTON

Pam Houston writes stories "that first get your heart racing, then pierce it with their truths about men and women—together and apart." The West takes on new meaning in her writing as she invites the readers to look at old experiences through new eyes. "What Shock Heard" is one of twelve stories in her collection Cowboys Are My Weakness.

What Shock Heard

IT WAS LATE SPRING, but the dry winds had started already, and we were trying to load Shock into the horse trailer for a trip to the vet and the third set of X-rays on her fetlock. She's just barely green broke, and after months of being lame she was hot as a pistol and not willing to come within twenty yards of the trailer. Katie and Irwin, who own the barn, and know a lot more than me, had lip chains out, and lunge ropes and tranquilizer guns, but for all their contraptions they couldn't even get close enough to her to give her the shot. Crazy Billy was there too, screaming about two-by-fours and electric prods, and women being too damned ignorant to train a horse right. His horses would stand while he somersaulted in and out of the saddle. They'd stand where he ground-tied them, two feet from the train tracks, one foot off the highway. He lost a horse under a semi once, and almost killed the driver. All the women were afraid of him, and the cowboys said he trained with Quaaludes. I was watching him close, trying to be patient with Katie and Irwin and my brat of a horse, but I didn't want Billy within ten feet of Shock, no matter how long it took to get her in the trailer.

That's when the new cowboy walked up, like out of nowhere with a carrot in his hands, whispered something in Shock's ear, and she walked right behind him into the trailer. He winked at me and I smiled back and poor Irwin and Katie were just standing there all tied up in their own whips and chains.

The cowboy walked on into the barn then, and I got into the truck with Katie and Irwin and didn't see him again for two months when Shock finally got sound and I was starting to ride her in short sessions and trying to teach her some of the things any five-year-old horse should know.

It was the middle of prairie summer by then and it was brutal just thinking about putting on long pants to ride, but I went off Shock so often I had to. The cowboy told me his name was Zeke, short for Ezekiel, and I asked him if he was religious and he said only about certain things.

I said my name was Raye, and he said that was his mother's name and her twin sister's name was Faye, and I said I could never understand why people did things like that to their children. I said that I was developing a theory that what people called you had everything to do with the person you turned out to become, and he said he doubted it 'cause that was just words, and was I going to stand there all day or was I going to come riding with him. He winked at Billy then and Billy grinned and I pretended not to see and hoped to myself that they weren't the same kind of asshole.

I knew Shock wasn't really up to the kind of riding I'd have to do to impress this cowboy, but it had been so long since I'd been out on the meadows I couldn't say no. There was something about the prairie for me—it wasn't where I had come from, but when I moved there it just took me in and I knew I couldn't ever stop living under that big sky. When I was a little girl driving with my family from our cabin in Montana across Nebraska to all the grandparents in Illinois, I used to be scared of the flatness because I didn't know what was holding all the air in.

Some people have such a fear of the prairie it makes them crazy, my ex-husband was one, and they even have a word for it: "agoraphobia." But when I looked it up in Greek it said "fear of the marketplace," and that seems like the opposite kind of fear to me. He was afraid of the high wind and the big storms that never even came while he was alive. When he shot himself, people said it was my fault for making him move here and making him stay, but his chart only said *acute agoraphobia* and I think he did it because his life wasn't as much like a book as he wanted it to be. He taught me about literature and language, and even though he used language in a bad way—to make up worlds that hurt us—I learned about its power and it got me a job, if nothing else, writing for enough money to pay off his debts.

But I wasn't thinking about any of that when I set off across the meadow at an easy hand gallop behind Zeke and his gelding Jesse. The sun was low in the sky, but it wasn't too long after solstice and in the summer the sun never seemed to fall, it seeped toward the horizon and then melted into it. The fields were losing heat, though, and at that pace we could feel the bands of warmth and cool coming out of the earth like it was some perfectly regulated machine. I could tell Zeke wasn't a talker, so I didn't bother riding up with him; I didn't want Shock to try and race on her leg. I hung back and watched the way his body moved with the big quarter horse: brown skin stretched across muscle and horseflesh, black mane and sandy hair, breath and sweat and one dust cloud rose around them till there was no way to separate the rider from the ride.

Zeke was a hunter. He made his living as a hunter's guide, in Alaska, in places so remote, he said, that the presence of one man with a gun was insignificant. He invited me home for moose steaks, and partly because I loved the way the two words sounded together, I accepted.

It was my first date in almost six years and once I got that into my head it wouldn't leave me alone. It had been almost two years since I'd been with a man, two years almost to the day that Charlie sat on our front-porch swing and blew his brains out with a gun so big the stains splattered three sets of windows and even wrapped around the corner of the house. I thought I had enough reason to swear off men for a while, and Charlie wasn't in the ground three months when I got another one.

It was in October of that same year, already cold and getting dark too early, and Shock and I got back to the barn about an hour after sunset. Katie and Irwin were either in town or in bed and the barn was as dark as the house. I walked Shock into her stall and was starting to take off her saddle when Billy stepped out of the shadows with a shoeing tool in his hand. Women always say they know when it's going to happen, and I did, as soon as he slid the stall door open. I went down when the metal hit my shoulder and I couldn't see anything but I could feel his body shuddering already and little flecks of spit coming out of his mouth. The straw wasn't clean and Shock was nervous and I concentrated on the sound her hooves made as they snapped the air searchingly behind her. I imagined them connecting with Billy's skull and how the blood on the white wall would look like Charlie's, but Shock was much too honest a horse to aim for impact. Billy had the arm that wasn't numb pinned down with one knee through the whole thing, but I bit him once right on the jawline and he's still got that scar; a half-moon of my teeth in his face.

He said he'd kill me if I told, and the way my life was going it seemed reasonable to take him at his word. I had a hard time getting excited about meeting men after that. I'd learned to live without it, but not very well.

Shock had pitched me over her head twice the day that Zeke asked me to dinner, and by the time I got to his house my neck was so stiff I had to turn my whole body to look at him.

"Why don't you just jump in the hot tub before dinner," he said, and I swung my head and shoulders around from him to the wood-heated hot tub in the middle of the living room and I must have gone real white then because he said, "But you know, the heater's messing up and it's just not getting as hot as it should."

While he went outside to light the charcoals I sat on a hard wooden bench covered with skins facing what he called the trophy wall. A brown-and-white speckled owl stared down its pointed beak at me from above the doorway, its wings and talons poised as if ready for attack, a violence in its huge yellow eyes that is never so complete in humans.

He came back in and caught me staring into the face of the grizzly bear that covered most of the wall. "It's an eight-foot-square bear," he said, and then explained, by rubbing his hand across the fur, that it was eight feet long from the tip of its nose to the tip of its tail, and from the razor edge of one outstretched front claw to the other. He smoothed the fur back down with strong even strokes. He picked something off one of its teeth.

"It's a decent-sized bear," he said, "but they get much bigger."

I told him about the time I was walking with my dogs along the Salmon River and I saw a deer carcass lying in the middle of an active spawning ground. The salmon were deeper than the water and their tails slapped the surface as they clustered around the deer. One dog ran in to chase them, and they didn't even notice, they swam around her ankles till she got scared and came out.

He laughed and reached towards me and I thought for me, but then his hand came down on the neck of a six-point mule deer mounted on the wall behind me. "Isn't he beautiful?" he asked. His hands rubbed the short hair around the deer's ears. It was hanging closer to me than I realized, and when I touched its nose it was warmer than my hands.

He went back outside then and I tried to think of more stories to tell him but I got nervous all over and started fidgeting with something that I realized too late was the foot of a small furry animal. The thing I was sitting on reminded me a little too much of my dog to allow me to relax.

The moose steaks were lean and tender and it was easy to eat them until he started telling me about their history, about the bull that had come to the clearing for water, and had seen Zeke there, had seen the gun even, and trusted him not to fire. I couldn't look right at him then, and he waited awhile and he said, "Do you have any idea what they do to cows?"

We talked about other things after that, horses and the prairie and the mountains we had both left for it. At two I said I should go home, and he said he was too tired to take me. I wanted him to touch me the way he touched the mule deer but he threw a blanket over me and told me to lift up for the pillow. Then he climbed up and into a loft I hadn't even noticed, and left me down there in the dark under all those frightened eyes.

The most remarkable thing about him, I guess, was his calm: His hands were quieter on Jesse's mane even than mine were on Shock's. I never heard him raise his voice, even in laughter. There wasn't an animal in the barn he couldn't turn to putty, and I knew it must be the same with the ones he shot.

On our second ride he talked more, even about himself some, horses he'd sold, and ex-lovers; there was a darkness in him I couldn't locate.

It was the hottest day of that summer and it wouldn't have been right to run the horses, so we let them walk along the creek bank all afternoon, clear into the next county, I think.

He asked me why I didn't move to the city, why I hadn't, at least, while Charlie was sick, and I wondered what version of my life he had heard. I told him I needed the emptiness and the grasses and the storm threats. I told him about my job and the articles I was working on and how I knew if I moved to the city, or the ocean, or even back to the mountains, I'd be paralyzed. I told him that it seemed as if the right words could only come to me out of the perfect semicircular space of the prairie.

He rubbed his hands together fist to palm and smiled, and asked if I wanted to rest. He said he might nap, if it was quiet, and I said I knew I always talked too much, and he said it was okay because I didn't mind if he didn't always listen.

I told him words were all we had, something that Charlie had told me, and something I had believed because it let me fall into a vacuum where I didn't have to justify my life.

Zeke was stretching his neck in a funny way, so without asking I went over and gave him a back rub and when I was finished he said, "For a writer lady you do some pretty good communicating without words," but he didn't touch me even then, and I sat very still while the sun melted, embarrassed and afraid to even look at him.

Finally, he stood up and stretched.

"Billy says you two go out sometimes."

"Billy lies," I said.

"He knows a lot about you," he said.

"No more than everyone else in town," I said. "People talk. It's just what they do. I'll tell you all about it if you want to know."

"We're a long way from the barn," he said, in a way that I couldn't tell if it was good or bad. He was rubbing one palm against the other so slowly it was making my skin crawl.

"Shock's got good night vision," I said, as evenly as I could.

He reached for a strand of Shock's mane and she rubbed her whole neck against him. I pulled her forelock out from under the brow band. She nosed his back pockets, where the carrots were. She knocked his cap off his head and scratched her nose between his shoulder blades. He put both hands up on her withers and rubbed little circles. She stretched her neck out long and low.

"Your horse is a whore, Raye," he said.

"I want to know what you said to her to make her follow you into the trailer," I said.

"What I said to her?" he said. "Christ, Raye, there aren't any words for that."

Then he was up and in the saddle and waiting for me to get back on Shock. He took off when I had only one foot in the stirrup, and I just hung around Shock's neck for the first quarter mile till he slowed up.

The creek trail was narrow and Shock wanted to race, so I got my stirrup and let her fly past him on the outside, the wheat so high it whipped across Shock's shoulder and my thigh. Once we were in the lead, Shock really turned it on and I could feel her strength and the give of her muscles and the solidity of the healed fetlock every time it hit the ground. Then I heard Jesse coming on the creek side, right at Shock's flank, and I knew we were coming to the big ditch, and I knew Shock would take it if Jesse did, but neither of us wanted to give up the lead. Shock hit the edge first and sailed over it and I came way up on her neck and held my breath when her front legs hit, but then we were down on the other side and she was just as strong and as sound as ever. Jesse edged up again and I knew we couldn't hold the lead for much longer. I felt Zeke's boots on my calf and our stirrups locked once for an instant and then he pulled away. I let Shock slow then, and when Jesse's dust cleared, the darkening sky opened around me like an invitation.

It wasn't light enough to run anymore and we were still ten miles from the barn. Jupiter was up, and Mars. There wasn't any moon.

Zeke said, "Watching you ride made me almost forget to beat you." I couldn't see his face in the shadows.

He wanted silence but it was too dark not to talk, so I showed him the constellations. I told him the stories I knew about them: Cassiopeia weeping on the King's shoulder while the great winged Pegasus carries her daughter off across the eastern sky. Cygnus, the swan, flying south along the milky way, the Great Bear spinning slowly head over tail in the north. I showed him Andromeda, the galaxy closest to our own. I said, "It's two hundred million light-years away. Do you know what that means?" And when he didn't answer I said, "It means the light we see left that galaxy two hundred million years ago." And then I said, "Doesn't that make you feel insignificant?"

And he said, "No."

"How does it make you feel?" I said.

"Like I've gotten something I might not deserve," he said.

Then he went away hunting in Montana for six weeks. I kept thinking about him up there in the mountains I had come from and wondering if he saw them the way I did, if he saw how they held the air. He didn't write or call once, and I didn't either, because I thought I was being tested and I wanted to pass. He left me a key so I could water his plants and keep chemicals in his hot tub. I got friendly with the animals on the wall, and even talked to them sometimes, like I did to the plants. The only one I avoided was the Dall sheep. Perfect in its whiteness, and with a face as gentle and wise as Buddha. I didn't want to imagine Zeke's hands pulling the trigger that stained the white neck with blood the taxidermist must have struggled to remove.

He asked me to keep Jesse in shape for him too, and I did. I'd work Shock in the ring for an hour and then take Jesse out on the trails. He was a little nervous around me, being used to Zeke's uncanny calm, I guess, so I sang the songs to him that I remembered from Zeke's records: "Angel from Montgomery," "City of New Orleans," "L.A. Freeway," places I'd never been or cared to go. I didn't know any songs about Montana.

When we'd get back to the barn I'd brush Jesse till he shone, rubbing around his face and ears with a chamois cloth till he finally let down his guard a little and leaned into my hands. I fed him boxes full of carrots while Shock looked a question at me out of the corner of her eye.

One night Jesse and I got back late from a ride and the only car left at the barn was Billy's. I walked Jesse up and down the road twice before I thought to look in Zeke's saddlebags for the hunting knife I should have known would be there all along. I put it in the inside pocket of my jean jacket and felt powerful, even though I hadn't thought ahead as far as using it. When I walked through the barn door I hit the breaker switch that turned on every light and there was Billy leaning against the door to Jesse's stall.

"So now she's riding his horse," he said.

"You want to open that door?" I said. I stood as tall as I could between him and Jesse.

"Does that mean you're going steady?"

"Let me by," I said.

"It'd be a shame if he came back and there wasn't any horse to ride," he said, and I grabbed for Jesse's reins but he moved forward faster, spooking Jesse, who reared and spun and clattered out the open barn door. I listened to his hooves on the stone and then outside on the hard dirt till he got so far away I only imagined it.

Billy shoved me backwards into a wheelbarrow and when my head hit the manure I reached for the knife and got it between us and he took a step backwards and wiped the spit off his mouth.

"You weren't that much fun the first time," he said, and ran for the door. I heard him get into his car and screech out the driveway, and I lay there in the manure, breathing horse piss and praying he wouldn't hit Jesse out on the hard road. I got up slow and went into the tack room for a towel and I tried to clean my hair with it, but it was Zeke's and it smelled like him and I couldn't understand why my timing had been so bad all my life. I wrapped my face in it so tight I could barely breathe and sat on his tack box and leaned into the wall, but then I remembered Jesse and put some grain in a bucket and went out into the darkness and whistled.

It was late September and almost midnight and all the stars I'd shown Zeke had shifted a half turn to the west. Orion was on the horizon, his bow drawn back, aimed across the Milky Way at the Great Bear, I guess, if space curves the way Earth does. Jesse wasn't anywhere, and I walked half the night looking for him. I went to sleep in my truck and at dawn Irwin and Jesse showed up at the barn door together.

"He got spooked," I told Irwin. "I was too worried to go home."

Irwin looked hard at me. "Hear anything from Zeke?" he said.

I spent a lot of time imagining his homecoming. I'd make up the kind of scenes in my head I knew would never happen, the kind that never happen to anyone, where the man gets out of the car so fast he tears his jacket, and when he lifts the woman up against the sky she is so light that she thinks she may be absorbed into the atmosphere.

I had just come back from a four-hour ride when his truck did pull up to the barn, six weeks to the day from when he left. He got out slow as ever, and then went around back to where he kept his carrots. From the tack-room window I watched him rub Jesse and feed him, pick up one of his front hooves, run his fingers through his tail.

I wanted to look busy but I'd just got done putting everything away so I sat on the floor and started oiling my tack and then wished I hadn't because of what I'd smell like when he saw me. It was fifteen minutes before he even came looking, and I had the bridle apart, giving it the oil job of its life. He put his hands on the doorjamb and smiled big.

"Put that thing back together and come riding with me," he said.

"I just got back," I said. "Jesse and I've been all over."

"That'll make it easier for you to beat me on your horse," he said. "Come on, it's getting dark earlier every night."

He stepped over me and pulled his saddle off the rack, and I put the bridle back together as fast as I could. He was still ready before I was and he stood real close while I tried to make Shock behave and get tacked up and tried not to let my hands shake when I fastened the buckles.

Then we were out in the late sunshine and it was like he'd never left, except this time he was galloping before he hit the end of the driveway.

"Let's see that horse run," he called to me, and Jesse shot across the road and the creek trail and plunged right through the middle of the wheat field. The wheat was so tall I could barely see Zeke's head, but the footing was good and Shock was gaining on him. I thought about the farmer who'd shoot us if he saw us, and I thought about all the hours I'd spent on Jesse keeping him in shape so that Zeke could come home and win another race. The sky was black to the west and coming in fast, and I tried to remember if I'd heard a forecast and to feel if there was any direction to the wind. Then we were out in a hay field that had just been cut and rolled, and it smelled so strong and sweet it made me light-headed and I thought maybe we weren't touching ground at all but flying along above it, buoyed up by the fragrance and the swirl of the wind. I drove Shock straight at a couple of bales that were tied together and made her take them, and she did, but by the time we hit the irrigation ditch we'd lost another couple of seconds on Zeke.

I felt the first drops of rain and tried to yell up to Zeke, but the wind came up suddenly and blasted my voice back into my mouth. I knew there was no chance of catching him then, but I dug my heels in and yipped a little and Shock dug in even harder, but then I felt her front hoof hit a gopher hole and the bottom dropped out and she went down and I went forward over her neck and then she came down over me. My face hit first and I tasted blood and a hoof came down on the back of my head and I heard reins snap and waited for another hoof to hit, but then it was quiet and I knew she had cleared me.

At least I'm not dead, I thought, but my head hurt too bad to even move.

I felt the grit inside my mouth and thought of Zeke galloping on across the prairie, enclosed in the motion, oblivious to my fall. It would be a mile, maybe two, before he slowed down and looked behind him, another before he'd stop, aware of my absence, and come back for me.

I opened one eye and saw Shock grazing nearby, broken reins hanging uneven below her belly. If she'd re-pulled the tendon in her fetlock it would be weeks, maybe months, before I could ride with him again. My mouth was full of blood and my lips were swelling so much it was running out the sides, though I kept my jaw clamped and my head down. The wind was coming in little gusts now, interrupted by longer and longer periods of calm, but the sky was getting darker and I lifted my head to look for Zeke. I got dizzy, and I closed my eyes and tried to breathe regularly. In what seemed like a long time I started to hear a rhythm in my head and I pressed my ear into the dust and knew it was Zeke coming back across the field at a gallop, balanced and steady, around the holes and over them. Then I heard his boots hit ground. He tied Jesse first, and then caught Shock, which was smart, I guess, and then he knelt next to my head and I opened the eye that wasn't in the dirt and he smiled and put his hands on his knees.

"Your mouth," he said, without laughing, but I knew what I must've looked like, so I raised up on one elbow and started to tell him I was okay and he said,

"Don't talk. It'll hurt."

And he was right, it did, but I kept on talking and soon I was telling him about the pain in my mouth and the back of my head and what Billy had done that day in the barn, and the ghosts I carry with me. Blood was coming out with the words and pieces of tooth, and I kept talking till I told him everything, but when I looked at his face I knew all I'd done was make the gap wider with the words I'd picked so carefully that he didn't want to hear. The wind started up again and the rain was getting steady.

I was crying then, but not hard, and you couldn't tell through all the dirt and blood, and the rain and the noise the wind was making. I was crying, I think, but I wanted to laugh because he would have said there weren't any words for what I didn't tell him, and that was that I loved him and even more I loved the prairie that wouldn't let you hide anything, even if you wanted to.

Then he reached across the space my words had made around me and put his long brown finger against my swollen lips. I closed my eyes tight as his hand wrapped up my jaw and I fell into his chest and whatever it was that drove him to me, and I held myself there unbreathing, like waiting for the sound of hooves on the sand, like waiting for a tornado.

ROSALEE VAN STELTEN

Rosalee van Stelten once worked on a ranch east of Calgary and was president of a cattle sales and management company. A widely published free-lance writer in both Canada and the United States, Rosalee entered the world of cowboy poetry with the poem "Didsbury Auction." She may have been straight from the city when she took the job, but she earned "country" the hard way.

Didsbury Auction

Right off the range, she was
tawny Charolais heifer
never before saw halter, heard
triple-tongued auctioneer.

Straight from the city, was I
drugstore cowgirl, fine
leather boots never tested
steel of the stirrup, stepped
in the steam of manure.

Didsbury auction stand:
four-foot counter, windows
behind, swinging gate
on the right, three steps down
to sawdust sprinkled floor.

Brown eyes crazed
the heifier bolted, leaped
on the left to the stand

Glass shattered
Blood spattered
She charged.

I kicked, swung, hung
on the gate above the arena
Horns, hide, grazed my side
hooves clipped my spine.

Off in the corner
she snorted and pawed
The crowd roared to its feet.

Is this how a cowboy feels
thrown by a bull?

Finally, they led her away
terrified Charolais
and I, cowed, swung back
for my last stand.

RODEO AND OTHER ARENAS

LENORE McLEAN

In the 1940s Lenore McLean grew up on the ranch next to Flores (or Florence) La Due Weadick on the Highwood southwest of Calgary, Alberta. All her life Lenore McLean has been involved with horses, an involvement that began as a little girl when she first met and came to know Mrs. Weadick. In "Mrs. Weadick and I," Lenore McLean writes of that memorable time.

Mrs. Weadick and I

"OH, LENORE," Mrs. Weadick would say, "It will make a lady out of you."

And because Mrs. Weadick said it, I would listen and somehow find it easier to leave the ranch, to return to school at the convent.

I wasn't sure I wanted to be a lady. I was raised on a ranch on the High Wood west of Longview and I liked the rough and tumble days of my childhood on the ranch but Mrs. Weadick could persuade me to do most anything she thought I should be doing.

You see, Mrs. Weadick was very special. Born Grace Maud Bensell in Montevideo, Minnesota in 1883 she ran away from home as a young woman and joined a traveling circus, taking the stage name of "Flores La Due." She had a natural talent for riding horses and fancy roping and she became one of the finest rodeo performers in America at the turn of the century.

Mrs. Weadick's father Charles Bensell was a noted criminal lawyer and later became a prominent judge. The life he had envisioned for his petite vivacious daughter was very different from the life she wanted. He was not in favor of vaudeville which involved horses and ropes and such, probably not in favor of show business of any kind.

But little Grace had other ideas. Whether she had seen one of the wild west shows or had just heard about them, as a child she determined to be a performer. Her father provided her with riding lessons at a local stable where the owners said if she wanted to really be a top notch horsewoman she would have to learn to do everything. So, Grace didn't just learn to ride she also learned to clean out the stables.

Grace spent more and more of her time with the horses, riding and learning the skills of roping. When she finally revealed her wish to be a performer to her father, she was rebuffed. That was when Grace decided to run away from home and planned her escape. During daylight hours, while her father was away at work, she had a stagecoach pick up her belongings, and take them to the site of the circus where she had persuaded the manager to hire her. Careful not to disclose her plan; she swept the tracks of the stagecoach away with a broom. Later, in the dark of night, Grace left home for good. Many years later she and her father were reconciled and he came to live with her in Alberta.

When she joined the traveling circus Grace Bensell took the stage name of 'Flores La Due.' After a season or two she left that job and toured the southern states with Colonel Cumming's vaudeville show. That was when she met Guy Weadick, a handsome young cowboy who also rode horses and roped with the show. They were married in 1906 in Memphis, Tennessee. By that time she was already well known as a performer and she kept the name of Flores La Due. It is said that Flores La Due could rope as many as eight riders with a single loop.

Guy encouraged Flores' natural talents for riding and roping and together they developed a special act and performed for audiences "all over the world," the so-called world really being North American and Europe. For several years they toured with Buffalo Bill's Wild West Show.

In 1912 the Weadicks finally came to Canada. Guy in partnership with H.C. McMullen, a livestock agent for the Canadian Pacific Railway and formerly a Montana cowpuncher, enlisted the aid of several prominent cattlemen of Alberta and the Calgary Stampede was created. With $1000 and a saddle as first prize in each event, the Stampede attracted cowboys from across the West. Rodeo was already flourishing in the American west and certain bucking horses were well known. Many of the cowboys had a string of bucking horses to help pay their way. If they couldn't win in the arena, they could make a few dollars with their broncs. Calgary Stampede attracted the best horses and the best cowboys.

The Stampede also attracted the best cowgirls—the best in North America. Fannie Sperry, Lucille Mulhall, Bertha Blancett and several others were there to win the money and the saddles in events that were listed for "ladies." All of these women were big names on the American rodeo circuit, having worked with shows such as the "101 Ranch show" out of Oklahoma or others. The fans had their favorites and the promoters made sure the Calgary fans were aware of their abilities long before the Stampede took place.

Of course, Flores La Due was one of the contestants. Roping was billed as one of the "cleanest and fairest" of all sports and roping was Flores' specialty. In fancy roping the rules stipulated that the cowgirls had to be ready to perform at any time during the show. They were judged on the greatest variety of tricks, both spinning and catching, both on foot and on horseback as well as ease, grace and skill.

The Stampede began September 2 and lasted until September 5. Each of the ladies who entered performed each day. After four days Flores La Due was judged first in Ladies Fancy Roping. Along with the prize money, she also received a special western saddle complete with engraved plaque on the back of the cantle. The saddle was made by Claude Mills.

In the Ladies' Relay Race, Flores lost out to a Mrs. H. McKenzie of Crossfield. All of the horses were to be saddle horses, meaning no race horses were allowed. The rider was to start and finish on the same horse and only two horses were allowed. In a two mile course the rider without assistance switched the saddle and blanket to the other horse each half-mile and at the end of the race also had to return the saddle to the horse she started out with. Stock saddles were to weigh at least twenty pounds. It was a grueling free for all. Although she was agile, Flores was also petite and that may have been to her disadvantage in such a contest.

In Ladies Fancy Roping Flores not only won the Stampede in 1912 but continued to dominate the event until 1919 at rodeos through North America.

During the winter the Weadicks toured on the Orpheum Vaudeville circuit in the United States and Canada. Their act was called 'Roping and Gab.' Besides Guy and Flores the act included brother Tom Weadick, Bill Sellman (Bridle Bill) and five trick horses—Blue Dog, Dandy, Keremios, Prince and Badger. Last but not least was their Boston Bull Terrier, Bum. When little Bum died he was stuffed and placed near the fireplace. To quote Flores, "a fitting tribute to a loyal pal who had helped pay for the ranch."

Flores retired in 1920 when the Weadicks purchased the Kuck Ranch on the High Wood which they renamed the Stampede Ranch with the brand TS. It was the first guest ranch in Canada and became successful under the sponsorship of the Canadian Pacific Railway. Guests were either housed in cabins or in the main ranch house where four bedroom doors carried the brands of the four sponsors of the 1912 Stampede: A.E. Cross' A7, Pat Burns' NL, George Lane's U and A.J. MacLean's CY. A gravity fed system of five or six showers was installed in one cabin. A tank of water above the stalls was heated by wood and coal and when the nozzles were turned, the water would flow.

During the years the Stampede Ranch operated the Weadicks entertained many famous people including Will Rogers, Charles Russell, Neil Hart, and Hoot Gibson. Cowgirls such as Bertha Blancett whom Flores knew from the circuit kept in touch. Postcards arrived from all over the world and Flores kept every one of them in a box. In 1934 the guest ranch closed. The Weadicks continued to live in the big house but otherwise it was like a ghost town.

I don't know when I first met Mrs. Weadick. She probably saw me when I was a new born babe as the Weadicks lived on the ranch next to that of my parents Joe and Josephine Bews. The Weadicks never went to town without stopping at my folk's place. Mrs. Weadick was just always there or so it seemed to me.

In 1939 when I was born the Highwood was still very much a wilderness. My father raised cattle and every summer the stock was moved to the high pastures in the foothills and every fall they were moved back to the home place again. World War II meant there weren't many young cowboys available for ranch work so my mother had to pitch in and help my father move the cattle. By the time I was two years old I was riding horses, following along behind the cattle. As babies my younger brothers rode along in the pack boxes. At age six or seven I was roping, wrestling and vaccinating calves at branding time. My father would let my brother and I try just about anything we wanted when it came to ranch work.

I was devastated when I was six years old. My parents sent me to a convent in Pincher Creek. In the days before my departure Mrs. Weadick talked to me saying, "Lenore, go to school. Get an education and then you will be able to do whatever you want."

Before I left she gave me a mother of pearl rosary. I did not know then that I would twine it in my wedding bouquet—the day I married Roy McLean. Her support encouraged me. Nevertheless I could hardly wait for summer holidays. The next summer or maybe the summer after that the Weadicks gave my brother and I two horses for show riding. Before that I rode Indian ponies. I'll never forget running to the barn the day my mare Trixie came. She was a brown thoroughbred and at last I thought I had a real horse.

I had learned to ride with an English saddle and I can remember hanging the stirrups up in the trees now and again when I helped with the round-ups. Even my brother Tom Bews who later became a bronc rider learned to ride in an English saddle. Before long we were riding in horse shows. The first time I took part in a show in Calgary there were more than forty contestants. Most of them had fancy saddles and stylish riding apparel. I had neither. Imagine my surprise when I won third. Mrs. Weadick was an excellent coach.

Mrs. Weadick also supplied me with western boots. Boots for children were not common and I probably wouldn't have had any but Mrs. Weadick had such tiny feet that hers fit me perfectly by the time I was about eight years old. I wore her boots until my feet grew larger than hers.

The Weadicks stopped to visit several times a week. They would drive up in their ivory car or maybe in the Stampede Ranch truck, the one with the TS brand on the side door and the wheels with the wooden spokes. Mrs. Weadick would always have some advice for me. One time she told me to learn as much as possible about housework. I replied, "When I grow up I'm going to have a maid."

She retaliated, "You must know all you can so you can keep a check on the maid!"

Mrs. Weadick and Guy had a truly good partnership. He was an organizer and had a vision. She was a stable business woman. I'm not sure why she took such an interest in me, but she did. Perhaps it was because she never had any children of her own. She told my mother that all the roping had twisted her internal organs.

In 1951 when Mrs. Weadick died I was twelve years old. Once after the war she bought me a bright red Mexican jacket, elaborately embroidered with silver thread and trimmed with a bright blue fringe. I wore it to her funeral and I did not respond to any of the sidelong glances at, what most would feel, was strange apparel for such a solemn occasion. When one kind lady commented on the beauty of the jacket, I quite simply burst into tears.

Later Guy Weadick came to our house. He was carrying Mrs. Weadick's leather riding skirt and jacket along with the saddle she won at the Calgary Stampede in 1912.

"Lenore," he said, "These are for you. Mrs. Weadick wanted you to have them."

Forty-five years later the saddle, the riding skirt and the jacket are still in my home. They have a place of honor and each day as I walk past them I am reminded of Mrs. Weadick, the incredible Flores La Due.

JEANNE RHODES

Jeanne Rhodes was Montana born and raised. She and Gwen Petersen of Montana were cowboy poetry partners for many years. According to Gwen, Jeanne was "a stickler for rhyme, meter and poetic feet." Jeanne's poems are included in a small chapbook called In the Sidesaddle.

Fannie Sperry

On the trail of Western History some figures stand up tall
For doing deeds the rest of us could not have done at all,
And we expect more heroines will surface now and then.
But the likes of Fannie Sperry we may never see again.

At an age when many children clutch a doll in either arm,
Fannie Sperry captured mustangs that ran wild behind their farm,
Brought them home and broke and trained them, sold them to the
folks around,
Who were sure that, trained by Fannie they were trustworthy and
sound.

First she rode at local horse shows where they passed the hat with
pride,
Cuz she stayed with bucking horses that the cowboys couldn't ride;
Then she rode in ladies' relays, racing finest thorobred horses,
Changing mounts and even saddles as they sped around their courses.

The Montana Girls with Fannie toured around the Middle West,
With Fanny giving all she knew for every show—her best.
And every now and then, as a spirited youngster would,

She'd still ride down a bucking bronc—because she knew she could.

Her reputation solid and her fame now spreading wide,
The budding sport of Rodeo sought her out to ride;
When Calgary, Alberta, had its first Stampede event,
The finest were invited, and Fannie Sperry went.

There among the riders from all the states out west,
And Canada and Mexico, who also sent their best,
She rode those snorting buckers that leaped and jerked and whirled—
And came home the Ladies' Bucking Horse Champion of the World.

In Winnipeg the following year, the title was renewed,
But the biggest news of that year was that Fannie was pursued
By old Bill Steele, who recognized a diamond from afar,
And soon proposed they merge their acts, with Fannie as the Star.

For ten years Bill and Fannie toured their own Wild Western Show,
And then retired as outfitters—showed hunters where to go;
And when Bill died in '40, Fannie ran the business still,
For *steel* was in her spine long before she met old Bill.

At 87, finally, she traded in her spurs
And went to live in Helena, a quiet life for her,
But she was not to be forgotten as a symbol of the West,
For in the Cowboy Hall of Fame, her name leads all the rest.

She never raced a barrel, she never tied a goat,
But the way she sat a bucker would tighten up your throat,
And we can hope to welcome more heroines now and then,
But the likes of Fannie Sperry we may never see again.

Berry Me Not

Chokecherries, chokecherries, purple and round.
How pleasant to live where these gems can be found.

My soulmate will love whatever I make,
Poured on a biscuit, or drowning a cake.

So, leaving a houseful of things to be done,
I grabbed up my buckets and vowed to have fun.

Off to the riverbank hot in pursuit
Of chokecherry bushes heavy with fruit—

I wasn't alone in the choice that I made,
Our cows were there too seeking water and shade.

Of course they had fertilized well where they lay,
So insects were thick on that scorching hot day.

But, darn it, I wasn't about to be licked
So I picked and I swatted and swatted and picked.

Then, both of my buckets heavy with loot,
I stepped in the mud as deep as my boot;

I followed it down with a face-forward sprawl—
Both buckets of chokecherries joined in the fall.

They silently sank in the cowpies and mud;
I picked up a few, they were covered with crud.

So back to the bushes, the heat and the bugs,
I picked them again, refilling my lugs.

Rushing back home, I started to cook,
Got dinner on somehow, by hook or by crook.

Washed all my berries and strained them for use,
Emptied my sugar sack into the juice.

It boiled for hours before it was ready;
I sterilized jars, I was getting unsteady.

I put on some supper, I cleaned up the mess,
And collapsed in a chair too tired to undress.

This morning my husband beamed over his plate
Of sausage and pancakes, and said as he ate,

"The best thing about this syrup to me
Is that these nice berries are utterly free."

To show that I'm tolerant and kind and forgiving—
The man that I live with is still with the living.

HELEN CLARK

For years Helen Clark traveled the West. She wrote nearly a thousand articles about the West for magazines such as True West. *In her travels she interviewed many ranch and rodeo women, including Fannie Sperry Steele, and helped them tell their stories. Helen Clark now lives in Butte, Montana, but she looks back fondly to a time when her boyfriend was a cowboy.*

A Horse Beneath Me . . . Sometimes

I WAS BORN MARCH 27, 1887 on a horse ranch at the foot of Bear Tooth Mountain north of Helena, Montana, and if there is a horse in the zodiac then I am sure I must have been born under its sign, for the horse has shaped and determined my whole way of life.

Perhaps it is odd that a woman should be born with an all-consuming love of horseflesh, but I have never thought so. It seems to me as normal as breathing air or drinking water, that the biggest thing on my horizon has been the four-legged critter with mane and tail.

If there are not horses in heaven, I do not want to go there. But I believe there will be horses in heaven as surely as God will be there, for God loved them or He would not have created them with such majesty.

When I was a small child, my parents could see how the twig was bent. One day a wild pinto of my father's came to drink at the spring that flowed by the house. According to my mother, I took a scarf for a lasso and toddled in its direction. Maybe it was significant that it was a wild horse I picked, for it is the wild horse that has held my heart.

How can I explain to dainty, delicate women what it is like to climb down into a rodeo chute onto the back of a wild horse? How can I tell them it is a challenge that lies deep in the bones—a challenge that may go back to prehistoric man and his desire to conquer the outlaw and the wilderness? . . .

"But you don't look like a rodeo rider," many people have said to me. I have never known for certain what conclusions I should draw from that remark. Should I be bowlegged? I'm not. Should I have had an enormous build, smoked cigars, waddled when I walked, cussed out of the side of my mouth, been uproariously loud? I wasn't. I was raised to be lady-like and refined, if rugged and wiry and independent, and I have remained so all my life. If I disappointed those who were expecting something like a three-ring circus, I'm not sorry. But I did, and do, dress differently from the average woman. . . .

"Mrs. Steele's own clothing spoke fully as emphatically of her disregard for convention and her opposition to the uncomfortable dress of the East, as she considers this part of the country. She wore a riding skirt of deep maroon that showed hard wear in the saddle. The sleeves of her orange shirt—it was not a shirtwaist—were held up by black elastic. Around her waist was a wide leather belt with gold buckle, a trophy won, together with $1,000 cash at Calgary, Can. On her breast was a medal presented to the 'champion lady rider of Montana,' while the stick pin in the red necktie had been won in a twenty-four mile relay race in Minnesota. A wide, high crowned sombrero covered her head, while two long braids of hair hung down her back. . . .

Relay racing was a part of rodeo I loved as well as bronc riding, and I rode a great deal in the Irwin Brothers rodeos as a relay rider. Among my pictures from their shows is one with Buffalo Bill Cody and a group of six women contestants. My costume was not very flattering in that picture, but neither were the clothes of the other females. That is because styles have changed so greatly since we were young. Today these clothes look a bit outlandish. . . .

Today I own no dresses. I never wore dresses on any of our rodeo trips across the country. I wore either divided riding skirts (no longer fashionable), or Levi's, or trousers. I wore a Stetson most of the time, or ribbons at my braids' ends. I have never owned a bonnet, but I wear a red hunting hat during hunting season.

I wear no jewelry except my gold wedding band and my silver or gold medals, selecting one at random to wear at rodeo appearances. On my wrist is a man's watch. My footwear consists of cowboy boots, hunting boots, packs, moccasins, and in deep snow, webs (snowshoes). Housedresses were never for me—I've never been that domestic, and an apron is something I never use.

I hardly saw men, yet let a horse go down the road and I noted all there was to see about it! Thank God that the man who did love me, and taught me in turn to love him, was a horseman or our marriage would have been doomed before it started. Bill Steele was eleven years older than I. He had been with horses all his life. He was a saddle bronc rider and rodeo clown, and he owned his own string of broncos. He produced a good many rodeos. We met for the first time when he came to engage me to ride in one of his shows.

A woman magazine writer embarrassed me one day when, during the course of an interview, she asked, "Did you love your husband at first sight?" I was so unprepared for the question that I got flustered. I answered, "Damn if I can remember." The woman looked askance. But she was to look more startled when, as the interview progressed, she asked, "How did you spend your honeymoon?"

"Rodeoing!" I answered, laughing. It was the truth. Even to me it now seems a funny thing, especially when the interviewer followed it up by logically saying: "But maybe you wouldn't have had any tomorrows. Maybe you might have been killed!"

How easily we could have been killed. But death didn't matter, somehow, because we met it so often day after day that, like life, it got to be commonplace. Once during a rodeo, my husband was knocked unconscious and taken for dead. There wasn't even time for me to go to him, for I had to get ready to make his ride for him. That may seem callous, but we were show people in our own right, and "the show had to go on." . . .

Rodeo broncs are numbered, and matching numbers on paper are put in a hat. From the hat, the contestants draw a number which determines the horse they ride. For years I stood in line with the men and drew a number, and rode the horse whose number I had drawn. But as the years began to creep up on me, I had to confine myself to riding my own picked broncs, or horses I knew.

I was still riding broncs when I was fifty, and I hope I shall ride a horse to the day I die. At sixty, however, I had to concede there would be no more buckers under my saddle. . . .

Now that I am what young people consider an old woman, and I look back at my life, I can truthfully say that if I had it all to do over again, I would live it exactly the same. From such a statement you gather that I have liked it. I have *loved* it, every single, wonderful, suffering, exhilarating, damned, blessed moment of it. And if, with my present arthritis, I must pay the price of every bronco ride that I have ever made, then I pay for it gladly. Pain is not too great a price to pay for the freedom of the saddle and a horse between the legs. . . .

There were many rodeo women as well as men that I liked, as Lucille Mulhall. She was a quiet woman. She was not only a good rider, she was a remarkable roper. There was Louise Thompson, a Wild West Show rider back in 1916 who still writes to me from California. . . .

Some of our rodeo women met a hard end, as Prairie Rose Henderson who vanished in a blizzard in Wyoming and whose body was not found until seven years later. Bonnie McCarroll and Marie Gibson, whose rodeo husband had hurt his back and who rode to support her four kids, both were killed by riding hobbled and having their horses roll on them. . . .

One time when Bill and I were in the East in one of Charlie Irwin's rodeos Bill was knocked out by a bronc that reared over backwards.

"What will we do? What will we do?" yelled Charlie, frantic at what had happened.

"Do?" said Wild Bill, stripping off his coat in case he would have to restrain Charlie. "By God, Fannie will ride these horses if Bill Steele is dead!"

When people ask me to list my favorite cities, I often put Calgary, Canada first. I notice that they smile, and I guess they are thinking it is because there I won the title for the first time of World's Champion Lady Bronc Rider, plus $1,000, plus a $250 hand-tooled leather saddle, plus a $300 gold buckle with hand-tooled leather belt. But the main reason for my choice is the city's friendliness, and its kindness to my mother.

In 1912, my parents saw to it that when I went to distant rodeos, I was properly chaperoned, for I was then unmarried. Mother did me the great honor of accompanying me to Calgary. It rained every day of the show except Monday, the opening day. It was a five-day rodeo. Mother was invited to sit in the Duke's box. That seemed more sensational on our return from Canada than my winning the World's Championship. My brothers and sisters kept asking over and over again for the details.

"Mother, did you sit with the Duke?" they questioned.

"With the Duke," said mother proudly, "in the Duke's box."

"What's his name, mother?"

"Duke d'Connought," replied Mother. It was one of her happiest memories.

The one woman in all my career I would have feared to contest against in saddle bronc riding would have been my mother, given back her youth and placed in the same age bracket as myself. I think she would have defeated me. She was a remarkable horsewoman. At the age of seventy-six, she sat in the saddle and roped a wild mustang.

SUE WALLIS

Sue Wallis was raised on a working ranch along the Powder River of Wyoming and presently keeps in touch with her ranching traditions by organizing and participating in the National Cowboy Poetry Gathering at Elko, Nevada. Her poems, including the following two, have been published in her chapbook The Exalted One.

Greenough Girls

Nineteen twenty-eight
Billings, Montana
Two slender, trim ladies
Flipping through a magazine
Quit the world of waiting tables
To fork the broncs
And spur their way around the world
In satin skirts they made at home

Alice tipped her hat to kings
Had tea with queens
Rode fighting bulls in Spain
Stayed Down Under
Went to cattlemen's picnics
Just to buck-jump
With no stirrups
In funny flat saddles

Marge married Heavy
Raised a baby in a teepee
On trains, in Model Ts

They bought Little Blue Rocket
In Canada
After that the boy rode with them
Up the arena ramp to the thrill and roar
Of Madison Square
Cheyenne, San Francisco, Boston
Red Lodge, Tucson . . .

There they are
Marge and Alice, Granddad's sisters
Two tiny trim ladies in neat clothes, big hats
Evidence that for a price
Plenty of will, the world can be won

As I've grown, their blood in my veins
Burns, and wants to

Nineteen thirty-four
Billings, Montana
Doris Corwin, college girl
Refined, determined, and lovely
Stepped off a train to marry her cowboy
In Hardin, in a square, bare room
With one brass spittoon
Granddad, cowboss, carried his bride to a teepee
Set a ways away at the wagon
And finished fall works

Already they knew
That there would be family
Fine homes, good ranches, and horses
And Grandmother built an empire of propriety and pride
Taught her daughters literature
Elegance—how to cook for thirty cowboys
With grace and honor in a genteel home

She frowned at daughters
Who cast eyes at aunts and glory
Who thought of a world not won
And with her determination, knowledge of right
Kept them at the house
Where she knew they belonged

My God, she is strong

There she is
Grandma Greenough, Granddad's sweetheart
Loving, true, deep-hearted and solid
Awesome as a mountain in a handsome woman way
Evidence that quiet dignity
Is priceless
And can be done

As I've grown, her blood in my veins
Runs deep, and proud, and calm
And wants to stand

So here I stand
And I look both ways
Wild adventure, and solid refinement
And I want both ways
Respectable pride and glorious fame
With only one path that I can ride

So I try
To weave between
To slip around and through
My models of life

To live up to
Those Greenough girls

Coyote Bitch

Tonight . . .
I feel like a Coyote Bitch
(in heat)
Do not annoy me, tempt me, or toy with me
I have been lonely too long.

An old bitch will wait with native intellect
Run just below the ridges
You won't see her 'til she catches
That first waft of
Rottenness

She'll linger ruthless
Over the carrion carcass
Of some uncaring
Wild Steer

Then drag the stinking skin
Back to her solitary den
To chew and slobber and maul the hide
Long after all hint of flesh is dried

Just for comfort
Mangling idle dreams of regal wolfish lovers
Strong and smart and beautiful

. . .Who never appear.

LINDA AKSOMITIS

Linda Aksomitis is a full-time teacher, part-time horsewoman and sometimes writer as she juggles a busy schedule in Qu'Appelle, Saskatchewan. She grew up with horses and married into a rodeo family, so she sees the rodeo arena from both sides of the fence.

A Rodeo Man

The Rodeo Cowboy:
well worn leather boots,
dusty denim jeans and shirt,
rain splattered felt stetson and
a kerchief knotted at the neck.
Cattle cutting, calf roping, bronc breaking,
cow ponies and cows,
his way of life.

Retired.
The past captured
in paintings and autographed pictures,
statues of the Quarterhorse and
the cowboy who rode him.
The recliner sways,
reminiscent of old Buck's smooth gait
as he sits amidst memories.
Faded blue eyes look back to
when a cowboy worked under
the burning prairie sun
branding and tending his herd.

He sees tanned leather faces,
quick to smile and slow to speak;
cowboy against cowboy—
the Rodeo.

From town to town,
through dirt corrals and weathered
fences, the crowds gathered
to cheer them.

The old cowboy
sits in new painted bleachers
at the rodeo, between
his friends,
missing that
which he desired most—
a son who'd fit the saddle
like he was born to it.
A Rodeo Man.

FLORENCE GATES

Florence Gates grew up on a ranch along the South Saskatchewan River. As a girl she rode long distances to school, broke horses and participated in rodeos. Her story is taken from her book of memoirs Back to the Coteau Hills.

A Horse Named Nancy

At break of dawn no shadows fall reflecting what's behind us.
All's clean and unpolluted.

WHICH PLAYED THE GREATER PART in the development of the west, man or his horse? The answer to that question, at best, would be a mere matter of opinion. Horses were here with the Indians when the first white man appeared in the west, and, although oxen were at first the main means of power for the prairie farmer, they were soon replaced by horses. The first draft horse was probably the Percheron, imported from France. Other breeds of heavy horses followed from various parts of Europe, until before too long, oxen were no longer used to pull the plow or the Red River cart. On the prairies, where waterways were scarce, transportation was also by horse. To supply this need, light breeds of horses were crossed with the native Indian mustangs which produced a tough and dependable animal. Bullee Rock was in all likelihood the first thoroughbred stallion to come to America. He was imported to Virginia in 1730. In 1765, Ranger, an Arab stallion, was brought to Connecticut, but the thoroughbred was the most popular type of light horse. Some good light horses came from Kentucky bluegrass country with the Turkey Track outfit, but Canada was backward in building really good strains of light horses. Accordingly, it was fortunate for the stockmen of the Coteau Hills when the

Canadian government purchased a registered thoroughbred stallion and stationed him at the farm of Geoffry Roffey a few miles west of Lucky Lake. He was a big horse, hunter type, and in his prime had been valued at fifty thousand dollars. Unfortunately, he became blind. However, the horse's misfortune was someone else's good fortune, for he now sold for a price which our government felt it could afford.

While I was teaching at Lucky Lake I had heard about this horse, and had gone to see him. He was the most magnificent animal I had ever seen. Although he was big, as hunters are, he was clean-limbed, long-barreled, and chesty. He was an unattractive, dull bay color, but it did not seem to matter. His eyes were obviously sightless, but he held his head high and long muscles rippled beneath the smooth skin on his shoulders and hind quarters. And I knew that, somehow, I had to get together enough money to breed my mare to this horse.

A year was to pass before I saw the horse again, but I had not forgotten him. By now I was teaching at Poplar Butte School and riding fifteen miles a day, return trip, in order to stay at home at the ranch. Good, fast horses were more than just a fancy to me; they were a necessity. But money was more scarce than ever for me since wages had not improved and I was now helping to put my brother Louis through the College of Engineering in Saskatoon. However, letting my heart rule my head, one evening late in May I dropped in at the Roffey farm to have another look at the big hunter.

I found Geoff at the barn grooming a long-legged bay filly. "Is she by the thoroughbred in the barn?" I asked. And when Geoff nodded, I asked her name.

"Nancy," he replied.

"Do you have her mother?" And when the man answered in the affirmative I asked another question. "Can I see her?"

The mother was an ordinary, dual purpose one, nothing one would expect to have such a racy looking filly as Nancy was. I ran my hands down her legs and rubbed her between the ears. She bent her head and nibbled on my coat sleeve.

"She likes you," Geoff said. And after a long look at the two of us standing there in his yard, he added, "Tell you what! If you'll take her out to the ranch this summer and train her for me, I'll pay you the amount of a breeding fee on the stallion."

Would I? I had loved the bay filly at first sight and would welcome the chance to work with her. Nancy was a small copy of her sire, spirited, but with width between the ears to indicate intelligence. She would be a joy to train. And, to boot, a foal from the only good thoroughbred stallion I had ever seen!

"I'll be glad to take her for the summer," I replied, and my face must have been wreathed in smiles. "I'll come for her as soon as school is out at the end of June."

And just so it happened. My father took me to the Roffey farm the evening of the last day of June. I put my saddle on Nancy and turned back west on the trail I had just travelled in the Model T Ford. We would take it easy. The filly was only three years old, and she was soft. Even though the June evenings were long, it would be dark long before we reached the end of the trail. Geoff had ridden Nancy a few times, but, as he had said, "She doesn't know anything."

She had never been off the farm, and I wondered how she would react to a passing car. Not that there would be many. Perhaps none would pass. However, I would be glad to reach the sanctuary of the hills.

It took considerable urging to get Nancy away from the barnyard where she had spent nearly all of her life, but once we had done so she travelled willingly enough. She had a long, easy stride and an alert way of looking at things. She pleased me. Sitting astride this young mare, I had a feeling of exhilaration, a sureness that here under my saddle I had speed such as I had never before had in horseflesh.

We were but a few miles on our way, right at Seven-mile Corner where the road turns south to Beechy, when the first car appeared on the crest of the hill behind us. I put Nancy in the ditch beside the road, but as the car came nearer to us I could not hold her there. However, she was not completely out of control, and leaped only a few yards into the plowed field before I was able to stop her flight. By now the car had stopped abreast of us, and I could see the driver was a stranger; at least, he was a stranger to me. He shut off the motor and stepped from the vehicle, making his way quietly in my direction, but he stopped when Nancy showed signs of backing away.

"That's a fine-looking mare you have there," he said. "Do you live hereabouts?"

"My father has a ranch west of here. That's where I'm going now."

"Is that the truth! Then I'll bet you can help me. I'm Johnny Hartwig and I'm promoting a stampede in Rosetown next month, July twenty-fifth. I've been scouring the country for bucking horses, and so far have had no luck in finding them. Does your father have any bucking stock?"

When I told him that indeed we had bucking horses at the ranch, the man asked if a deal might be made with my father for him to rent the horses for the Rosetown show. The horses had been rented to the stock contractor of the Clearwater Lake Stampede on more than one occasion, so I felt free to say that I was sure a contract could be made. The year was nineteen thirty-seven, one of the worst of the depression years, and I knew that a few extra dollars would be more than welcome. Hartwig wanted the horses delivered and mentioned a sum of one hundred dollars for twenty head of bucking horses. There were no facilities on the ranch for hauling stock, but I told him that I was sure something could be arranged. Probably I would help to drive the horses across country to the stampede grounds a day or two before the show.

The deal made, pending Leslie's approval, he shook my hand and turned toward his car. I had dismounted to adjust my saddle blanket, and Hartwig stopped to watch me as I tightened up the cinch and prepared to remount.

"You're a good rider," he said. "You wouldn't want to make a little money yourself at the stampede, would you? I would contract you to ride an exhibition bronc at my show. It would help the gate receipts if I could advertise a lady bronc rider. I'll give you twenty-five dollars to ride one horse."

I was almost sure that I would be one of the riders to drive the bucking stock to Rosetown. In other words, I would be there anyway, so why not? What was one bronc to ride anyway? I was riding them all the time at the ranch. It took only a moment to decide.

"You can advertise a lady's exhibition ride. I'll be there." Then I turned Nancy's head in the direction of the ranch and let her trot on down the road.

That night I told my father of the chance encounter and of the tentative deal I had made with Hartwig. Leslie would have liked more money. As he said, the hundred-mile return trip would take a lot of flesh off his horses, not to mention the experience of being put through the bucking chutes. But horses were not selling at that time, and the sum offered would be clear money and better than nothing. So, some three weeks later, on the morning of July twenty-third, twenty head of unbroken horses were cut out of the herd of more than three times that number. Late in the afternoon of that day, so as not to travel in too much heat, Louis and I started the horses on the fifty-mile crosscountry drive to Rosetown. I was riding Nancy.

Just before darkness closed in on us that night, we got reluctant consent from a farmer in the Glamis area to pen the horses in an enclosure in his barnyard, and to put our saddle horses in his empty barn. We also got a feed of oats for them, but there was nothing for the bucking horses. I was offered a bed in the house, but Louis was to sleep in the barnloft. The old feud between farmers and ranchers was still more or less alive, and there was a feeling in our minds that this farm family had no kindness in its heart for us because we were from the hills where only ranchers lived. Between my worry over the horses who had nothing to eat after a hard drive, and chagrin that my brother had to sleep in the barn, I did not sleep well. I was glad to arise before anyone else was awake, slip out to the barn and waken Louis, who had slept in the loft better than I had in a bed in the house. We had plenty of time to get to our destination this day and could have let the horses graze in the ditches along the roadway, but they were keyed up and would stop for only an occasional bite as they trotted on.

It was not yet noon, but the heat was already oppressive as we skirted the eastern perimeter of Rosetown.

We knew that we had not done the job we had undertaken until the herd of wild horses was in the corral at the stampede grounds, and we knew also, that getting the horses in would be a tricky task. Like the steers Leslie and his brother-in-law had driven down the main street of Saskatoon thirty years before, one false move would have sent the bucking horses flying in every direction. And if even one had panicked and broken back, the whole herd would have followed. The closer we got to the corrals and the stampede arena, the harder the herd was to handle, until finally, closely bunched, it stopped altogether. To make matters still worse, men were working with hammers and saws, putting up the last of the chutes for the show the next day. Louis and I reconnoitered. We had to have help. That much we knew!

Fortunately, one of the workers at the arena saw us, and Hartwig, who did not want to lose the horses any more than we did, ordered the men to lay down their tools and line up on the opposite side of the gate through which we would have to drive the horses. There was not a mounted man to help us, but we had to force the reluctant herd into action. Yard by yard, jumpy step by step, we approached the gate, until finally we were there. The lead horse looked at the gate. While all of us held our breath, he looked a split second at the opening, then leaped through the gate and into the enclosure. The others scrambled after, shouldering one another in their haste to get to the freedom that seemed to be ahead.

Thankfully, we unsaddled, watered and fed our mounts, and made sure that the bucking stock we had just delivered was also well fed and, more important, that the horses had plenty of water. Only then did we think of our own needs, remembering that we had not eaten since the night before. Hartwig offered us a ride downtown, where we registered in adjoining hotel rooms, washed sunburned faces, combed down our sunbleached and windblown hair, and went out to eat. We were still at the restaurant when Johnny Hartwig found us. He sat down at our table and began to pour on his charm. Already he had his eye on me. He was a virile man, quick, almost nervous in his movements. He was suntanned, muscular, a former saddle bronc rider, the kind of man I had known and lived with all my life. Or so it might seem. But there was something about this cowboy that made me wary. There was a bold aggressiveness, a familiarity that I did not find flattering, that I did not like!

When he asked, "Which hotel are you staying in? I want to talk to you," I did not answer. Seeing my set lips and unsmiling face, he should have been warned, but he persisted. "I have another problem, and I think you can help me."

Then, knowing he would find out anyway, I told him where we had our rooms. But to this information I added, "I'll meet you in the lobby of the hotel after supper."

Later, he found me sitting near the big window facing the main street of the town, watching the people on the street below. Johnny sat down and went right to the point. "I still haven't found any horned steers for the bulldoggin'. You know this country. Can you help me find some? There isn't much time left."

Nearly all the ranchers dehorned their cattle, but I could think of one, not too far distant, who did not.

"About forty miles south of here, at Clearwater Lake, there's a rancher who I think has horned cattle. His name is Laurence Ohmatch. He might rent you some horned steers."

"Jump in the car and we'll drive there right now." His steel-grey eyes seemed to see right through me as he said, "We'll get to one another before this show is over. And when it is, you can come with me to the 53 Ranch north of Prince Albert where we hole up between shows." And when I did not answer, he said, "Oh, come on now! I've never seen a girl yet that I couldn't get if I wanted."

My eyes looked deep into his as I answered, "You're looking right at one now."

But he laughed and changed the subject back to the steers he so badly needed, and soon. "You'll have to show me the way to those steers, and we haven't any time to lose."

"Find my brother and take him too. Otherwise I won't go."

Johnny coaxed. He accused me of being afraid of him. He tried everything except threats. In turn, I laughed at him and did not budge. Finally, ungraciously, he went to find Louis.

While I waited for them to return, I chuckled to myself. I was young, unsophisticated, a hillbilly schoolteacher. All this he had seen. But I was not a fool, and this he had not seen. He had warned me, not meaning to do so, and I was not tempted to ignore the implications of what the man had said. I had not turned down good men only to fall prey to a handsome rake.

The day of the show, July 25, 1937, was a hot one, but there was a good crowd of spectators. There were contestants enough, but only one of them, Slim Gates, from Weyburn, Saskatchewan, had brought either a rope horse or a bulldogging horse. There was, therefore, only one horse for all the calf ropers and bulldoggers to mount. Slim's horse could not carry all the ropers and doggers to their stock. Besides, two horses were needed, one for the bulldogger and one for his hazer, for each contestant in that event.

Desperate for another horse, the cowboys eyed Nancy, and they came to me, asking to use her. "Can I rope off your horse?" And "Will you let me haze off your mare? She looks like she could run."

I knew that Nancy could run, but I doubted that she would perform to their satisfaction. She had never been in a rodeo arena before. She was by now well-mannered, but this was expecting too much. I refused to let any of them use her.

As one of the cowboys turned away from me, I heard Hartwig say, "I told you she was just plain silly about that horse."

The remark was all I needed to make me change my mind. I walked to where the men were standing in a disconsolate group, and told them I would let as many mount her as I thought she could stand, but I also warned them that she probably would not work well, especially as a calf roping horse. "You will ride her, knowing she is not trained for the job, and if anyone mistreats her, he will have me to settle with. And it won't be easy!"

I made the exhibition ride on a grey gelding. To make it an extra thrill for the crowd, he was eared down in the arena in front of the chutes. Lady bronc riders were in the habit of hobbling their stirrups, tying them together under the horse's belly, but my father would not let me ride that way. He said it was better to get bucked off than to be tied to a horse. This one did not buck hard, but afraid that I might get hurt, two pick-up men flanked me on each side and lifted me off the horse before I was ready to let him go. They did not know how tough I was, seeing only a little country girl who had just ridden fifty miles, bareheaded in the sun.

When the show was over, the cowboys kept coming to me with a quarter of what they had made while riding Nancy. They had to press me to take their money, for I had done it only to help them out—and to spite John E. Hartwig. Perhaps, too, I was remembering years before when Louis and I had been reprimanded because we took money for helping a man out of a mudhole.

Louis did not like to dance, but wild horses could not have kept me away from the one held the night after the stampede was over. It was a noisy affair, not rowdy, just everyone having a real good time. I do not remember his asking me to, but it seemed natural that I should go with Slim Gates, owner of the only trained ropehorse at the show. Perhaps Nancy and Tex, paired in the bulldogging event and sharing the calf roping, had a little to do with it. I recall other names from that night, however. Ben Jahnke was there, and there were two other Slims—Slim Hill and Slim Bjorklund, both of them well over six feet tall. Slim Hill had been hurt at the afternoon performance, so did not dance, but the other one liked to dance with me, mainly, I thought, so that he could look down at me and ask, "How's the weather down there?" The top of my head did not reach much above his belt buckle.

After the dance was over, Slim Gates drove me to my hotel. "You and your brother will start back with the bucking horses tomorrow?" he asked.

"No," I replied. "Louis will go back to the ranch with them alone. Once out of the corral and away from the edge of Rosetown, they will head straight for home. Louis will simply have to follow them and open the gate into their range. I'll turn Nancy loose with them. My father will take my gear back in the car. I'm taking the bus to Watrous to spend a couple of weeks with people I stayed with when I went to Normal School in Saskatoon, the Arch DeWolf family. I'll be taking the Greyhound there tomorrow."

By this time we were parked on the street in front of the hotel. We sat there, relaxed and happy, for a long time. I told him about my father's ranch, where it was in the Coteau Hills, how beautiful it was, how peaceful the valley within the halfcircle of buttes, and how much I loved it all. I talked about the deep, steep-sided coulees that lay between the buttes, and of the deer that found seclusion there beneath the maple trees. I told, too, of the shy, little brown bush rabbits that lived their lives out there among the brambles. I recalled the hooting of the owls at night and the happy lovesongs of the redwinged blackbirds who nested among the rushes. It was summer, I was young and in love with the world.

"The wild roses at the foot of the Big Coulee," I said, "They are not as beautiful anywhere else on the prairie."

Finally, before we said goodnight, I invited him to come and see it for himself, and as I climbed the now deserted stairway to my room, I thought to myself, "I like him. I like the way he took it slow."

Next morning the tall, slim roper from Weyburn accompanied me to the bus bound for Saskatoon, thence to Watrous. As he took my hand in parting he asked, "Can I write to you?"

"Of course," I answered. "I'd like you to."

From then on things did not move slowly. Three weeks later we met for the second time at Clearwater Lake Stampede. Slim arrived a day ahead of the rodeo. Leaving his rope horse at the lake in the care of another cowboy, he made his way through the hills and along the cowtrails to Maple Butte Ranch. It was less than a month from the date of our first meeting, but already we both knew what it was we wanted. The raspberries that Rachel Giauque had preserved a quarter of a century ago were soon to be opened.

On September 12, 1937, Slim came again to the Coteau Hills, this time with a diamond ring. The year following, on July 25, exactly one year from the day of our first meeting, Slim Gates and I were married.

CHRISTINE EWERT

Christine Ewert has been running the barrels in the rodeo arena many times. Along with her sister Karen, she has appeared on stages across Western Canada singing her rodeo songs, the ones she started writing and singing as a teenager. "I'm in the Money" is just one of many songs Christine has written with, she says, a little help from Mom.

I'm in the Money

I'm in the money; rodeo's in me
I just won a big show, Honey, can't you see.
Hello brand new saddle
Good-bye rusty truck
Now I can pay buddy; I still owe him a buck.

Chorus
I'm on cloud nine
I'm feeling fine
Drunk without the wine
Happy all the time
I'm wearing a smile
Cheerful all the while
Can go another mile
And I'll travel in style.

I'm in the money; rodeo's in me
I just won a big show; Honey, can't you see.
Hello brand new Stetson
Good-bye crumpled straw

Gonna buy new Ropers
Might even call my Pa.

I'm in the money; rodeo's in me
I just won a big show; Honey, can't you see.
Hello steak and lobster
Good-bye sour dough
Won't have much tomorrow
Today is all I know.

YVONNE HOLLENBECK

Yvonne Hollenbeck ranches with her husband, Glen, at Clearfield, South Dakota. On a warm day, Yvonne might be found herding cattle to the pasture some twenty-five miles west or timing events for the Clearfield Rodeo. Winter days find her at the quilting frame, stitching the quilts that have won prizes across the West. Between these activities, she somehow finds time to write down some of her thoughts, creating her one-of-a-kind cowgirl poetry.

Roper's Wife's Lament

The faucet drips and the drain won't drain
  'cause papa has a rope horse to train.
I'm a-feeding the cows and a-milkin ole' Bess
  all papa does is roping, I guess.

It's early to bed and early to rise,
  . . . gotta get goin', gotta rope with the guys;
There's no time for dining nor goin to shows
  for all of his spare time's for more rodeos.

There's ropes in the closet, ropes under the chair,
  open the oven, there's one dryin' there;
there's ropes on the dresser and under the bed
  there's more in the basement, and out in the shed.

Him help with the lawn or the painting out-doors?
  He don't have the time, gotta tune on his horse.
There's no extra money for shopping, you see
  'cause we'd better just save for the next entry fee.

For meeting my kinfolk, there's no time, of course
    but he knows every pedigre of every rope horse.
When I look at my daughter, all I do is hope
    that she marries a feller who don't like to rope!

J. ANNETTE GRAY

"Warm chinook winds blowing across the foothills, cattle and horses grazing in the valleys of the North Saskatchewan River, branding crews, haying time, rodeos and parades—I loved every minute of my life as a rancher's wife." (Jayne) Annette Gray spent much of her life on a ranch near Rocky Mountain House, Alberta. Twisted Heart *is the title of a manuscript she has just completed.*

Twisted Heart

(EXCERPT FROM THE NOVEL)

THE PARADE had barely reached the end of the route when Penny slid out of the saddle, smacked old Zeb smartly across the side of the head, sent a few choice words in Rick's direction and disappeared in the crowd. Rick doubled up in a fit of laughter. *Revenge—it had tasted so sweet in his mouth!*

Cam stayed just long enough to pull the saddle off Zeb, tether the gelding out, then left without a single word, but for the first time in his life, Rick didn't care what any of his friends thought. Fair was fair, she'd asked for it.

He was still grinning to himself and brushing down Breeze, when Casey Adams came bounding up.

"Man alive! Am I glad to see ye, Haynes," Casey exploded, hauling off with a smack to the shoulder that sent the brush out of Rick's hands. *A little bit of Casey went a long way.*

Rick rubbed the sore spot with his fist and eyed the two-hundred and fifty pounds that loomed in front of him. "So help me, Adams . . . one day, I'm getting you drunk and putting your saddle on backwards," he snarled. He picked up the brush and tossed it at the trailer, then shoving his hands on his hips, he turned to glare, "What now, Adams?"

Casey was balancing a stock saddle on his shoulder as effortlessly as if it was made of foam. A roll-your-own dangled from his mouth. "Well, I got me some tough luck an' I'm hopin' you'll help me out. Ol' Russell, my ropin' partner, couldn't make it today. He's got woman problems an' stayed home. An' I've paid all my entrance fees, an' every-thin'. I see ya got yerself a new horse . . . an' I'll lend ya this stock saddle if you'll head an' haze fer me today." He flicked a spray of ashes to the ground, then looked up to see Rick eyeing him suspiciously. "Come on, Haynes, ya ol' coyote. Ya can't let a feller down. I need ya bad this afternoon."

"Is this going to be a repeat of last year?" Rick asked. "If I remember rightly, you were the joker who talked me into riding that Brahma. Don't shake your head at me, Adams. You know damn well you were, and I'm still wearing a scar . . . and a grudge. I said right then, that would be the last time I'd listen to any of your crazy schemes." Rick gave Breeze a slap on the neck as he held up a water bucket. "Come on girl, drink."

"Don't know what yer whinin' about, Haynes. Ya did okay . . . and ya never split the prize money with me, either . . . like we planned."

"And you never got two dozen stitches in you, like I did . . ." Rick said, motioning to his arm. "Where were you when that snorting bugger turned, and came back for me?"

The bull ride had been one of Rick's proudest moments. A million times, he'd relived that ride, a million times he'd admired that jagged scar. It was far more prestigious than any salon tattoo, a fact Casey Adams would never hear from his lips.

Even now, as he grumbled, his mind was way ahead of Casey, his adrenaline racing at the prospects of roping, reasoning that this would be a good time to try the new mare out. Her foal was old enough. It wouldn't hurt her. *If dingle-fingered Murray roped off Breeze last year, like everyone claimed he had, well, then why couldn't he?* "Okay," Rick said, giving a deep sigh, ". . . but what about the prize money. If we hit a winning streak, I want at least half." He tipped his head allowing his black

Stetson to shade his eyes. Casey wasn't known for being overly generous when it came to opening his wallet. "A third . . ." Casey bargained.

"Half . . . or it's no time for you," Rick said digging his heals in. Never again would he allow someone to get the jump on him. Not Jo, nor Penny—and for sure not Casey.

Casey's voice was lost in a mutter. "Okay then . . . but for half I'll head . . . you'll heel."

"It's okay by me . . . if the officials allow it."

Rick loaded the foal into the trailer and closed the door, then threw the stock saddle on Breeze. So, he hadn't told Casey he'd never roped off the mare before today. He laughed out loud as he thought about it. It was more than a little ridiculous, to say the least. Granted he'd been practicing roping all spring on the home-made roping dummy—but this mare—it was only word of mouth, no more than rumor, that said she had been ridden in competition. He didn't even know if she would take to cattle. She's likely bolt and rear on him the first time he swung a rope. *Well, then ol' Adams wouldn't need to worry about splitting the prize money, would he?*

Rick mounted and rode to the infield. He spotted Casey over at the announcer's box checking him in with the officials. It was easy to recognize Casey. It took a good horse to support him, and the bald-faced bay stood taller than most, and was as heavily coupled as Casey himself.

"I put in a good word fer ye, Haynes . . . so they'd accept you." Casey gloated as he jogged back to where Rick sat scowling. *That was the most annoying thing Casey could think to say—that and the way he bellowed it out. Like Rick Haynes wasn't up to par or something. Like the officials needed Casey's endorsement. It wasn't as if this was pro-rodeo or something. It was just a two-bit amateur show—no big deal.* Rick was still fuming as he entered the arena, vaguely aware that the loud speaker was announcing the next team roping event. *But, What? What was the announcer saying? Oh, no! Leave it to Casey!*

"Here's Rick Haynes, folks . . . and it's an honor to introduce this top performing cowboy. He hails from Stanton. They tell me that in spite of an injury here at Dexter last year, he still took home most of the prize money . . . and I've just been informed that the tall appaloosa Rick's riding this afternoon is a Champion roping mare out of Montana. So be prepared, folks . . . you're going to see some real professional riding and roping here this afternoon. Please welcome Stanton's Top Cowboy . . . Rick Haynes."

Above the noise of the bawling cattle, Rick heard the roar of the largest crowd that Dexter had ever entertained—felt the blood rush to his cheeks. *The announcer hadn't even mentioned Casey's name, just his. These people were expecting some kind of star performer. Curses on Casey or whoever started this wild rumor, lying and bragging around, telling everybody this mare was a Champion. They'd set him up to look like a fool. Breeze—a champion? Really!*

The crowd was still yelling and clapping. He was glad to be this far away, they couldn't see the color of his face right now. He tipped his Stetson in the direction of the grandstand and Breeze hunched backward beside the wooden chute where a good-sized animal bawled and crashed about, anxious to escape. He could feel the mare's nervousness, see ripples trembling down her withers. Lord help him! What a time to be riding a brood mare!

"Easy girl!" He quieted her with a pat.

He saw Casey give the chute handler a nod. Instantly, the gate flew open, the steer was free, the rope barrier fell, and they were away. Casey got his rope over the steer's horns a second after they'd cleared the barrier. Rick flicked his rope at the steer's back heels, got both feet and the steer stayed upright. *Perfect!* Breeze did her whirl about and Rick threw his hand up.

It was the fastest time of the day, and it surprised Rick how quickly the mare had responded. She had positioned herself without any direction from him. He shrugged it off. *Beginner's luck.* After the team roping, Rick filled in for Casey's friend in the bull-dogging event. Again the announcer gave Rick a glowing introduction and to Rick's surprise both he and Breeze lived up to it.

"Rick Haynes, Folks! A good solid run—give the cowboy a big hand."

Rick looked up at the grand stand. He could see familiar faces, old friends and neighbors from Stanton cheering him on, wishing him well, and Breeze was working like a real Champion. It was hard to believe!

Rick was dallying his rope back to his saddle horn, when Casey came loping over from the chutes.

"Look Haynes," he yelled, ". . . some farmer brought in a rank roan over there. Calls him 'The Crusher.' There's a hundred bucks for anybody that will ride him out of the chutes."

"Go for it, Adams," Rick said, keeping his eyes on his lariat.

"I wuz thinkin' of you, Haynes. That could be an easy hundred. It don't have to be no qualified ride, either. Just get the sucker out of the chutes."

Rick thought for a minute, then cantered Breeze to the corrals in back where Ray Lott was working the pens. Sure enough a wiry looking long-legged roan was on the outside of the bunch. Its ears were laid back and it came up with its hind feet as Ray rode past.

"Adams says you're riding this stallion, Haynes," Ray called over to him. "Want me to cut him out of the bunch for you."

"Hundred bucks?" Rick shouted above the drumming hooves and bawling cattle.

Ray swung his horse in closer and reined up. "Heard the tallies up to one-seventy-five, now, and you don't need to stick with him for all eight seconds. I'll warn you though . . . they don't call him the crusher for nothing. He's got a habit of throwin' himself in the chutes. The devil's already broken a guy's back up at Drayton."

Rick bit his lip, then nodded and Ray beckoned another wrangler. They were running the roan in as Rick turned away.

There hadn't been much time to think about it. *Maybe that's the way it should be, when you're facing death head on. There's no time to worry and there's worse ways to go.* Just the same, Rick felt the blood pounding in his veins as he tied Breeze to the end of a corral and reached for his leather gloves, then decided against them as some guy threw him a pair of loose-rowel regulation spurs.

The roan was in the chute in no time, snuffing and pawing like a Burlington freight. Rick scaled the metal chute. In the July sun, the metal rails were scorching hot, and the dust hovered in clouds as he lowered himself into the chute. The smell of sweaty hair mixed with the acid taint of stallion dung cleared his head. And above the thrashing horse, Rick heard the loud speaker announcing his name. A fellow by the name of Randy, something or other, in a bright orange shirt was leaning over, giving him a hand. "Bail off if he starts to go down," Randy screamed into his ear as Rick nodded and the gate flew open. Rick brought his spurs high into the stallion's neck, felt the horse snort, rear and for a second Rick was sure he was going over—backward—in the chute, horse and all. He threw his weight forward, his left spur deeper into the horse's neck and then with half twist the horse shot out, hitting the ground so hard it jarred every bone in Rick's body. What a ride! Everything out of perspective. The leather handhold cutting into his left hand, the right hand fanning the air, his dark hair flying loose, but he leaned back, kept spurring, toes out, legs straight and high on the neck, as the stallion squealed, the klaxon sounded the eight seconds he didn't need. Still they twisted and slammed across the arena, and the next thing he knew a pick up grabbed him and he landed on his feet. He found the rigging and his Stetson and waved them both in the air.

The crowd went wild.

"Well, Haynes, let's see what we got," Casey said, a puff of smoke rising from his cigarette as he crouched in front of the cattle chutes at the end of the afternoon. He was scratching a few figures in the dirt to tally their day's winnings. "Team ropin', cattle pennin', steer-wrestlin' . . . and seconds in decoratin' . . . an' that silver dollar thing. That means . . ." he concluded, wiping a mosquito from his cheek and leaving a smear of dirt, ". . .we'll have around three or four hundred bucks with what ya made on ol' Crusher. That's not too shabby a day's pay. And ya know what that means . . . we'll have to stick around fer tonight's show an' pick up a belt buckle or somethin'."

That suited Rick just fine. A quiet break before the evening's show. Yes, it was turning out to be quite a day—a day of nice surprises.

"See you later, Adams," Rick called back, as he loped Breeze to the horse trailer. He was dusty, but happy as he made his way from the infield to where he knew the foal would be anxiously waiting for her mother.

To say the least, Breeze had put on an incredible performance. Any horse, even Red Bar Z, would be hard pressed to match her lightning speed and willingness to please. She was the kind of a horse that would have made Gramp's eyes sparkle with pride—a real Champion. George Haynes had always said a good horse was any color. *Guess Gramps was right.*

Rick dismounted, kicked open the trailer door and in a flurry of long black legs, the filly came flying out, found Breeze and began nuzzling and nursing to the mare's soft nickers. The sight of the colored foal brought a small crowd of admirers, some children, a few dude cowboys . . . and . . .

"No!" *It couldn't be—but it was. "Mara!"*

She was standing by the horse trailer watching him. He could see by the lights in her eyes that she could scarcely contain herself. A brisk puff of wind had worked its way down from the treed bank above her, making her long black hair billow over a white eyelet blouse—and there were those snug-fitting red denims, again.

"Mara." He saw her cheeks pucker, then in an instant he was besides her, catching her arm roughly with one hand, his other hand still holding the horse's reins. "You, you little . . ." He couldn't seem to think of the right word. He wanted to kiss her right there and then, and might have, if it hadn't been for all those gaping people. It seemed like years since he'd seen her. He hadn't realized you could miss somebody you barely knew. "Where have you been?" He caught his breath, let his eyes rest on her. "Mara, it's good . . . real good to see you. I mean . . . I was wondering where you were when you didn't show up that night." How could he tell her he'd been worried sick, without appearing to sound like a blundering idiot. "How have you been, girl?"

The sun had just come out from behind a cloud and leaf patterns danced on her cheeks as she burst out laughing. "First things, first," she said, just as saucy as ever. "I heard you tell some children over by the grandstand that you named your foal after an opera star. Which opera star, Mr. Haynes? Or were you just teasing those innocent little girls?"

Rick grinned. "Any similarity to that name and any living person is strictly coincidental. Isn't that what those smart-mouthed lawyers would have me say? Yes, strictly coincidental. Well, that is, unless I want to be sued, or something." His face grew serious as he tightened his grip on her arm. "Do I want you to sue me?" he asked, glancing down, his eyes mocking her. "I called her Mermaid because she's cute, kinda reminds me of some lil' ol' opree gal who might invite me to dinner if I confess to stepping on her toes, again." He laughed and brought his boot down to threaten a white string sandal. "Come here, girl. Let me tromp on those toes." His voice was husky and he could see her face turning pink as she looked over her shoulder. Some more of his curious fans were back, staring, pretending to pass by, wanting to see who had ridden the Crusher.

"I came to see your horses, not you," she said, but he felt her tremble when he squeezed her arm.

It was Breeze's nudge that made them step apart. Mara immediately caught Breeze's chin strap, pulled the horse's head between them, began stroking the horse's damp black neck. "You've got a nice way with children," she mused. "I thought that was so sweet, the way that tiny tot came up to ask about the filly. You must have looked like a giant to her." Rick hadn't forgotten the incident. He gave Mara a sideways grin as she continued her trend of thought. "You like little girls, don't you?"

"Like big girls better, especially girls who don't play games, who don't stand men up. Girls who phone and let a fellow know where they are." He reached for the lariat hanging on the saddle horn, "I've a notion to hog tie you until I get some straight answers . . . like when do we go for that date you promised me?" He was just kidding around when he shook the lariat free and made a gesture as if he was going to throw the rope, but she took him quite literally and ducked farther behind Breeze.

"Put your rope down," she said, tilting her chin. The smile had disappeared and all that old arrogance was back. It was both an irritation and a challenge that Rick couldn't resist. He pushed the mare to one side, gave an exaggerated flip of the wrist like he intended business, then pitched a lazy rope, one that wouldn't hurt. She stopped it easily with the palm of her hand. then stepped to the safety of the horse trailer, peering back at him and smirking. "Now, put the rope down," she repeated.

His wolf whistle cut the air and her head disappeared as he twirled the rope. Breeze was still saddled, still bridled, and without worrying about the consequences, he leapt for the saddle, gave the mare a kick, and shot around the trailer, swinging his loop as he went. She was obviously surprised. He heard her let out a little squeal, then set off runing. The head start he gave her only added to the excitement. With a war hoop, he bore down on her, flipped his rope over the white lace top and sprung like a cougar from the saddle. Before the rope pulled tight, he had her in his arms, pulled her with him to the ground. With a half hitch he secured her kicking ankles, another half hitch bound her wrists, then crouching above her, he tossed his hands in the air and someone from the brow of the hill bellowed, "Time . . . two seconds flat."

Her hair made a pretty web of dark waves across her face; there was a smudge on her chin; grass stains on her white lace blouse and her top buttons had let go. Gees! She was beautiful. He winked as he saw the shocked look in her eyes.

"Untie me," she demanded, panting hard.

"Please, untie me." Rick mimicked and wiggled his eyebrows, "Pretty please."

"People are laughing," she hissed. Well, she was right there. He'd drawn another small crowd, and he heard a robust sounding voice croak, "Way to go Haynes." And somebody else cackle, "You got you a pretty lil' buckaroo, there Haynes. Keep 'er hog tied."

With a knee poised above the tumble of hair, Rick let his eyes drift over her. And he knew his looking made her struggle all the more. She was just as feisty as he'd ever want. *Oh, that it was legal to keep her tied.* "If you promise not to yell, I'll untie you," he said, bringing the other knee down beside her. He, too, was breathing hard, but not from exertion.

He waited for a second, but when he could see she clearly wasn't enjoying the game, he loosened the lariat and she shot to her feet, buttoning her blouse, rubbing her elbows, dusting off her red jeans, but she didn't fuss. He'd expected she might and in front of this many spectators it might have looked real bad.

"I'm going to get even with you," she said between clenched teeth, combing her fingers through her hair and tossing it back. They walked together to the horse trailer. She with shoulders thrown back and head up, striding out with the dignity of a Roman goddess. Rick with a cocky smile, walking and leading Breeze. The colt straggling behind; the onlookers still craning their necks.

The trailer was only a few meters away. She marched to the front of it, slid down and sat cross-legged, panting in the shade. He watched her out of the corner of his eye. She was concentrating on the ground, her lips trembling. What was she thinking, he wondered?

He thought he knew. *She wasn't used to this kind of rough and tumble, was she?* The rodeo life—she wasn't a part of his world. He sensed her feelings, her shock, the indignity she'd felt in front of this audience. This was not like the audiences she knew, the elite opera fans with their dignified adulation, smooth handshakes, restrained nods, bundles of cellophane-wrapped roses. No, these were rodeo folks—his fans. They meant no harm, but they were coarse and vulgar and they had laughed at her.

He wanted to comfort her, still he couldn't risk an apology just yet; didn't think he could pull one off with this many ears still bent on listening.

With a sense of guilt, he busied himself, pulling the saddle off Breeze's sweaty back, then giving the horse a quick brush and tethering her out. A middle age man came by, tried to make conversation, but Rick discouraged it, and now, as he finished his chores, the onlookers were finally straggling away. He threw the currycomb and brush in the trailer's tack compartment, then stepped over to where Mara was sitting and slid down beside her.

"I'm sorry, Mara. Guess that was a stupid thing to do." He picked a blade of grass, tossed it in the air, watched it fall between them. "But it was fun . . ." he said, giving her a twisted grin. She had barely looked up and he saw her lips pucker. " . . . well . . . fun for me," he said, leaning to flick a long stem of timothy in her direction. "Don't take it so hard." She flinched as the grass connected, a flinch that gave him a disturbing view of her arm. A fresh welt, bright pink and sore-looking made a smooth line across her forearm—a rope burn. Immediately, he was wide-eyed, stammering and apologetic. "Oh, no . . . no Mara. Don't tell me I did that. Here, let me look. I didn't do that. I didn't . . . ? Oh, hell, I did . . . didn't I?"

His heart sank. It wasn't serious, and he knew it. Heaven knows, he'd had his share of rope burns, they burned for a while like a mild kettle scald and healed fast. They just looked bad and made a fellow feel like hell, if he put one on somebody he was trying to impress. "I'm sorry, really sorry. I surely didn't mean to do something like that." Her look of reproach softened and he could see a smile beginning to grow in her eyes. "I've got some stuff in the truck. Stuff Gramps always put on rope burns. Heals real good."

"Okay," she said, leaning back against the blue trailer. He was going to tell her not to lean back; she'd get that white blouse dusty, but then he realized he'd already done a pretty good job of that.

It took no time at all to retrieve the round tin of salve from Sheba's glove box It was battered with age and took some force to work the lid off, but she let him apply the yellow cream and it was good—good to have this excuse to touch, to feel her soft skin under his own rough finger tips, to see her eyes, dark as night, light up again when she looked at him, like stars that flashed bright on the range on a moon-less summer evening. Her lips twitched and had begun to curl at both edges. "What's funny?" he asked.

"Oh, nothing. It's just that you look exactly the way I imagined you would. Black hat, black shirt, spurs and . . ." Her voice was soft. She showed no signs of malice. "Did you know I was watching you ride today . . . ride that bucking horse?" She was certainly different, this girl—so much different than any other woman he'd ever known—so forgiving. For a hoity-toity opera star, she was one hell of a lot different than he'd ever expected her to be. He was listening intently now as she went on. "It's just like those old re-runs with you dressed like . . ." She faltered as he let his fingers twirl little oily circles at her wrist, heard her catch her breath. ". . . like John Wayne . . . or . . . or maybe the Lone Ranger. You know, one of the good guys?" she said, studying him, like he was turning into a memory she intended to hold on to.

"Flattery . . . will get you everywhere," Rick said feeling the need to lift her hand and drop his lips to it. He felt her muscles tighten.

"I didn't mean that," she said, wrenching her hand free with a force that blistered his lips and made him wish she'd been more explicit. She clasped her hands, locked them together, moved the sore arm away before he could started re-daubing. "That's enough," she said, indignantly. "You may look the part, but that doesn't mean you can. . ." Her expression was all serious-Sue again as she fumbled for words, ". . . that you can . . . can . . . start throwing ropes at me."

That wasn't what she meant and he knew it. It only made his blood heat, made him want to grab the lariat from where he'd just thrown it on the iron peg, make her stop yoyoing between come-hither, and stay back.

"Boy, am I going to have a lot of explaining to do, when I get home," she said. "Which reminds me . . ." She straightened the watchband on her wrist, looked at the watch and now, the familiar ruby stones seemed to glisten a protective aura around her whole body, ". . . I'd better get going, before they send the search party after me." Making a move to stand, she uncrossed her legs, then curled sideways. He watched the tight red denims wiggling dangerously close, momentarily touch his own, sending an electric tingle up his dangling leg. Automatically he swung a hand out, caught her knees and pinned them down. *He'd be a fool to let her go.*

BETTY LYNNE McCARTHY

Betty Lynne McCarthy and her family recently moved from a Montana ranch to a New Mexico ranch. She attends gatherings when she can, but often the ranch keeps her busy at home. The following poem, "Just Call Me Cactus Blossom," is pure fun, as is most of her cowgirl poetry.

Just Call Me Cactus Blossom

Out upon the windswept reach
A cactus blossom grows,
A tender sunburst, colored peach
Or yellow, like a rose.

This flower far from hothouse lights,
Thrives on summer rays,
And drinks the dew of warm June nights
On hills where cattle graze.

I marvel at this hardy bloom
While riding down the trail,
And catch a whiff of soft perfume
From petals pink and pale.

I stop my saddlehorse awhile
And slack his bridle reins,
To gaze at buds that are the smile
That light the lonely plains.

I dare to think I'm like this flower

That grows there all alone,
A splash of joy in life's brief hour
To all the friends I've known.

But keeping secret is a must.
My kinship with these plants,
For every bucked-off cowboy's cussed
The cactus in his pants.

EDNA ALFORD

Edna Alford is widely known among Canadian writers, but not necessarily for her ranch writing (although she was raised on a farm in Saskatchewan). As a young practical nurse she worked at various lodges for the elderly, where she met retired school teachers, stenographers and, yes, ranch women. She fictionalized their lives and her observations in a book called A Sleep Full Of Dreams. *"Half-Past Eight" is taken from that book.*

Half-Past Eight

TESSIE BISHOP TOOK HER TUBE of "Scarlet Fire" lipstick and removed the lid. The lipstick was old and stale and had that sickly sweet smell peculiar to the cosmetics of the aged.

The mirror on the dowager dresser was adjustable, swung on ornate brass hooks, and Tessie tilted it so she could see as much of herself as possible. She wished she had a full-length mirror like the one she had hung on the bathroom door of the apartment she lived in before she had to come to the lodge, before the money ran out and the time with it. She wanted to check the hem of her dress, get the overall effect of the outfit she was wearing to the Stampede Parade.

The mirror on this dresser was tarnished and wavy—like all the others in the lodge, Tessie supposed. Her image was distorted in this mirror, unreal in the bronze shimmer. She couldn't believe she really looked like this, her skin old and wavy and discoloured, mapped with cracks. But what could you expect, she thought. Time passes, doesn't it, and all things considered, she had held her own, didn't look nearly as old as she was, she assured herself, in spite of the mirror.

Mirrors weren't trustworthy, regardless of the fairytales. "Mirror, mirror on the wall, who is the *oldest* of us all?" she mocked the white-haired woman trapped in the yellow glass. Then laughing she said, "See, you can't tell, you silly old bitch. You don't know a goddamn thing—and in a few minutes you'll know even less."

She stretched her lips thin, into a false smile. Then she slowly, meticulously spread a thick, bleeding layer of lipstick horizontally across her mouth, right to the tapered corners—first on the top lip, then on the bottom. She replaced the lid on the tube and laid it on the dresser top. She took a piece of Kleenex and patted her mouth several times, gingerly.

Next she took a round clear plastic container from a small top drawer of her dresser. The brown-stained label on the bottom read "Pomegranate Blush." She unscrewed the lid and dipped the tip of her right index finger into it. Then she smeared a round high blotch of "Pomegranate Blush" on each cheek.

The rouge was pink and had the same sweet sickening odour as the lipstick, like rosewater and glycerin gone rancid in sun and age. The bright pink cheeks clashed violently with her "Scarlet Fire" lips and together with white, heavily powdered skin in wrinkles, made her look like a clown.

She applied eyebrow pencil in thin black arches over her almost browless eyes and in conclusion, brushed mascara thickly on her short white lashes. It dried lumpy.

When she had finished, she smiled with satisfaction at the mirror. She began to hum to herself. She went to the long window of her small dark room and was delighted to see the summer sun already climbing high and hot in the eastern sky. There were only a few roguish tufts of cloud drifting easily through the blue whiteness.

She had been hoping for weeks now that there would be no rain today. She and Flora Henderson had crossed their fingers in unison yesterday—at the supper table, in the tea room, and at prayer meetings when everyone else was singing "Rock of ages cleft for me, let me hide—" they would both look out at the sky, then back at each other, hoping the weather would hold for the parade.

The weatherman on CFCN Radio last night had reported that a fine day *was* expected for the parade, that there were clouds moving in over the Rockies but they weren't expected to reach Calgary till late tomorrow. Tessie put her face close to the warm green shimmer of the window screen and breathed a satisfied, and at the same time, excited sigh of relief.

She had on her best summer dress, a flowered cotton print with huge pink and red and orange mums with black stems and leaves frolicking all over it. A thin black patent leather belt sat squarely on her hips. A very classy number, she thought. A perfect dress for a parade. She wore a navy straw hat with a small brim and last week she had bought an orange chiffon scarf to lace through the brass holes in the hat and tie pertly under her chin. The scarf perfectly matched the orange mums in the dress print.

When she brushed her hair, she flipped a small white curl on either side of her face to fall sultry against her cheeks. Her hair looked exactly as she had worn it in what she called her "hey-day," in the early twenties. Tessie had been one of the first to bob her hair and she wore it now in the same short-cropped style. Admiring herself in the wavy mirror, she remembered that she had been a very beautiful young woman. Everyone had told her so and she herself had thought that it was true.

When she was finished putting on her make-up, she put the lipstick along with her comb, some Kleenex, and her clutch purse in a small black bag she had crocheted.

Although she could barely make ends meet on the small pension she got from the Veterans' Affairs Department, she had managed to save a little over twenty dollars for today. It hadn't been easy but she had cut down on wool for crocheting last month and she made do with the meals at the lodge which, she thought, was a sacrifice, to say the least. And she hadn't bought a drop of liquor in all that time.

One good thing about today was that she didn't have to worry about Flora. Flora was game to go and always had lots of money. In fact, she was more excited about the parade than Tessie, could talk of nothing else. You'd never know she was eighty-six. Nothing could keep her down—a lot like me, thought Tessie. Age meant nothing to her, which was probably why they chummed around together, not because of the drinking, which was the opinion of most of the old biddies who lived here. And Flora always paid her own way.

There were all sorts of rumours about Flora. Some said she won the "Pot of Gold" at the fair one year and that was why she could stick her old age pension cheques under her mattress and not worry about cashing them. But Tessie knew that Flora and old man Henderson had owned a hotel up north in British Columbia and that they had catered to the men from the logging camps. Flora spent a good deal of her time supervising the girls on the top floor. "There was good money in them girls," Flora told Tessie confidentially.

Today's the day, all right, Tessie thought. Today we'll go out and see the parade and eat and kick up our heels for a change.

Leaving her bed unmade, she picked up her straw sun hat, her black bag, and a sweater just in case. She locked the door, trying the lock afterward and then walked down the hall and knocked on Flora's door, number twenty-three. She frowned down at her brown oxfords which were not beautiful and didn't match her dress. But they were sturdy, she thought, for all the walking they would have to do today.

Flora opened the door a crack. Then, finding it was Tessie, she flung the door back against the jamb. "Yah, come on in," she bellowed.

Flora, too, had high rouge blotches on her cheeks and her hair stuck pin-curl fuzzy out from under a wide-brimmed mannish straw hat. For all her money, thought Tessie, Flora might at least buy a new summer hat. That one, Tessie was sure, must have been old man Henderson's fifty years ago.

Flora wore a long-sleeved, shapeless dress of grey-striped arnel her daughter-in-law had helped her pick three years ago. But she had new shoes, handsome sturdy white sandals. Tessie felt a slight twinge when she saw them.

"Good day for a parade, eh Flora?" she said. She was not about to let on to Flora how envious she was of the new sandals.

"Good day for a parade, eh Tess?" Flora hadn't heard Tessie speak. That was another thing that irked her about the older woman. She was partially deaf. But at least she wasn't afraid to go. So Tessie smiled patronizingly at Flora. I may not have fancy sandals, she thought to herself, but at least I'm not deaf—yet.

Flora smiled back, picked up her purse and sweater, and they left the room, Flora locking the door of room twenty-three behind them. She tried the lock twice.

They passed several ancient ladies with canes, shuffle-feeling thick routes along the walls of the hallway on their way to breakfast. The hoyer stood in the middle of the lower hallway outside Miss Bole's room and Tessie edged her way around it as if she were afraid it were alive, as if it might reach out and grab her. But Flora stuck out her foot and gave the hoyer a shove and sent it rolling into the wall, clanking when it hit the baseboard, its canvas straps swinging foolishly.

"You'll never get me inta that goddamn thing," she bellered at the metal hoist used to transport bedridden lodgers to and from the bathtub. "Goddamn stupid nurse," Flora continued, "leaving that contraption out in the hall so's one of us'll fall and break our bloody hips. No more of a nurse than a pig's foot," she yelled. "She hasn't got the brains she was born with. I wouldn't hire her if ya paid me, Tess."

Tessie raised her eyebrows and smiled. Flora guffawed. "Oh Christ, Tess. She ain't fit for that kinda work!" Tessie giggled.

At breakfast Tessie and Flora had to sit with Mrs. Morrison and Mrs. Popovich because there were no spaces left at the other tables by the time they got there. Tessie had hated Helen Popovich ever since the fight over the big brown rocker on the sun porch. Tessie had lost that one, but only because Helen Popovich called in the matrons. And Mrs. Morrison wasn't much better— "Yes Helen this" and "Yes Helen that"—a spineless old bat if there ever was one.

But she tried to ignore the other two women and she and Flora talked about their plans. Would they take the bus as far as the stadium or would they walk while it was still cool? Better take the bus, they decided. No sense risking being late and missing the Parade Marshall. Tessie would definitely be upset if she missed Prince Charles.

Mrs. Popovich's forehead furrowed cynically. "Why you'd want to fight them crowds is beyond me," she clipped the remnants of a fractured voice, "and on a day like this! Good Lord, Flora, you'll shrivel up in the heat. What if you have an attack? Things aren't like they used to be you know. Nobody'll pick you up from the street now—they just leave you lying there. I know an old woman who lay for five hours, I say, on the street and her leg was broke and nobody helped her. She died too."

"We all do," Flora interrupted, "but Tessie and me ain't dead yet." She winked at Tessie and Tessie winked back.

"We won't strain ourselves, Helen," Tessie compromised. "We're just going to have a look. We don't plan to be gone long. After all, we're not going to be on the street you know. We do have seats in Mewata Stadium and we do have our hats."

"Suit yourself," Helen clucked with finality. She didn't speak to them again but when Tessie and Flora gathered their things together and strutted out of the dining room, Tessie whispered loudly, not only for Flora but so Helen could hear.

"You know what they say, Flora—mind your own business, eat your own fish—not to mention the dog in the manger." She looked around to make certain Helen had heard her and smiled with satisfaction. Helen was staring furiously at the porridge in the thick porcelain bowl on her plate. She was jabbing it viciously with the wrong end of her spoon.

Outside the building and walking on the sidewalk toward the bus stop, Tessie and Flora were a peculiar and somewhat amusing couple. Flora, although eighty-six, was still tall and raw-boned, her heavy body lumbering like a large grey-striped animal from side to side with each step. Tessie, on the other hand, was a little like a bird, very small and colourful beside Flora. The steps Tessie took were Lilliputian and energetic which produced a kind of hopping effect as she dodged Flora's large body, like a bright pecking bird on the back of a hippo.

When they boarded the bus it was already packed with an uproar of parade people. Tessie and Flora had to cling desperately to the chrome rods along the top of the seats because there was no place to sit. They didn't mind, except when the teeming vehicle lurched.

"Take it easy you old sonuvabitch," Flora called up to the driver, although he couldn't have been a day over fifty, Tessie thought, and not half-bad looking. To Tessie's embarrassment, Flora continued heckling, "I been in bloody buck-boards made better time than this and was smoother too, yah, you bet—they give a better ride!" Some of the passengers nearest them giggled or muffled their laughter but one man laughed right out loud.

"What the hell's the matter with *you?*" Flora turned on him. "Ya drunk or just off your rocker?" The man laughed again and so did Flora this time.

Tessie inspected the clothing worn by the other passengers, mentally rated the parade outfits on a scale of one to ten. A zero, she thought, that one is definitely a zero. Pausing tentatively, her eyes scanned a young girl from the waist down.

"If I had legs like that," she said to Flora, "I wouldn't be caught dead in shorts, even if I was sixteen-years-old."

"Yah, you bet," said Flora, "she'd be scrubbin' floors in my place." She winked at Tessie. "Not like you Tess," she added. Tessie blushed and cupped her hand over her eyes, pretending to look out the window to see where they were.

The ride to the stadium wasn't long but when they slowly and awkwardly disembarked all the while jostled and shoved by the swarming young, the two old women were relieved to breathe more deeply, even though the air was full of exhaust from the back of the bus. By now the near-noon sun was very high and the heat wafted around the women. But instead of making them sluggish or uncomfortable as it did most old folk, the heat only served to increase their excitement. Along the way to their seats, Flora openly rebuked the rude, both drivers and pedestrians. She broke a ten-dollar bill to buy them two revels and two paper cups full of Orange Crush. "Why don't you watch where you're goin', ya dirty bugger," she cursed when a young man bumped her elbow, making her spill the drinks so that her hands were sticky when they arrived at their seats.

From where they sat they could see the whole spread of the city centre—the Calgary Tower, a dull one-legged crane with a red crown, half-surrounded on one side by tall lean office buildings, the head offices of banks and oil companies, like confident prehistoric monsters with thousands of glass eyes glittering in the high hot sunlight. For a while they both stared at it, intently, as if their city were a foreign country they had never set foot in—they were not afraid, but were not exactly sure what they could expect.

They were soon distracted. Tessie first heard the off-key din of horns and the tremor of drums in the air as the great parade wound its way along farther up the route. Flora, being hard of hearing, had to be told that it was very near the stadium and then they both fidgeted, straining to catch their first glimpse of the leading entourage.

Finally the Parade Marshall rode into view. He was none other than Prince Charles himself, the Crown Prince of England. He was mounted on one of the magnificent dark RCMP stallions, just as his Uncle Edward had been so many years before. It didn't seem that long a time ago. Tessie tallied the years in her head. No doubt about it. Fifty. Half a century. It hardly seemed possible, but there it was.

Prince Edward was a doll and she hadn't been the only girl who thought so. And Charles was a fine looking young man, too—but just a boy really. Nevertheless, Tessie was impressed. He carried himself well, exactly the way Tessie thought the Crown Prince of England should. From the time he was a baby, Tessie had kept a scrapbook of newspaper clippings, pictures and stories about his arrivals and departures all over the Commonwealth. That was how she learned he was going to lead the parade. There had been big spreads about him in the newspapers, both the *Herald* and the *Albertan,* several weeks before.

Tessie was more than impressed. Other than Edward, there had been only one Marshall who had excited her more and that was Bing Crosby. He rode in a low, sleek convertible, but because Tessie had watched that parade from the street, she had been almost close enough to touch the man with the dreaming voice as he passed. "Where the blooo of the night / Meets the gold of the day (babababababa) / Someone—waits for—meeee," Tessie crooned. In her memory, Bing had waved directly to her and at the very thought of it, she could feel a warm flow of blood flush her pomegranate cheeks. Flora never could get too worked up about the Royal Family and Bing Crosby seemed somehow after her time.

Behind the Crown Prince rode the Royal Canadian Mounted Police. To Tessie they looked like a flock of red birds, flag wings fluttering. There were white hats scattered all along the parade and the hats looked like white gulls on dark waves. And there was the waving of hand wings from the procession to the crowd and the wing-waving back from the white-hatted bleachers which to Tessie looked for all the world like an island of white birds in the middle of the city.

There was a wide assortment of Indians with red and yellow and white and blue beadwork. Riding and walking, they looked like beautiful and mystical doomed birds, feather headdresses swaying on their backs and feather plumes totter-waving from the tight headbands.

Among them walked a riderless horse with a sign hanging on its side. The sign identified the horse as the one Nelson Small Legs should have been riding. He was the young Indian man who had just taken his own life, Tessie remembered, the young man who couldn't go on with his battles with bureaucracies and reservations, the newscaster had said. Tessie pointed his horse out to Flora and reminded her who he was. "Yah, yah, yah, I know," Flora replied in a sad low voice.

Tessie hoped the riderless horse wouldn't dampen Flora's spirits. She always liked the Indian section of the parade best of all and looked forward to it every year. Tessie remembered their talks about the Indians in the North who sold their beaded moccasins to the loggers who came to the hotel. And Flora talked especially of a raven blue beauty who had worked in her house, on the top floor of the hotel. Tessie thought there was more to that part of the story than Flora let on by the far away look in her eyes when she spoke of the girl. Tessie had been around too. Flora didn't need to think she could pull the wool over *her* eyes.

But Flora soon perked up and the two old women quickly became intoxicated with the colour of the parade and the sound and with the smell of fresh horse droppings randomly and indiscreetly released by the great beasts on the pavement. The hot sun ricocheted off the trumpets and the cymbals of the strutting bands and off the majorettes' batons thrown high and gleaming into the summer sky.

Floats of paper flowers glided miraculously by themselves, dream-like, their tractors hidden under more paper flowers. Flora and Tessie both disagreed with the choice of the judges as to which floats should win the first and second prizes and they argued with each other about the way it should have been.

They drank the spectacle whole and undiluted while the sun played on their gleaming wrinkles which collected small droplets of sweat in the heat. Tessie's mascara ran and blackened the already prominent bags of skin under her eyes.

Long after the last float had passed the stadium, they sat watching the crowd clear, watching the parade trail away along the route. They were sorry it was over and only after a cleaner arrived pushing his long-handled bristle broom down their aisle, did they stand laboriously and gather their things. They started down one of the aisles of the bleachers. There were only a few people wearing white stetsons left, picking up thermoses, cushions and left-over lunches.

When they got down to the street Flora said her tongue was stuck to the roof of her mouth—that's how thirsty she was. And Tessie agreed. "You have to take it easy when you get to be our age, Flora," she said, "dehydration, you have to be careful of dehydration at our age." Flora looked shocked. "I *mean,* Flora, that we old folks need a lot of rest—and liquids—say at the Palliser Hotel, for example."

Flora laughed. "Yah, you bet, Tess. This here Rimrock Lounge—now that's what I call a nice quiet place. We should have brought the other old dames with us, Tess. Be good for 'em." Tessie hailed a Yellow Cab and they set off toward the city centre.

In the old days, Tessie remembered, the Palliser had been the tallest, most impressive building in the city, a testimonial to the indisputable might of the Canadian Pacific Railroad. But in recent years it had been dwarfed by a six-hundred-foot concrete tower which hovered over it, and by the sleek new shopping complex which appeared to be nudging the old hotel slowly toward the curb, toward the subway. She remembered when the tower had been built by the Husky Oil Company. At first it was called the Husky Tower but they had already renamed it the Calgary Tower. Why, Tessie didn't have the faintest idea, but they had done it, down in City Hall she supposed. Anyway the tower looked to Tessie like a man's you know what and she couldn't resist telling Flora that it was the biggest one she'd ever seen—and she had seen a few in her time.

The heat was beginning to work on the women as they climbed and their feet grew heavy and slow. Inside, the hotel was large and cool and bright. An enormous old chandelier glittered with amber light near the high ceiling of the lobby. The two women went directly to the Rimrock Lounge and sat down in luxuriously upholstered red velvet chairs at a small round table. Tessie ordered a Shanghai Sling with a red maraschino cherry and a piece of pineapple on top and Flora ordered a shot of whiskey, straight.

After their second drink an old man in a brown straw cowboy hat, a western tie and a big belt with a large brass horsehead buckle came over to Flora and Tessie's table. The ladies were boisterous by now and asked him to join them. He swept his cowboy hat off his head, harlequin-tipped it to the ladies and introduced himself as Hank. Hank had a lumpy hooked nose like the warted beak of an old hawk. He bought two rounds and Tessie, especially, was grateful.

"Well wha' did you ladies think of it this year?" asked Hank.

"Stacks up, I'd say," said Tessie. "Better than last year's if you ask me."

"Didya ever see so much *horseshit* in all yer life?" Hank shook his heavy hawk head.

"Never," Tessie replied, emphatically.

"Seems to me it don't all come from a horse's ass neither," Hank continued. "Every bloody politician in the city was there and some come all the way from Ottawa to ride over the turds—" he paused. "On second thought," he said, "maybe some of it *do* come from a horse's ass."

Tessie covered her mouth with her hand and laughed till her face turned red. Flora just threw her head back and let the laughter roll up from her belly. Her hat fell off and landed on the carpet behind her chair. Satisfied with the effect his commentary had on his new companions, Hank stretched out his legs and clasped his gnarled brown hands behind his head, slowly lifted one enormous, scuffed Texas boot and crossed it deliberately over the other boot.

"I'll tell you what I like," he drawled. "I like them majorettes with their baa–tons."

"You mean their legs don't you, Hank?" Tessie volleyed.

"Yah, you bet," said Flora who had her hand cupped to her best ear and had caught the word "legs." "Not too bad, not too bad at all. You and me, Tess, if we had a couple of them peaches, we could buy and sell that Pine Mountain hole ten times over. Get ourselves a fair-sized house, one of them old fellas across from Maunley Park. We'd live on the first floor and set up shop on the second. Whadaya say, Tess?" Flora's voice, low and hoarse, rumbled along like an old train.

"Why *not* Pine Mountain?" snickered Tessie. The "not" was high-pitched, a little girl's squeal. She put her hand on Hank's arm and said, "That's where we live, Hank, in the lodge," and turning to Flora, continued, "God knows it's old enough—lots of rooms. You and I could live in the Maunley Mansion, Flora, in style, like the matrons."

"Yah, you bet. Be nice and quiet. The girls could take the fellas out inta the park, under the trees—be nice in the spring, eh Tess?" She winked at Tessie and Tessie winked back.

"One small problem," said Tessie, "what do we do with all those old ladies? As you would say, Flora, they sure as hell ain't fit for work."

"Yah, you bet," Flora laughed, "as far as I can figure half of 'em don't even know where they are. Seems to me things could go on pretty much as usual, Tess, and nobody'd know the difference—but for the matrons, I guess. We might have a little trouble bringing them around."

Hank, who had finally come to appreciate the nature of Tessie's and Flora's plan, rolled his eyes toward the ceiling, then bowed his head and, tipping his hat low over his brow, drawled, "Ah-haa—I didn't know you was that sort of ladies." Then he raised his head and stared directly at Tessie who blushed and looked down at her drink. Gingerly, she slid the maraschino cherry from its plastic green arrow and popped it into her mouth. It was sweet, deliciously sweet.

Late in the afternoon the three tottered into the hotel dining room and ordered steak sandwiches. Tessie ate too much and had stabbing gas pains for some time after the meal. Flora had trouble chewing the meat with her false teeth but she enjoyed the blood beef flavour and ate everything on her plate.

When they finished their meal the three went back to the bar. Flora had to stop at the washroom on the way. There was a line-up and Hank and Tessie could hear Flora cursing from all the way across the lobby. Once in the bar they drank beer from pitchers and sang along with a man who played a honky-tonk piano in a dark corner of the lounge. The words of the songs were projected on a white square of wall and a little ball bounced from word to word along the lyrics so they could know where they were and what to sing.

"Roll out the barrel," Flora bellowed, "we'll have a barrel of fun," not always in tune or in time with the piano.

Tessie's hands fluttered and she leaned her old body, covered in orange and pink and red mums, languorously toward Hank as they sang together and whispered ripe jokes which Flora couldn't hear but laughed at anyway.

Once, while asking "What'll the ladies have?" when buying another round, Hank slapped Tessie's thigh and left his hand on one of the large orange mums that clung to the cloth of her dress. He left it there for what seemed a very long time to Tessie and she felt the blood rise to the rouge on her cheeks. She winked at him. Flora didn't see any of this and Tessie didn't let on to her what had happened.

After awhile, Flora began to doze and snore intermittently. Twice, she nearly fell off her chair. The second time, she almost tipped the chair over and that seemed to startle her, perk her up. Tessie had to admit she was a bit disappointed in Flora for petering out so fast, but then she was so much older than Tessie.

Hank had just come back from the washroom and had poured himself another glass of beer when Tessie felt the hand on her stocking, moving up her thigh. She leaned toward Hank, then straightened abruptly. Both of Hank's hands were occupied—a half-full glass of beer in one and a Player's cigarette in the other. She had just watched him light it. She turned on Flora.

"Jesus H. Christ, Flora!" she yelled. "That's the limit! We're going home!" She blushed. The people at the next table all turned and looked at her as if she'd lost her mind. Hank was looking at her that way too.

"Oh come on, Tess," Flora cajoled, "I didn't mean nothin' by it. The party's just beginning."

"I say it's over, Flora. Come on." Despite Hank's slurred protests, Tessie went out to the lobby and called a cab. When she came back, she picked up Flora's hat and their purses and they left. Hank walked out to the lobby with them. Before Tessie passed the doorman, she turned and pretended to look back at the glittering old chandelier. But she couldn't see Hank. He must already have gone back into the bar.

Tessie was furious with Flora, plunked the older woman's hat on her head, put her in the back seat of the cab, and climbed into the front with the driver. But after they had been driving for awhile, she began to calm down. No point in looking back, she thought to herself. She shouldn't have done it. It never worked. And there was no sense spoiling the whole day because of what Flora did, not over a little thing like that. Flora was drunk. That was the problem. But they'd gotten drunk together before and there was none of this nonsense. Must have been the parade, thought Tessie, all those bloody majorettes and all those Indians. She thought about that for a moment. Well, at least Flora would go with her, wasn't afraid of a little fun, and there was no harm done after all.

Instead, Tessie began to worry that the matrons would be up, or that the night nurse would catch them coming in. With any luck Mrs. Tittler would be asleep, but if she wasn't—. Tessie sighed deeply, then belched. Her stomach was full of gas again because of the beer. Not only that, she was pretty sure she would be hung over in the morning.

Flora began to sing in a subdued, broken voice, "Roll out the barrel, we'll have a barrel of fun—," then stopped abruptly in the middle of the first verse as if she had just remembered something vitally important. She laughed and launched into a rollicking chorus of a different song, sung to the tune of "The Dark-Town Strutters' Ball"—

> OOOH—there's gonna be a ball
> the mother-fuckers' ball.
> The witches an' the bitches

gonna be there all.
Now honey, don't be late
'cause we'll be passin' out
pussy 'bout half-past eight

I got fucked in France,
fucked in Spain,
I even got a little on the coast of Maine—
but the best damn piece of all
was my goddamn mother-in-law
last Saturday night
at the mother-fuckers' ball.

The cabbie tipped back the brim of his hat, looked over his shoulder and grinned. "That's a new one on me," he said. "I thought I'd heard 'em all."

"Huhaw!" Flora guffawed. "Do I look like I'd be singin' a new song?"

That wasn't very likely, Tessie thought, regarding her old friend with amusement and a fair amount of admiration, but then Tessie had never heard the song before either—and she had been around.

"Oh yah, we sung it in the bar all the time, years ago, up North in my old man's hotel." She paused, remembering.

"Yah," she said quietly, "that's an old dog."

As they climbed the steps toward the dark building, Tessie could hear the roll of thunder in the black west. She smelled something dank, like mildew, in the air. That's all right, she thought. Let her come down in buckets—all night if she wants to, and all day tomorrow. As long as it didn't rain today.

At the top of the steps, Flora rattled her throat, dragged up a patch of phlegm and spat it into the flower bed beside the lodge where it hung white and bubbly on a purple petunia. Tessie winced. They snuck in through the sun porch door which, luckily, had not yet been locked. In all likelihood, Mrs. Tittler had completely forgotten about it again, Tessie thought.

In the feeble light of the porch, Tessie noticed that Flora's straw hat sat awry and saucy on her head. Someone might get up. Maybe Mrs. Tittler would come out and see the tilt and suspect. "Stand still a minute will ya, Flora," she said. She reached up and straightened the hat and fuss-tucked the fuzzy grey strands of hair under the brim. Flora pretended to stand at attention.

But no sooner had they started up the hall when Flora began to wander from one side to the other, banging on each door and roaring, "Wake up ya deaf old coots! C'mon now, outa the sack!" Then she began to sing—"Oh, there's gonna be a ball, the mother—"

"Shshshsh," Tessie pleaded, her right index finger poised dramatically stiff and vertical over her red-crusted lips.

"You'll wake 'em up for shhure, you crazy old drunk!"

"What's a matter with ya, Tess?" Flora bellered to the lodge of aged sleeping ladies. "I'd rather be fuckin' drunk than this." She wheeled and staggered, raised her right arm, waved it around in the air and, fisting the fingers, resumed weaving back and forth across the hall, banging on bedroom doors and singing—

> "The witches and the bitches
> gonna be there all.
> Now honeee, don't be late
> 'cause we'll be passin' out—

"Jesus Christ," she interrupted herself, "most of these old dames don't even make it to seven-thirty let alone half-past eight—and the worst of it is they wouldn't know what to do with it even if they could get holda some."

Tessie, who was now standing in the stairwell at the other end of the hall, stopped tapping her foot. Though she was half-hidden in shadow, her moon white face appeared to project itself out of the dark, like a mask on a stick. Her eyes were rimmed in black where the mascara had run in the hot afternoon sun and met the thin black arches pencilled on her brows.